Pulp Sonnets

For Bob the Leaf Master, wizard of Nature! With friendship

ALSO BY TONY BARNSTONE

POETRY

Beast in the Apartment (Sheep Meadow Press, 2014).

Tongue of War: The Pacific War from Pearl Harbor to Hiroshima (BKMK Press, 2009). Winner of the John Ciardi Prize in Poetry, the Independent Publisher Book Award (Silver Medal), and the Poets Prize.

The Golem of Los Angeles (Red Hen Press, 2008).

Sad Jazz: Sonnets (Sheep Meadow Press, 2005).

Impure (University Press of Florida, 1999).

Naked Magic (chapbook, Main Street Rag, 2002).

MUSIC RECORDING

Tokyo's Burning: World War II Songs (Stormbarn Music, 2012). Music by Genuine Brandish, with lyrics by Tony Barnstone, John Clinebell, and Ariana Hall.

ANTHOLOGIES

Dead and Undead Poems (Everyman Press, 2014). Co-editor with Michelle Mitchell-Foust.

Human and Inhuman Monstrous Verse (Everyman Press, 2015). Co-editor with Michelle Mitchell-Foust.

TRANSLATIONS

River Merchant's Wife by Ming Di (Marick Press 2013). Co-translator with the author and Neil Aitken, Afaa Michael Weaver, Katie Farris, and Sylvia Burn.

Erotic Chinese Poems (Everyman Press, 2007). Co-editor and translator with Chou Ping.

The Anchor Book of Chinese Poetry: The Full 3000-Year Tradition (Anchor Books, 2005). Co-editor and translator with Chou Ping.

The Art of Writing: Teachings of the Chinese Masters (Shambhala Publications, 1996). Co-editor and translator with Chou Ping.

Out of the Howling Storm: The New Chinese Poetry (Wesleyan University Press, 1993).

Laughing Lost in the Mountains: Selected Poems of Wang Wei (University Press of New England, 1991). Co-editor and translator with Willis Barnstone and Xu Haixin.

TEXTBOOKS

The Literatures of Asia (Prentice-Hall, 2002). Editor.

The Literatures of the Middle East (Prentice-Hall, 2002). Co-editor with Willis Barnstone.

The Literatures of Asia, Africa, and Latin America from Antiquity to Now (Prentice-Hall, 1998). Co-editor with Willis Barnstone.

FOREIGN EDITIONS

Laughing Lost in the Mountains: Selected Poems of Wang Wei (Beijing: Panda Books, 1989).

FOREIGN TRANSLATIONS

The Art of Writing: Teachings of the Chinese Masters, translated, edited, and introduced by Tony Barnstone and Chou Ping, translated into Arabic by Dr. Abed Ismael (Damascus: Al Mada Publishing Company F.K.A., 2003).

Buda en llamas: Antología poética (1999–2012), bilingual selected poems by Tony Barnstone, translated into Spanish by Mariano Zaro (Mexico City: Ediciones El Tucán de Virginia, 2014).

PULP SONNETS

Poems by

TONY BARNSTONE

Drawings by

AMIN MANSOURI

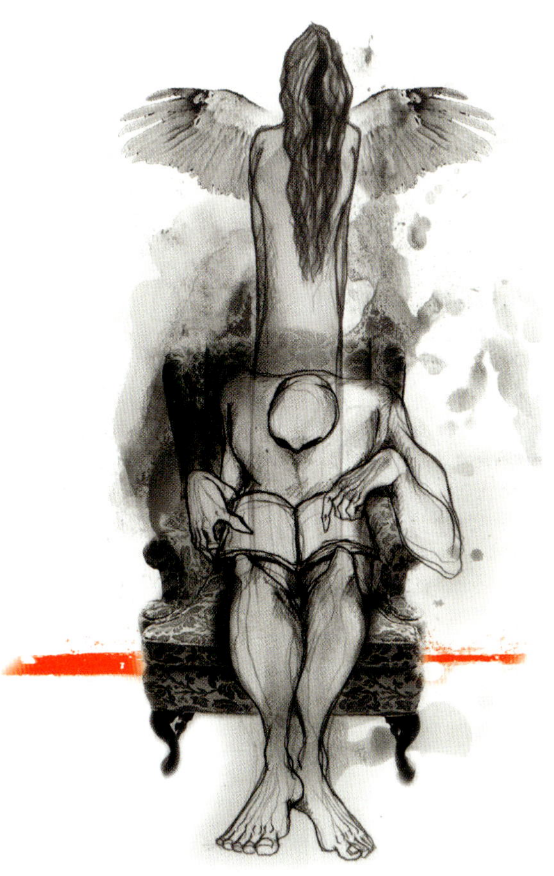

T|P

NORTH ADAMS, MASSACHUSETTS

Pulp Sonnets.

Library of Congress Cataloging-in-Publication Data
Barnstone, Tony.
[Poems. Selections]
Pulp Sonnets : poems / by Tony Barnstone; illustrated by
Amin Mansouri. First paperback edition.
pages cm
Includes bibliographical references.
ISBN 978-1-936797-62-2 (pbk. : alk. paper)
I. Mansouri, Amin, 1984- illustrator. II. Title.
PS3552.A7215A6 2015
811' .54--dc23
2015017619

Cover and text designed by William Kuch. Cover art: Amin Mansouri.

First paperback edition: September 2015.

Tupelo Press
P.O. Box 1767, North Adams, Massachusetts 01247
Telephone: (413) 664–9611 / editor@tupelopress.org / www.tupelopress.org

Tupelo Press is an award-winning independent literary press that publishes fine fiction, nonfiction, and poetry in books that are a joy to hold as well as read. Tupelo Press is a registered 501(c)(3) nonprofit organization, and we rely on public support to carry out our mission of publishing extraordinary work that may be outside the realm of the large commercial publishers. Financial donations are welcome and are tax deductible.

This book is in memory of Roger Zelazny, brilliant and irreverent writer of fantasy and speculative fiction, and my first creative writing teacher — he was kind enough to allow me to sit in on his writing workshop at Indiana University in 1977, when I was sixteen years old.

CONTENTS

PULP: A MODERN MYTHOLOGY XI

1 KILLERS and TRAMPS

The Cat Lady 2
The Chemist 3
The Lover 5
New York Blues 5
Night Has a Thousand Eyes 6
A Woman Like a Bullet 6
Mexican Movie, 1939 8
The Chop Shop 9
1. A Stand-Up Guy 9
2. Italian Sandwich Meat 9
Insects and Cigarettes 10
1. A Fat Black Tick 10
2. Revelation 11
3. The Metamorphosis 11
4. One Cigarette 12
The Ballad of Dottie and Pete 13
1. Greased Chicken Breasts 13
2. Red Pickup 14
3. Chopped Meat 14

15 OPERATION RAGNAROK

1. A Back Alley in Honningsvåg 16
2. Wet Work 16
3. Death and the Author 17
4. At the Fishhouses 18
5. The Job 19
6. The Man with the Glass Eye Speaks 20
7. God Complex 21
8. The Hermeneutics of Spycraft 23
9. The Poetry of Murder 24

JACK LOGAN, FIGHTING AIRMAN:

THE CASE OF THE RED BORDELLO

1. Acquainted with the Night 26
2. Tricks and Stag Flicks 27
3. The Name of the Rose 28
4. The Trick Turns 29
5. The Act 30
6. Two Black Books and a Stack of Cash 31
7. Angels and Buttercups 31
8. Angel Face 32
9. A Heap of Broken Images 32
10. A Rose by Any Other Name 33
11. Tough Act to Follow 34
12. The Kiss 34
13. The Distressed Rose 37
14. Tough Guise 37
15. The Death Trap 39
16. The City Dead-House 39
17. Dressing the Meat 40
18. From Tempest to Othello 41
19. Spider Cat and Bad Eye 42
20. When It Rains, It Pours 43
21. Animals 44
22. Note Left Pinned to the Pillow (Signed "Violet") 45
23. Small Fry, Big Fish, and the Dish 46
24. Angels Falling from the Sky 46
25. Taxes and Death 47
26. A Bouquet of Violence 48
27. Violets are Black and Blue 49
28. Untouchable 50

51 THEOGONY

Fortress of Solitude 52
Wonder Woman and the Gravity Monster 52
The Living Flame 53
The Human Torch 54
The Bent Adventures of India Rubber Man 55
1. India Rubber Man's Credo 55
2. The Origin of India Rubber Man 56
3. India Rubber Man at the Temple of Sin Adult Novelty Store (the Origin of Miss Elastic) 57
4. The Anthem of Miss Elastic 58
5. Miss Elastic Rescues India Rubber Man from Evil X-Girlfriend 59
6. India Rubber Man and the Fear and Trembling and Sickness Unto Death 60
7. India Rubber Man's Buddhist Christmas 61
8. India Rubber Man and the Anorexic Doll 62
9. India Rubber Man and Miss Elastic in the Morning 63
10. India Rubber Man and the Bath 64

65 BESTIARY

The Monster Speaks 66
Thing 67
A Stranger's Newspaper 68
The First Dark Knight 69
The Blowfly Thing 70
The Two-Headed Man 71
The Sphinx 72
Ways of Looking at a Vampire 73
1. I Am Legend 73
2. The Revenant 74
3. The Flea 74
4. The Lurker at the Window 76
5. The Second Death of Dracula 77

Snake People . . . .
1. The Worms of the Earth 78
2. Claws in the Darkness 78
The Werewolf of Green Knolls. 79
1. Pooch 80
2. Snarl 80
3. Little Piggy 81
4. That Time of Month 82
5. Wolf's Best Friend 82
6. Whine 83
7. Rabbit's Revenge 84
8. Feeding Time 85
. 86

87 THE HORROR OF HAUNTED VALLEY

1. Red Glow in the Woods (Case 001: Dan Weiss, 13, Andrea Troyer, 14). . 88
2. Bagged Cats (Case 002: Anthony Miller, 18, John Fitzgerald, 19) . . . 89
3. The Fire Sacrifice (Case 003: Sheriff Kim Oja, 37) 90
4. Picnic in the Woods (Case 003, Addendum: Sheriff Kim Oja 37, Dan Weiss, 13, Andrea Troyer, 14, Anthony Miller, 18, and John Fitzgerald, 19) 91
5. No Refunds, No Returns (Case 004: John Fitzgerald, 19, Kathy Strong, 20) 92
6. Priest of the Strange (Case 005, Bilal Shaw, 33, Proprietor, Golden Dawn: An Esoteric, Theosophical and Masonic Bookstore). 93
7. Unholy Ghost (Case 005: Addendum, Bilal Shaw, 33) 95
8. Illegal Alien (Case 006: Ronaldo Alcalay, age unknown) 96
9. Lost Girl (Case 007: Nathan Potter, 26, Linda Goldman, 33) 97
10. Revelation Now (Transcript: NSA Radio Intercept, Speaker Thought to Be Bilal Shaw, 33). 98
11. New Under the Sun (Case 008: Brian Turner, Infantry Team Leader, 40) 99
12. Diary Entry: Brian Turner, in the Bunker 101
13. Diary Entry: Brian Turner, in the Bunker 101
14. Final Diary Entry: Kim Oja, in the Bunker. 102

103 CAPTAIN FANTASTIC WIZARD OF SCIENCE AND THE QUEST FOR THE NEW UNIVERSE

1. Captain Fantastic in "Among the Flat Earthers!" 105
2. Captain Fantastic in "Mutiny in Space!" 105
3. Captain Fantastic in "Lost in Space!" 106
4. Captain Fantastic in "The Wreck of the Space Cruiser Santa María!" . 107
5. Captain Fantastic in "Trapped in Sargasso Space!" 108
6. Captain Fantastic in "The Paradise Planet!" 109
7. Captain Fantastic in "The Savages of Paradise!" 110
8. Captain Fantastic in "Cannibal Planet!" 111
9. Captain Fantastic in "Strange Gods!" 112
10. Captain Fantastic in "Return to the Paradise Planet!" 113
11. Captain Fantastic in "The Planet of Women!" 114

115 the TOMB in the WOODS

1. Prologue 116
2. In a Forest Savage, Rough, and Stern 117
3. Each Open Archway Breathes Out Clutching Dread 118
4. Just Puppets on a Stage of Darkness 118
5. I Hear the Darkness Whispering 120
6. Giant Coils of Darkness Winding 121
7. The Climb Out of the Underworld 122

123 THE PEOPLE IN THE WALL

1. The Doors of His Face 124
2. Library of Fear 125
3. The Turn of the Screw 126
4. My Boyfriend Was a Zombie 127
5. The People in the Wall 128
6. Mirror House 130
7. The Inbred Fools! 131
8. The Death Bed 133
9. The Mirror Vampire 133
10. The Escape 134
11. Hypocrite lecteur,—mon semblable,—mon frère! 136

ACKNOWLEDGMENTS 138

PULP: A MODERN MYTHOLOGY

Pulp Sonnets is based on decades of research into Victorian sensation novels, Gothic literature, pulp narratives, B movies, and comics, from which came so many genres of popular fiction. What is great about such "lowbrow" genres is that they are unrepentant fun. I've tried to make my sonnet sequences fun as well — but repentant fun. After all, what was enjoyable in 1930 in *Weird Tales* or *Amazing Stories* can be rough fare for a contemporary audience. So in these poems I turn the mirror back on the act of storytelling to cross-examine space-opera colonial narratives, hard-boiled gender stereotypes of the femme fatale and damsel in distress, and sexualized horror-movie violence.

I do so because these stories are still important reflections of our culture. They reveal deep workings of the American psyche. And they are our modern mythology: the epics, divinties, and heroes of Greece may have largely faded from popular consciousness, yet mythic tales remain the stuff of our dreams. For cunning Odysseus, we substitute the picaresque adventures of Dashiell Hammett's wily Continental Op and his case-hardened progeny. For Hercules, we have Conan and the Incredible Hulk. For Oedipus solving the riddle of the Sphinx, we have the modern detective, Sam Spade. The gods of Mount Olympus have reincarnated as superheroes in tights and capes. The minotaur, hydra, and harpies have given way to successive monstrous generations, from Mary Shelley's Frankenstein and Bram Stoker's Dracula to the fiends of H. P. Lovecraft's Cthulhu circle of horror writers. The creators of these works were aware that they were creating a new mythology. In fact, the subtitle of Shelley's *Frankenstein* is *The Modern Prometheus,* and the underpinning of Hammett's classic detective novel *Red Harvest* is the Arthurian myth of the Fisher King and the Wasteland. What blockbuster movie or imaginative television series does not have its roots in the classic pulp genres?

In his article "Caviar and Bread Again," William Carlos Williams writes that the poet can through "a magnificent organization of those materials his age has placed before him . . . recreate it — the collective world. . . ." The poems in *Pulp Sonnets* seek to strike the pop-culture materials of our age against the flint of the sonnet form, to see what sparks will fly.

Tony Barnstone
Whittier College, 2015

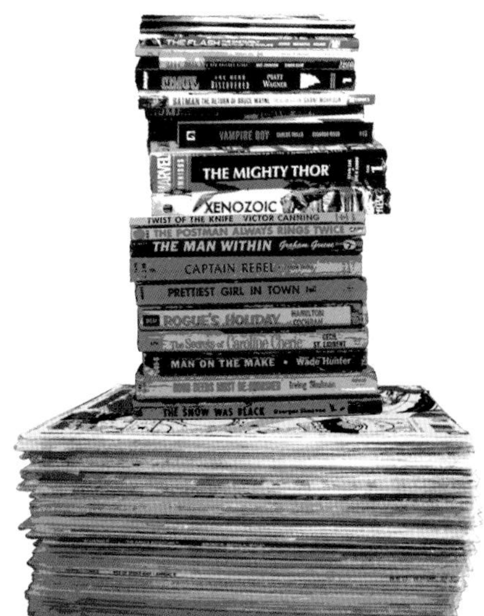

"We should have hanged him long ago," gibbered Publius. "No good can come of poets . . ."

—from "The Phoenix on the Sword"
by Robert E. Howard

KILLERS *and* TRAMPS

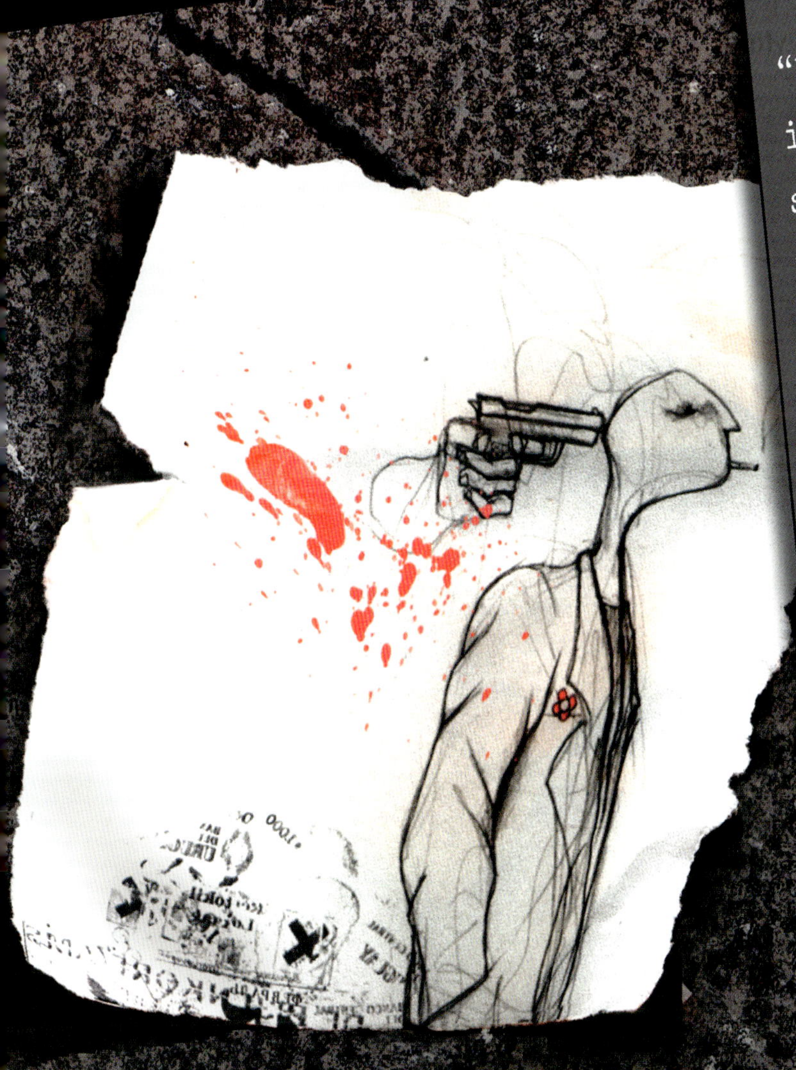

"What sense does it all make? What sort of God would put us here in this goddamned, stinking slaughterhouse of a world? Some guy that likes to tear the wings off flies?"

—from ***Nightmare Alley*** by William Lindsay Gresham

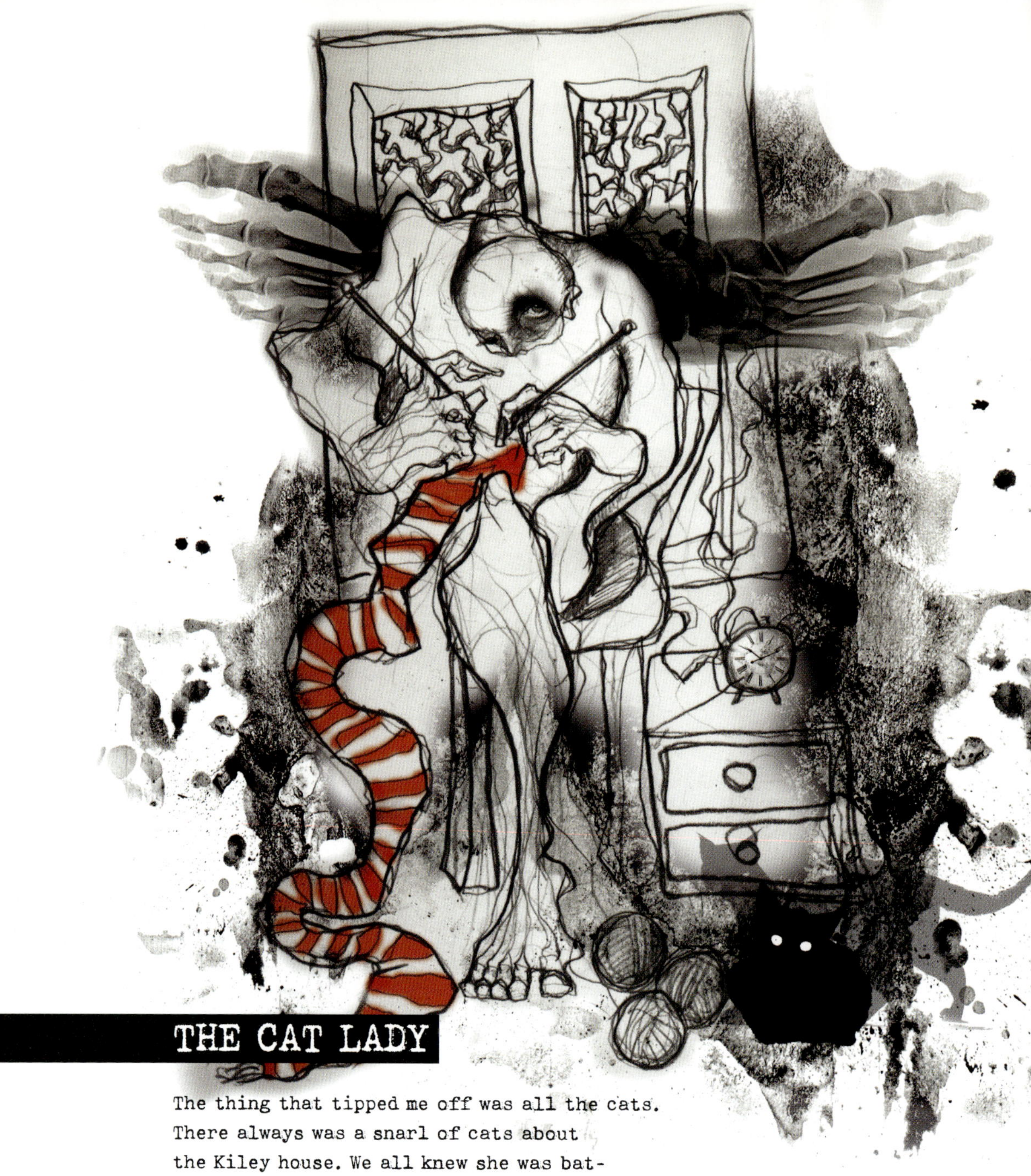

THE CAT LADY

The thing that tipped me off was all the cats.
There always was a snarl of cats about
the Kiley house. We all knew she was bat-
shit from how she let plants and grass grow out
until the place was Africa, with ways
worn through savannah grass. I doubt
that anyone went through that tangled maze
up to the house for months until the rude
caterwauling began. After five days
I knocked. The door swung open. The cats had chewed
and clawed the cupboards, but they were shut fast,
had picked squirrel bones among the sealed canned food.
And other bones. One thing I'll say for cats,
they love you so much, they will eat you last.

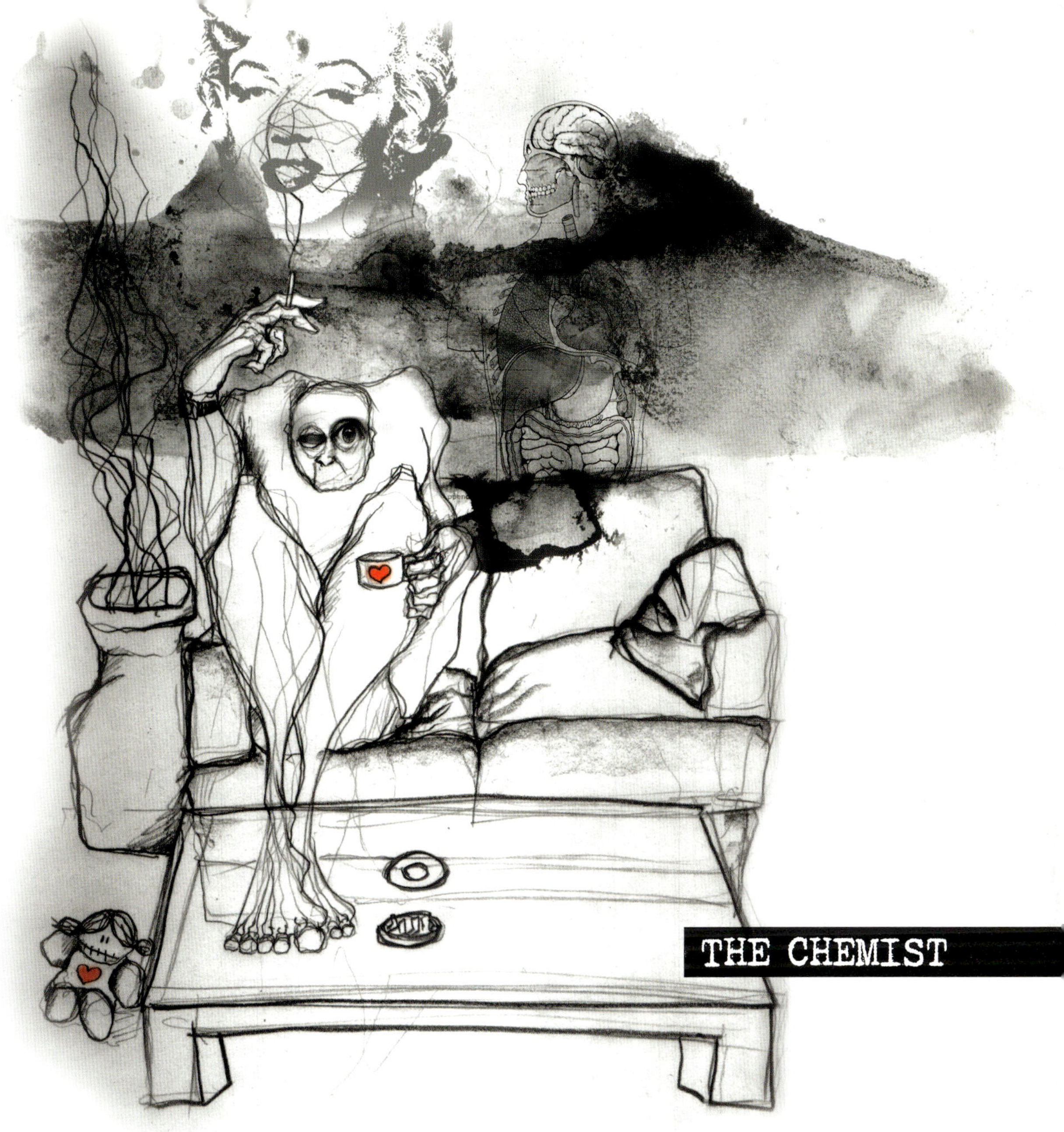

THE CHEMIST

With my glass mask tied tightly, I grind,
I grind away, and moisten, mash up paste,
pound at the powder, while smoke twirls. I taste
the almond scent right through the mask, and find
my mouth is watering. Invisible
death: it resides in baths where you might drown,
and copper wires, careening cars are full
of it, and guns. There's death throughout this town.
He is with her; and they know that I know
where they are, what they do: they believe
I cry at home, while they laugh, laugh at me.
He says he wants divorce, just wants to go.
I sift the fine white powder through a sieve
into the sugar bowl. I'll set him free.

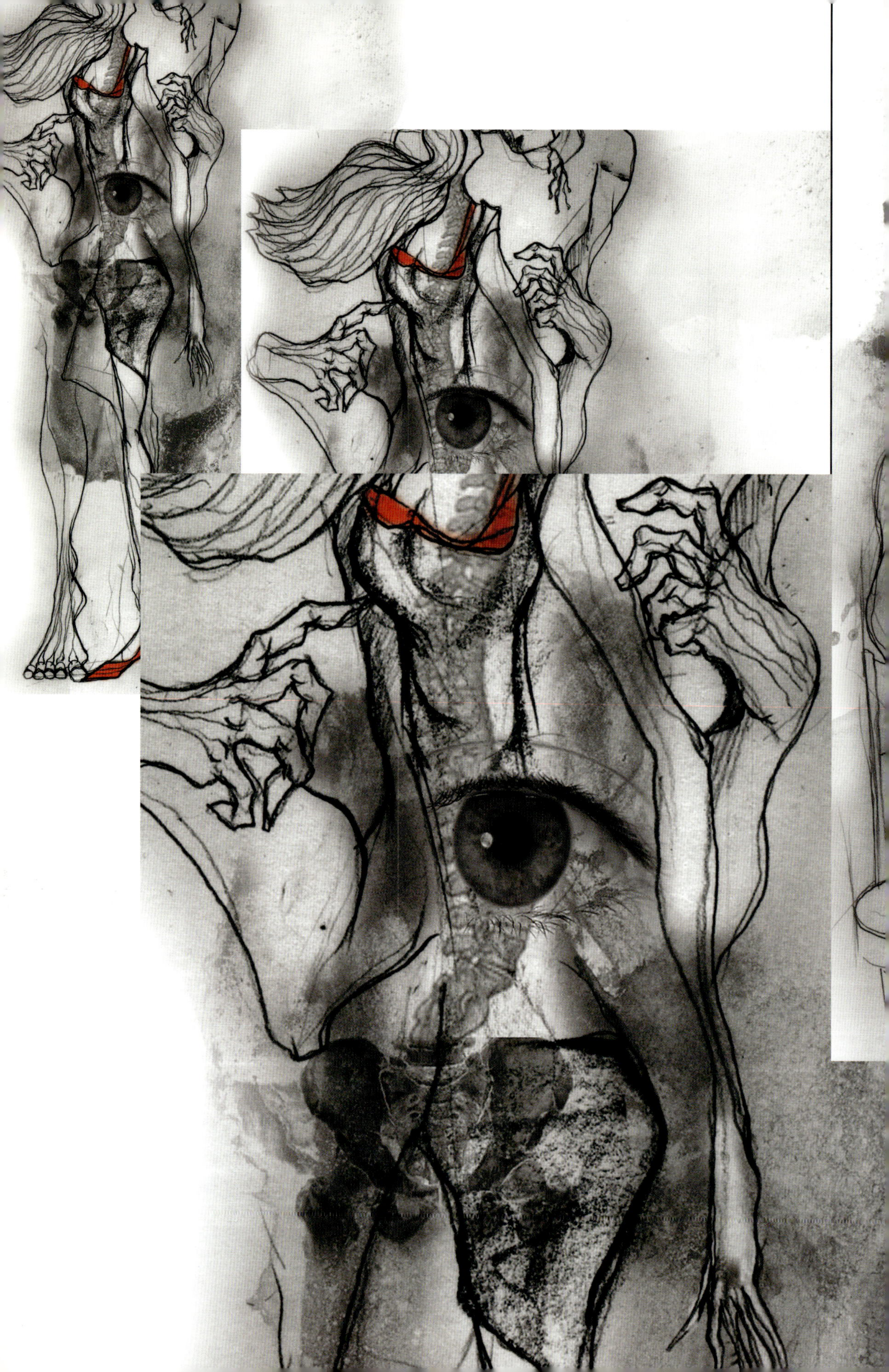

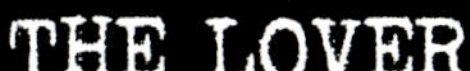

THE LOVER

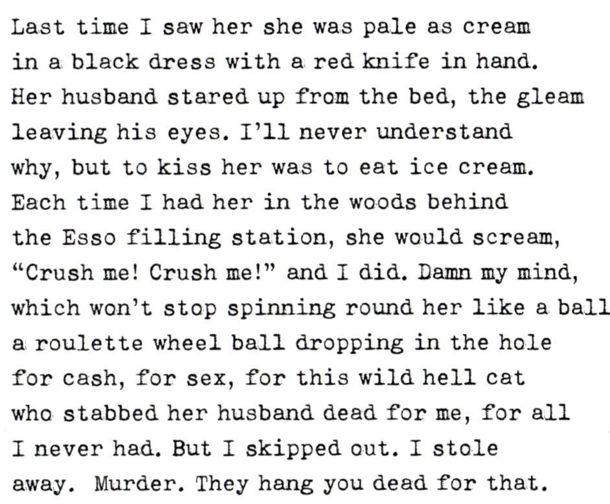

Last time I saw her she was pale as cream
in a black dress with a red knife in hand.
Her husband stared up from the bed, the gleam
leaving his eyes. I'll never understand
why, but to kiss her was to eat ice cream.
Each time I had her in the woods behind
the Esso filling station, she would scream,
"Crush me! Crush me!" and I did. Damn my mind,
which won't stop spinning round her like a ball,
a roulette wheel ball dropping in the hole
for cash, for sex, for this wild hell cat
who stabbed her husband dead for me, for all
I never had. But I skipped out. I stole
away. Murder. They hang you dead for that.

NEW YORK BLUES

I listen. Listen to the city sing
New York, New York, helluva town. I hear
through the thin wall a radio simmering
The Bronx is up, the Battery's down, and tear
a nail off with my teeth, send my mind
out through the keyhole like a giant ear
and listen: not here yet; peer through the blind:
a taxi's headlights rake the street, two people
embrace in a dark doorway. Will they find
her body soon? I am in a deep hole.
She's underneath the garbage in a bin.
I listen. Whispers. Shapes flit by the peephole.
There's one fix for the sort of fix I'm in:
I gulp down all the pills, chase them with gin.

NIGHT HAS A THOUSAND EYES

Going home, he walked along the river,
looking at the stars and at the water.
It made the stars seem brighter when the water
caught them upside down and made them shiver.
They must have brought out the reserves: such light,
woven like a gleaming fish-scale cloth.
Something winked as though a star had dropped.
He pinched at the small spark and snagged a bright
diamond ring, large stone, and of good water.
Leaves rustled round his feet—no, dollar bills.
And there: a lady's handbag. Then the chills:
By a stone plinth, on the bridge, a woman tottered.
Rushing, he snatched her back. He asked, "But why?"
She looked at him as if in pity and,
"They're watching," she sighed. "You won't understand,
will you? Oh, shut them out. The eyes. The eyes."

A WOMAN LIKE A BULLET

I switch the light bulb off but dreams keep streaming
from dark eye bulbs, just nerve-sparks, neural specters.
And somewhere in those fires of shape and seeming
is you, a woman shaped in beauty's vectors,
a pistol in your silk-gloved, fine-boned hand
pointed approximately right at my left
ventricle. Femme, why be so fatal and
so beautiful? Why let the mortal heft
of steel in hand compose the denouement
of our dark romance? Yes, I know you are
just nerve-sparks cast upon the eyelids' screen
—you left this life, this man, this tenement—
but dreaming makes "you were" become "you are."
I feel you still: a bullet in the spleen.

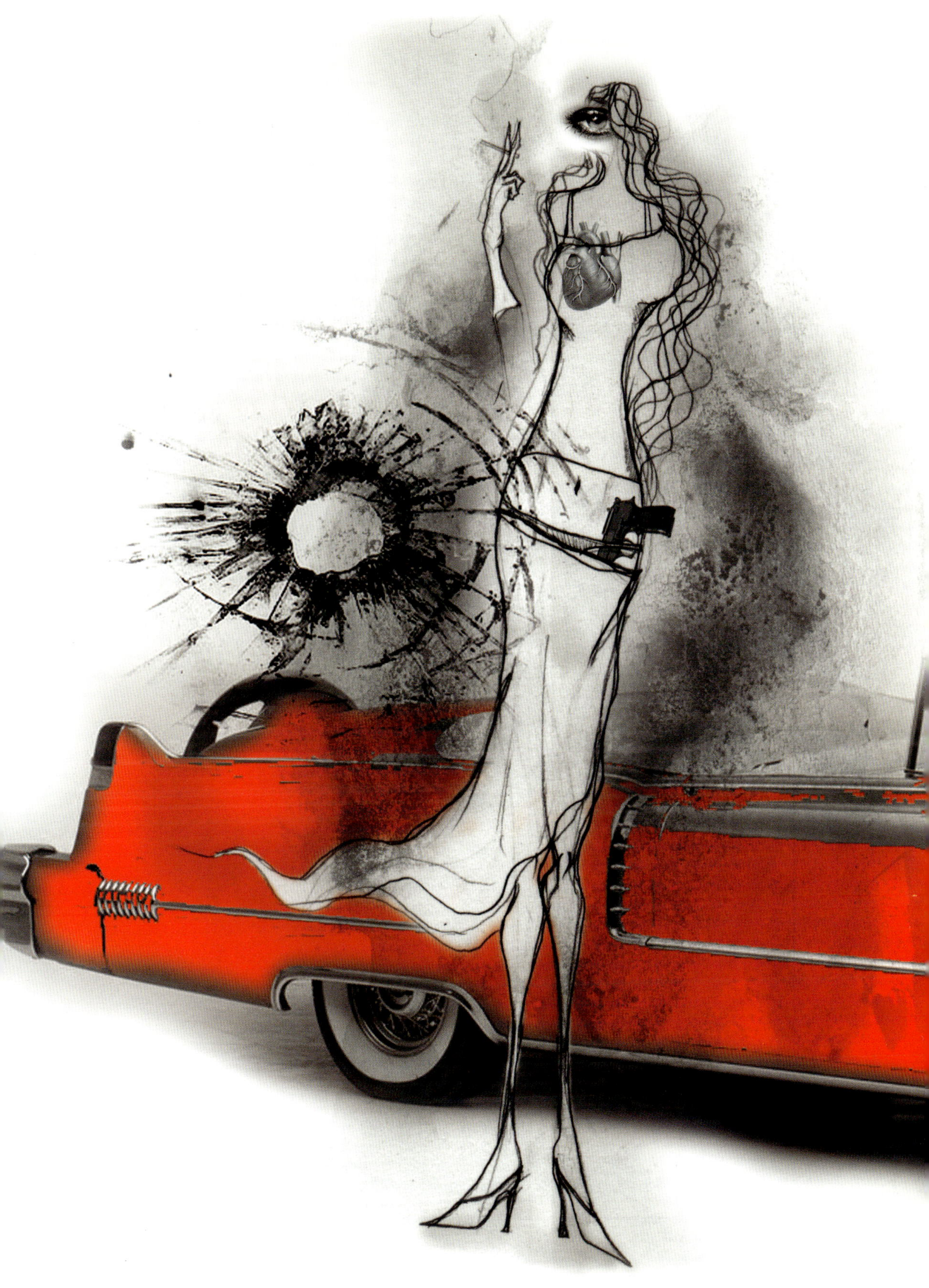

MEXICAN MOVIE, 1939

In dubious light we see the villain, El
Diablo, riding on a pale white horse.
A Devil lives inside this villain; hell
is Gila monsters coiled inside the bell
of the dead church, the late sun's bloody force
that casts a dubious light on Villa El
Descanso Rojo, by whose ochre shell
Diablo reins his horse, and sighs. A worse
Devil lives inside: our villain's hell
is named Rosita Cruz, for whom he fell
in lust, for whom he took the villain's course.
In dubious light we see the villanelle
Diablo witched up, hoping it would spell
the end of her resistance, but of course
the Devil lives inside this villa; hell
is beauty dead to poems, to him: *Why, tell*
me, Dios, why so much pain? Are you the source?
In dubious light, who knows the villain's hell?
What Devil lives inside this villanelle?

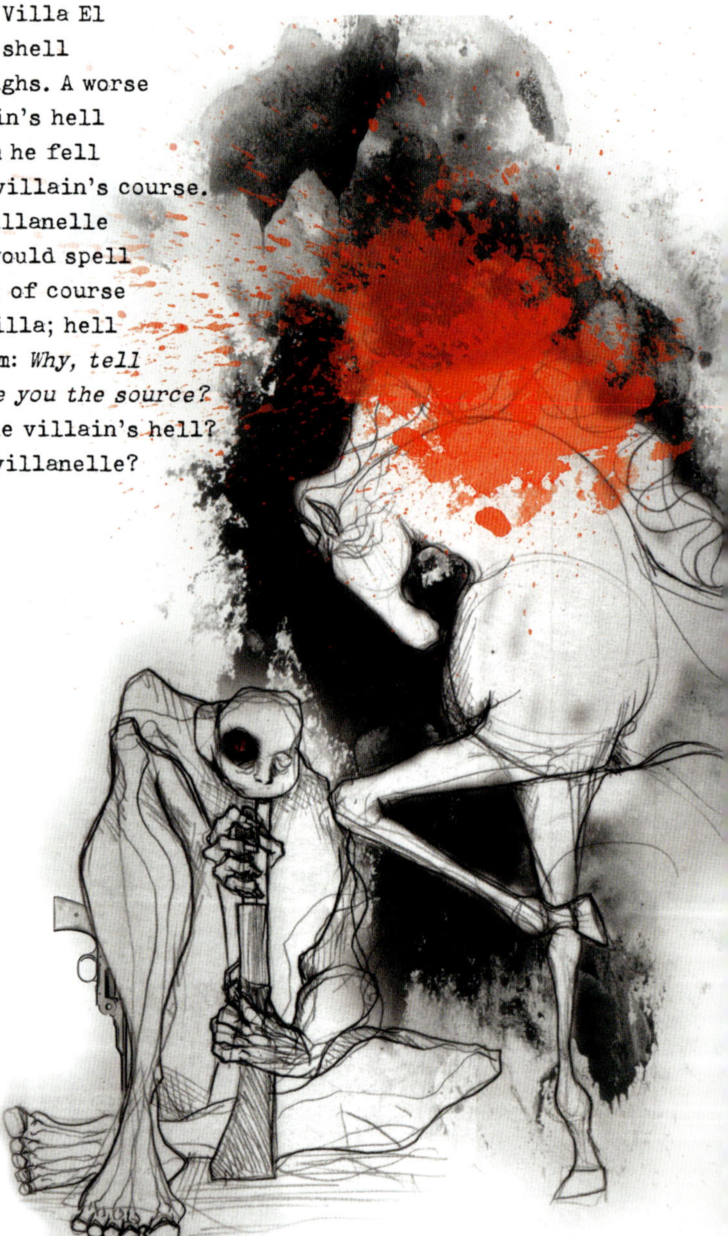

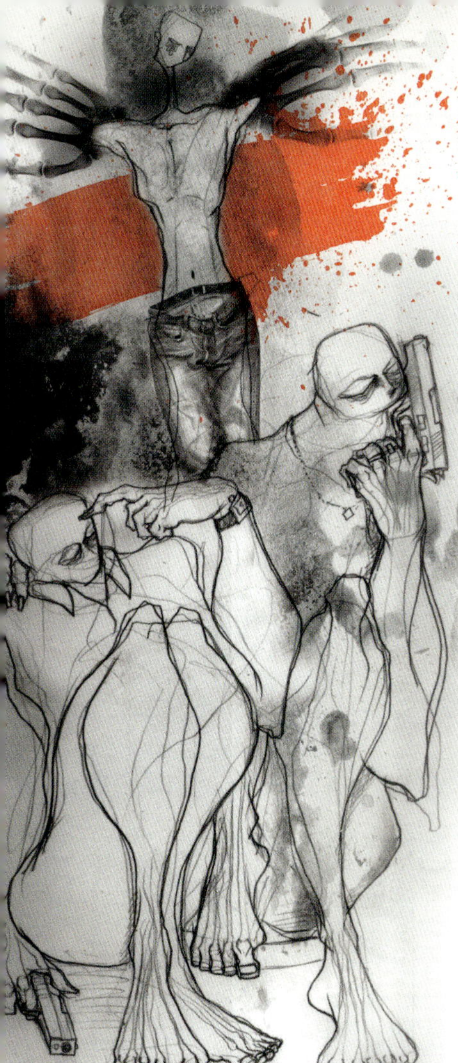

THE CHOP SHOP

1. A Stand-Up Guy

"You want a hand with that?" I ask and plop
the thing down on the bench in front of Bill.
He jumps back, cursing, though in our chop shop
we've both seen enough hacked off hands to fill
a wax museum. "Fuck. You fuck," Bill says,
"Not everything's a joke." Nick made us kill
one of our crew from in the glory days,
though I told Nick he wouldn't have confessed,
that he was stand-up. Nick gave an ice gaze,
imagining an icepick in my chest,
I guess, and so I joked, "He won't be stand-
ing long." "We killed a *friend,*" says Bill, unmanned.
"I *know,*" I snap. "You want me all depressed?"
I trim the fingers from the other hand.

2. Italian Sandwich Meat

My job was trimming fingers from the hand
while Bill was bagging up the head and feet,
saying, "Shit-fuck!" The thing to understand
is this: the torso in a plastic sheet
with the heart knifed to stop the pump, the head
shot twice then wrapped up in a towel, were meat,
just meat, not Joey Scars. Joe Scars was dead,
and swearing wasn't going to bring him back.
"Which sandwich do you want to have?" I said.
Bill still was cursing at the bench. "We whack
our best friend and you're thinking ham and rye?"
His hands was shaking, fumbling for his pack
of Kents. Just one more job: "Bill, you know I
like you," I said, and shot him in the eye.

INSECTS AND CIGARETTES

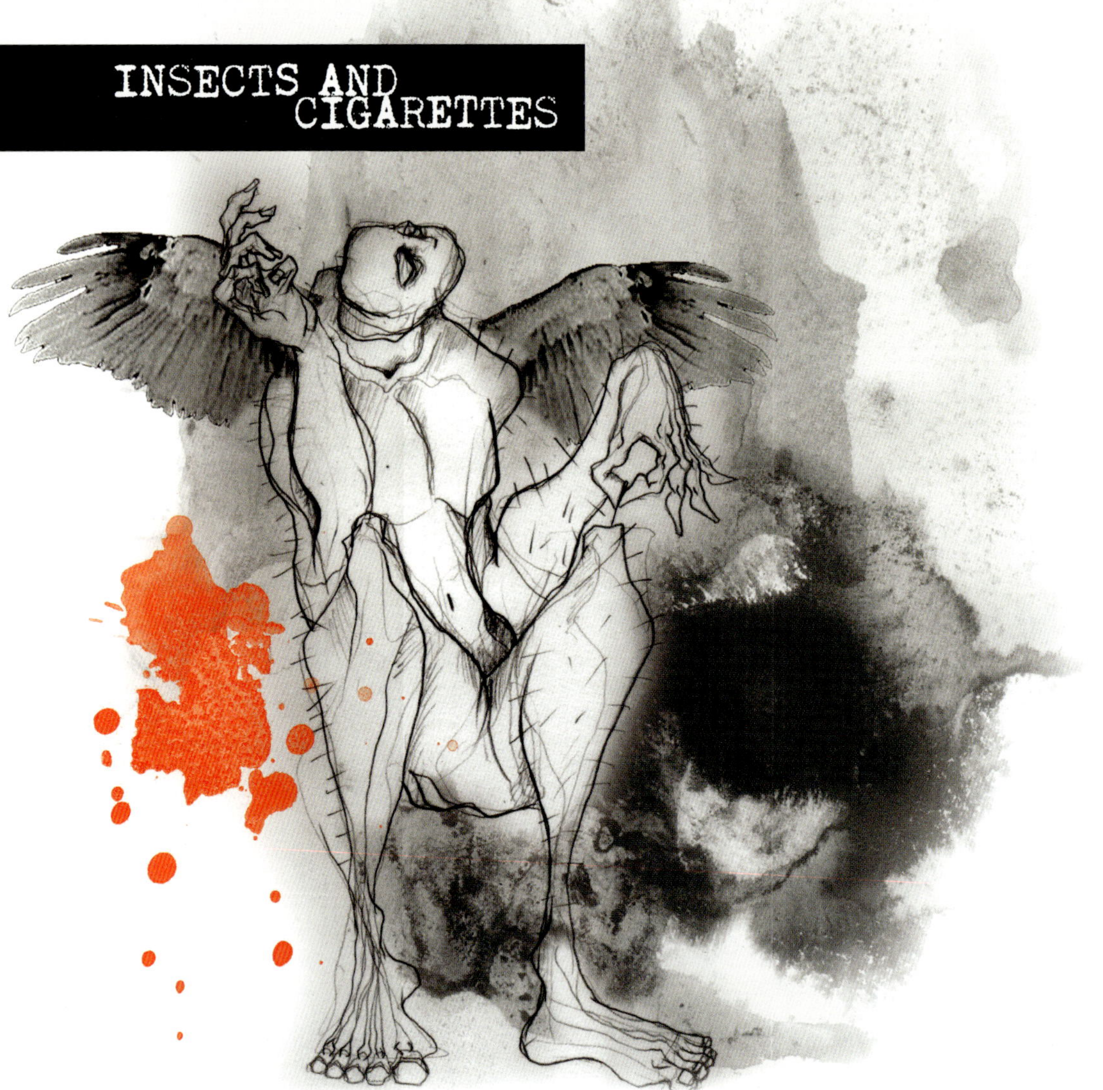

1. A Fat Black Tick

Out of the hair on my forearm I pick
a fat black tick and hold it in my nails,
crushing in slowly while the small legs kick.
I crush it harder till the armor fails
then rub the bloody shell into my pants.
It's instinct from way back when we had tails
—to kill the crawling insects, fleas and ants
and cockroaches that try to scurry free
to safety while the giants do their dance
and, godlike, roar incomprehensibly.
And God? That sadist. Stay out of his reach.
He pulls the wings off dragonflies. A flea
like you or me, he'd smush then flick the meat
away, the way a fat man picks his teeth.

2. Revelation

I flip a cockroach on its armored back.
Its legs keep scrambling, try to grip the air,
and it will run like that till Christ comes back
because there's nothing solid to grip there
and Christ ain't coming back. Just smush the thing,
I think. Just snuff its tiny light. Somewhere
good people live, and they have everything
to keep them good. They're kind because their kind
don't hold their one true love imagining
the skin peeled back, the skull inside. My mind
can't get a grip, cockroach on its back.
I poke the thing and watch it spin. Some kind
of God has killed the lights. We'll run through black
till Christ comes back, and Christ ain't coming back.

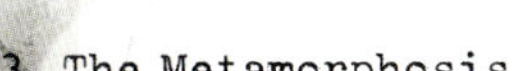

3. The Metamorphosis

I put a cockroach in my mug and watch
it scrabble at the glass that keeps it trapped,
and think, yeah, there I am. I'm a wet match,
spilled beer, an insect. All my life I've tapped
against the glass and climbed and slid back in
and scrabbled on my back. I still am trapped
when I walk out and like the Little Match Girl, thin
and cold, watch all the mink coat people pass.
A cockroach climbs the glass and slides back in;
no exit for a bug. But to break glass,
a man can swing a rock. Now let's take us.
I'm cold. Hand me your fur coat, buddy. Pass
me the purse, miss. I've got a gun. No, shush.
No tears. I know it's hard. Be generous.

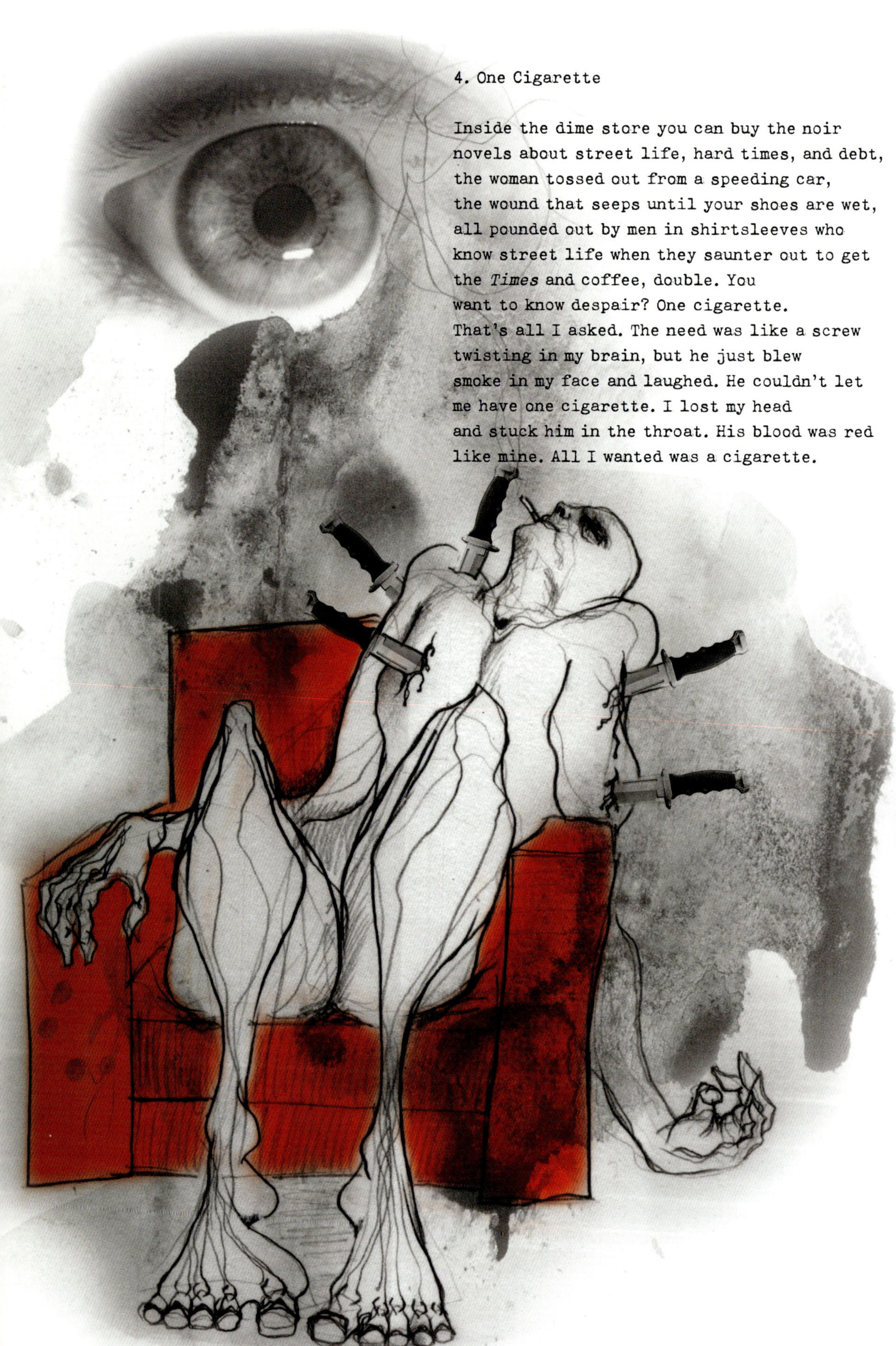

4. One Cigarette

Inside the dime store you can buy the noir
novels about street life, hard times, and debt,
the woman tossed out from a speeding car,
the wound that seeps until your shoes are wet,
all pounded out by men in shirtsleeves who
know street life when they saunter out to get
the *Times* and coffee, double. You
want to know despair? One cigarette.
That's all I asked. The need was like a screw
twisting in my brain, but he just blew
smoke in my face and laughed. He couldn't let
me have one cigarette. I lost my head
and stuck him in the throat. His blood was red
like mine. All I wanted was a cigarette.

THE BALLAD OF DOTTIE AND PETE

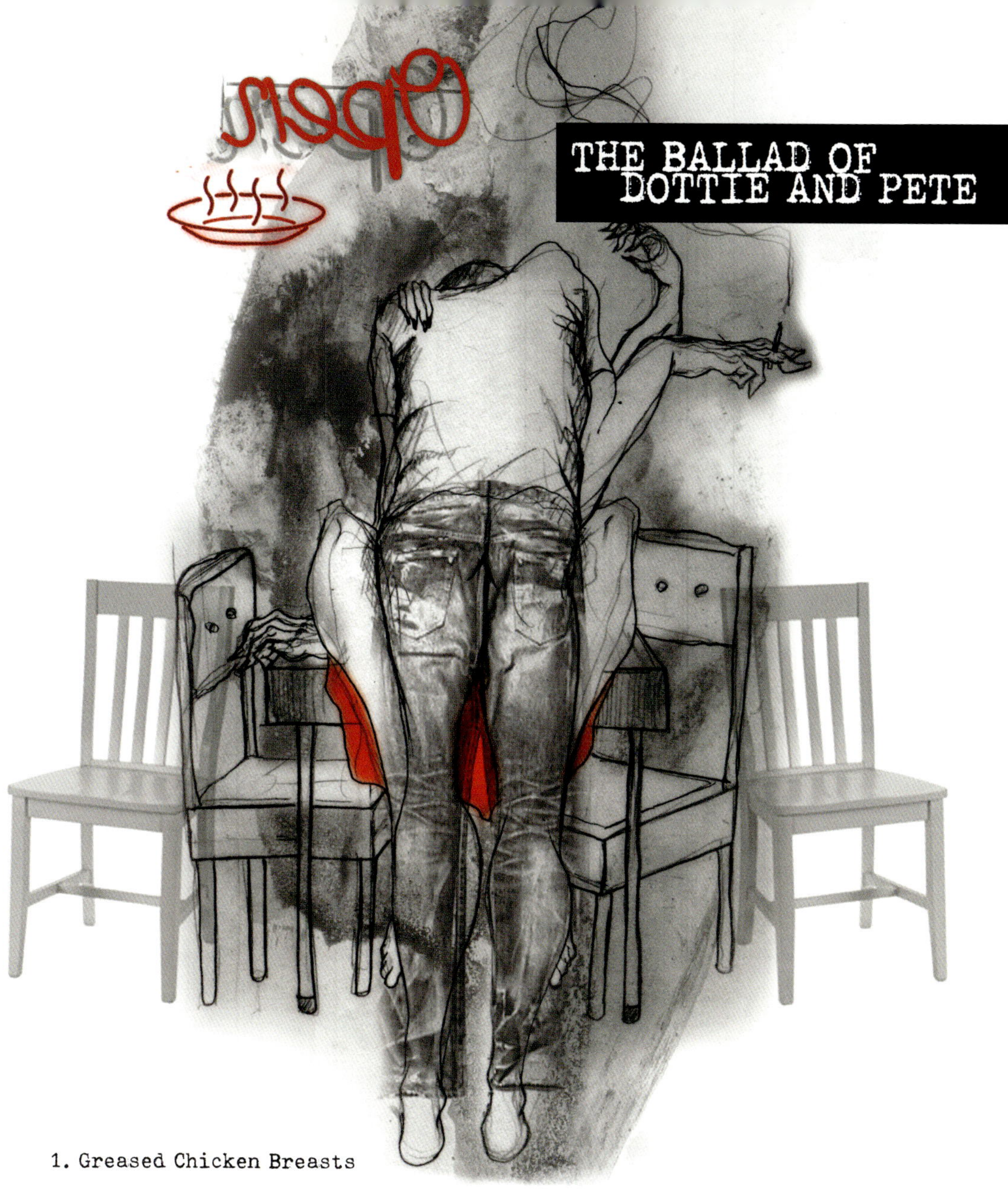

1. Greased Chicken Breasts

I let the fry chef take me on the table,
there in the grease. Honey, it was fantastic,
like root canal. You find out what you're able
to stomach. Would you act enthusiastic
while some slob with a chicken chest was rutting
you in the grease, honey, and say, *Fantastic,*
Bill, if you'd starved like I have? When Bill's cutting
meat to fry up, the man's sexy enough.
I don't eat slop; it's chicken breasts for rutting.
Sure, I might stand on principle, and tough
it out, sure I might say, *I'm not a piece*
of meat, might say *No man's sexy enough*
for that. Sure, honey. But I've made my peace.
So I lie back, and take it in the grease.

2. Red Pickup

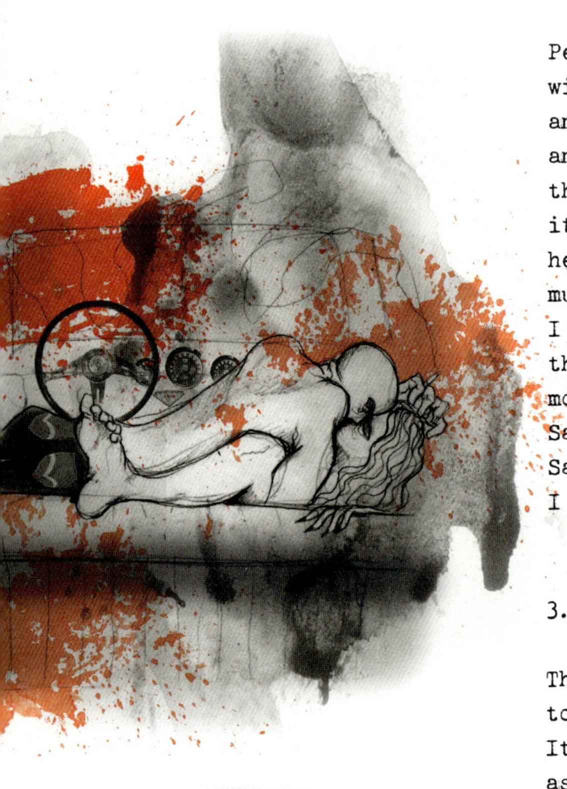

Pete clattered up in a red pickup truck
with rusted rims and blood across the dash
and seat. I knew right off that he was stuck,
and rolled the garage open so to stash
the pickup till nighttime when we could hose
it off and not be seen. "You got some cash?"
he asked and crushed my bosom against those
muscles of his I always liked back when
I was his girl in Texas. Then I chose
the straight life, shacking up with Bill. Now ten
months later who shows up and grabs my meat?
Same repeat-trouble Pete I left back then.
Same handsome, crazy-look-in-his-eyes Pete.
I let him have me on the bloody seat.

3. Chopped Meat

The thing that does us in is Pete decides
to chop his head off with a spade. The creep.
It's not enough we killed old Bill? Besides,
as far as I's concerned, the man can keep
his head, so long as we can have what fills
the cash box. Cash box, that's a joke. We reap
the whirlwind for four crinkled dollar bills
and change. And that's when Pete go gets the spade
from out the back. I lean against the grill
and cry while Pete goes at him with the blade.
Pete laughs and says, "I guess he lost his head,"
and lifts Bill's by the hair. I was afraid.
That's why I phoned the cops on Pete, then fled.
Why do that when the man's already dead?

OPERATION RAGNAROK

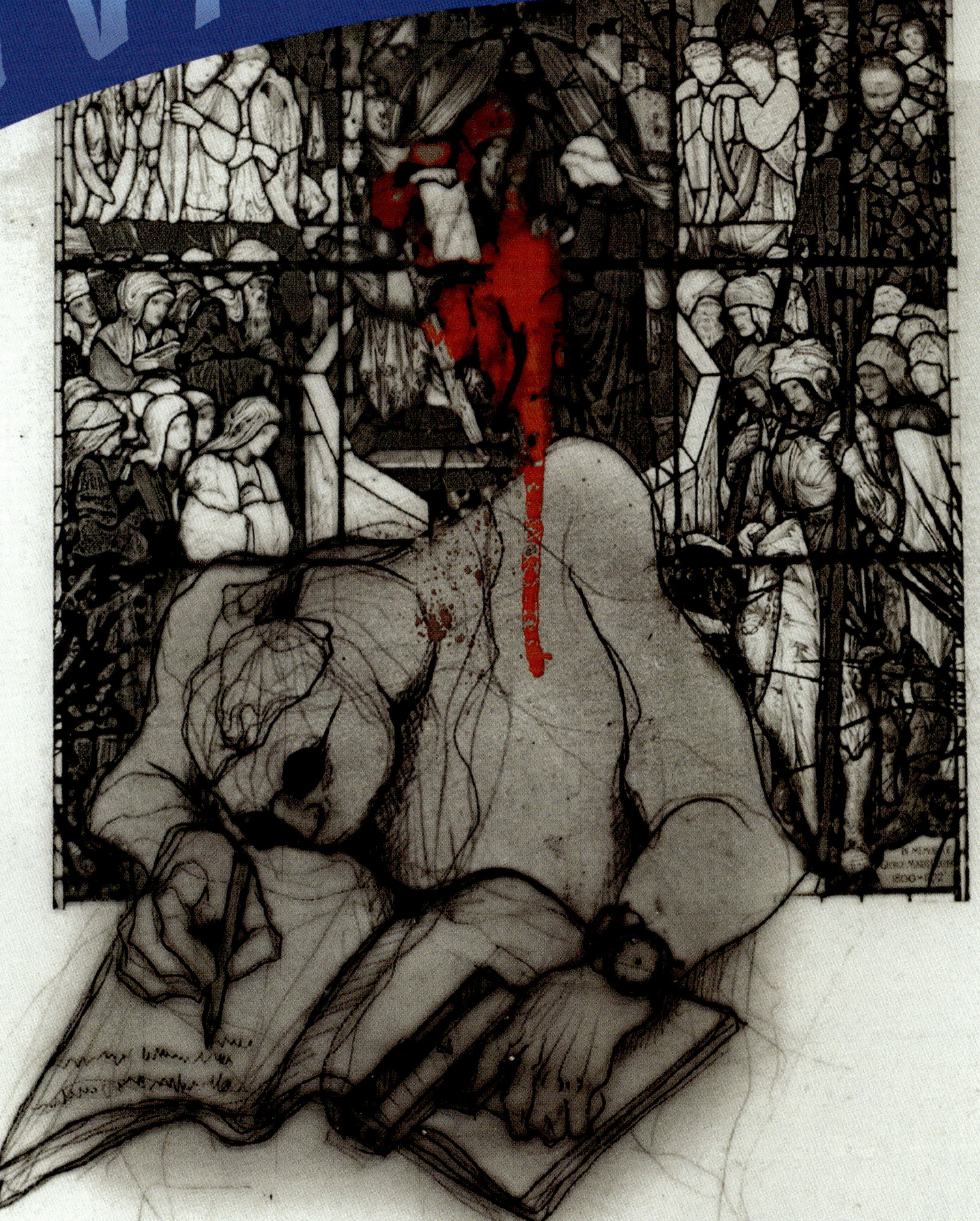

"It's not an easy thing to meet your maker."

—from *Blade Runner*

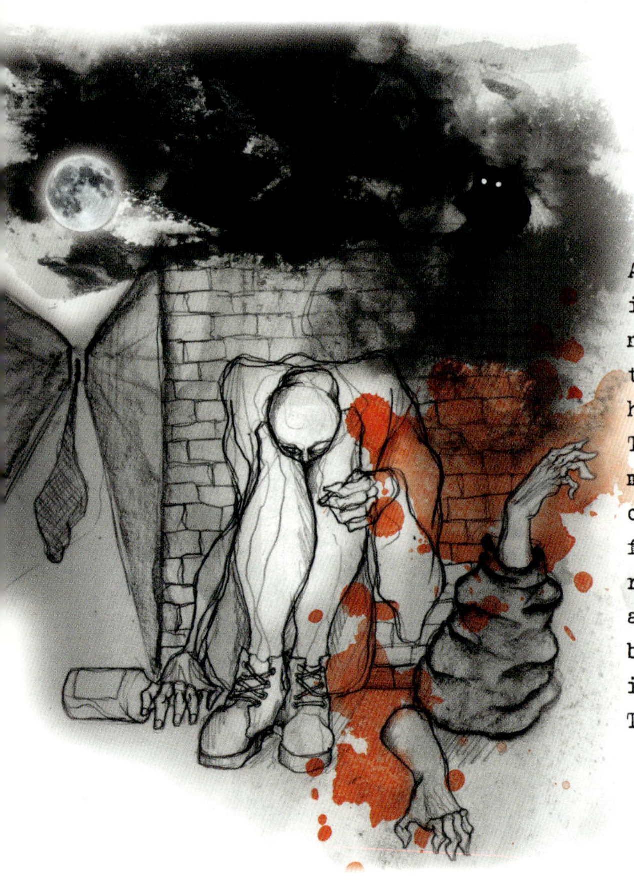

1. A Back Alley in Honningsvåg

An old drunk sailor, sleeping in his boots,
is catching tigers in red weather, while
nearby a squalling yellow kitten roots
through black-bagged garbage. I try to dial
headquarters on my secret wristwatch phone.
The signal's dead, as dead as Sven and Jan,
my contacts, sliced like reindeer meat. Alone
of all my crew, I got out of Sudan,
for what? To die in Norway? One more body
run through the saws inside the factory
and canned? I'd like to understand. I'm nobody,
but who are you, assassin? Mystery,
it's all a mystery. The film is cut.
Thrashing awake, the sailor mumbles, "What?"

2. Wet Work

"What's next?" I ask the sky. No answer, but
I detect motion: Sigrid in a door-
way. "Come in quickly or . . ." The rest is cut
off suddenly. She turns, a long-necked deer,
and leaps into my arms in fright. Behind
her I sense something dark, and there, an eye
that gleams with borrowed light, and so I find
both enemy and sorceress. I spy
the swift dark flight and dodge the knife. For miles
we run through rain. On the white yacht, I ask,
"Where is the microfilm?" Sigrid just smiles
and drops her robe. Wet skin, and it's my task
to dry her off. I put down my martini
to solve the riddle of her black bikini.

3. Death and the Author

Her arrogance of breasts in black bikini
nearly busts free of the vestigial cloth
as she dives for the gun. Too late. The teeny
flat black Beretta's in my hand. A moth-
like thought is fluttering inside my skull:
I have forgotten something — what? Of course,
the man with the glass eye! I must be dull
from loss of blood, can't dodge the sap's blunt force.
I turn and spin, falling. The moth's aflame
behind my eyes, two wings of fire that spread
till all the world is red. "Sigrid, you bitch!"
I groan. But still, why fall for her then blame
her for the fall? Who writes the tale I read?
With cheek to floor I watch my fingers twitch.

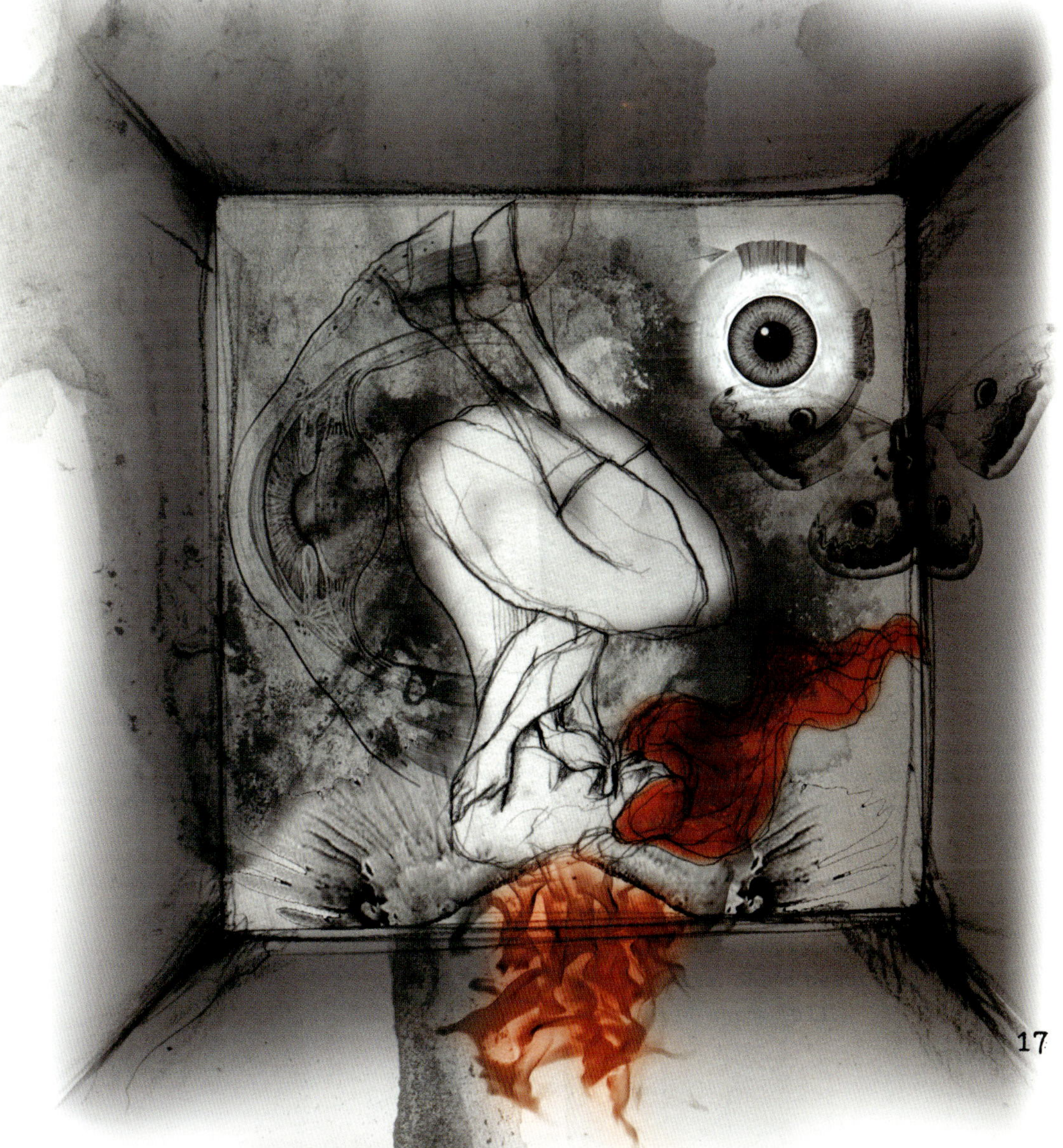

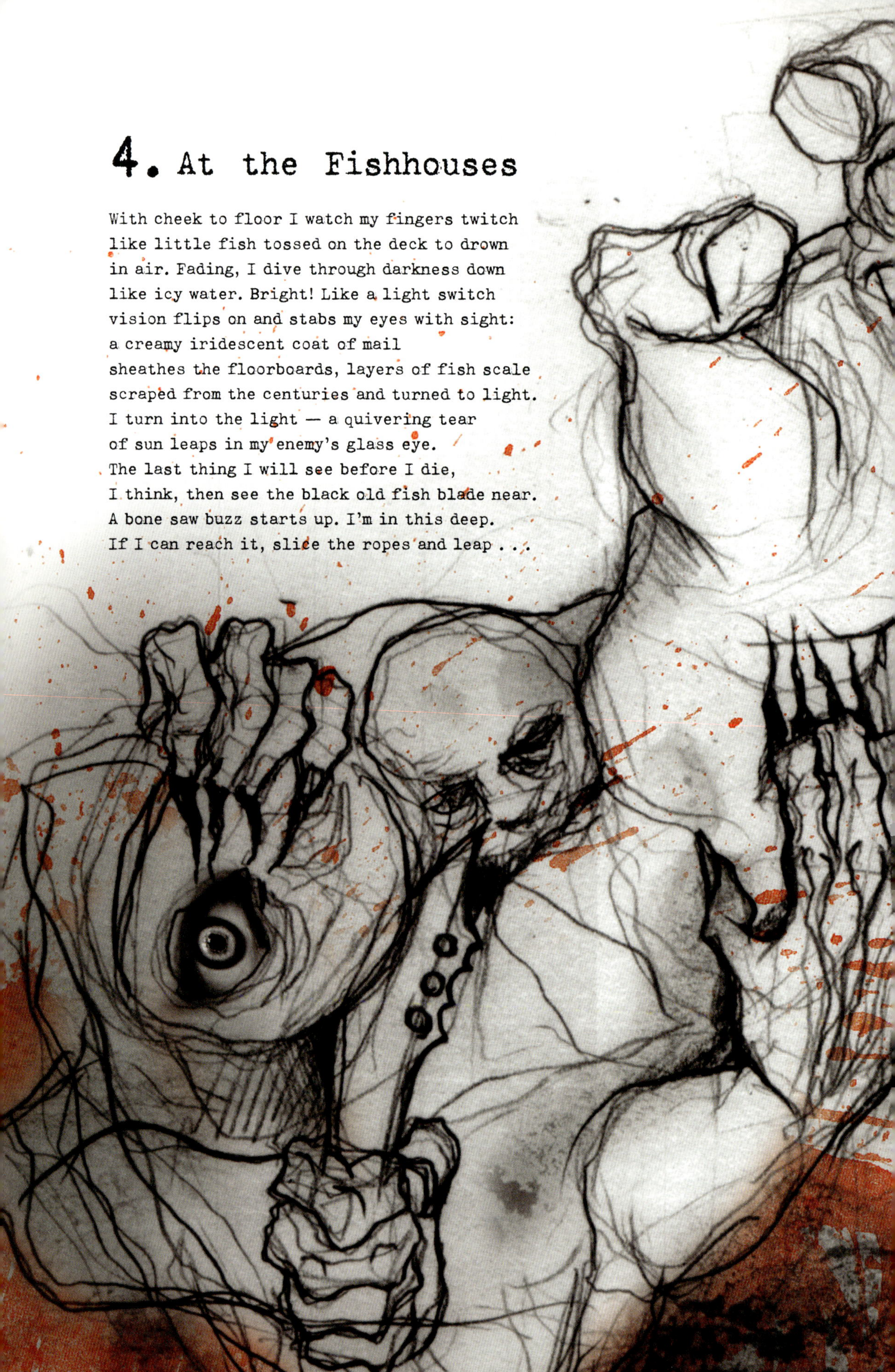

4. At the Fishhouses

With cheek to floor I watch my fingers twitch
like little fish tossed on the deck to drown
in air. Fading, I dive through darkness down
like icy water. Bright! Like a light switch
vision flips on and stabs my eyes with sight:
a creamy iridescent coat of mail
sheathes the floorboards, layers of fish scale
scraped from the centuries and turned to light.
I turn into the light — a quivering tear
of sun leaps in my enemy's glass eye.
The last thing I will see before I die,
I think, then see the black old fish blade near.
A bone saw buzz starts up. I'm in this deep.
If I can reach it, slice the ropes and leap . . .

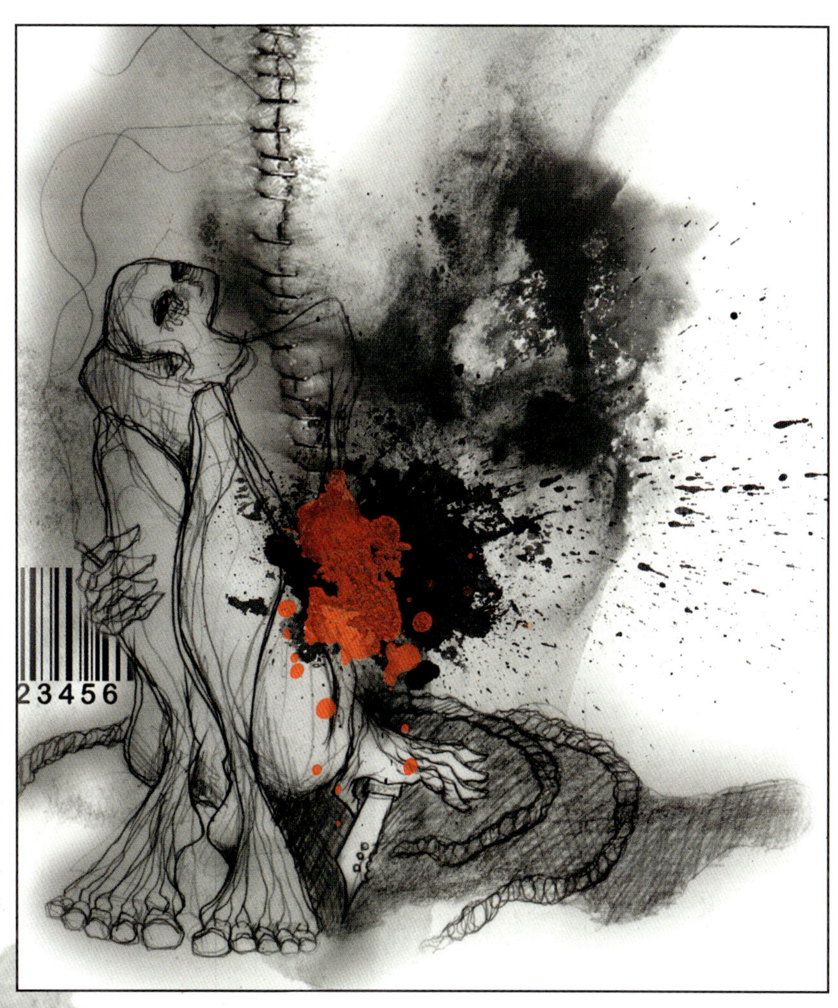

5. The Job

If I can reach it, slice the ropes and leap
with the slim worn fish blade, I might just live
through this part of the plot. There is no give
in the tight rope, but I still my breath, keep
as still as death, and use an ancient trick
I learned in Bangkok, wriggle to the knife,
breathe out, then slice, leap, fight — and save my life.
The man with the glass eye with a small flick
of light departs and leaves me with fish skin,
the stink of salmon, bright flecked herring scales
stuck to my arms. Leviathans, fish tales,
strange destiny, hair-breadth escapes, hairpin
plot twists, hair-raising peril — it's my job
to suffer at your hands, assassin, God.

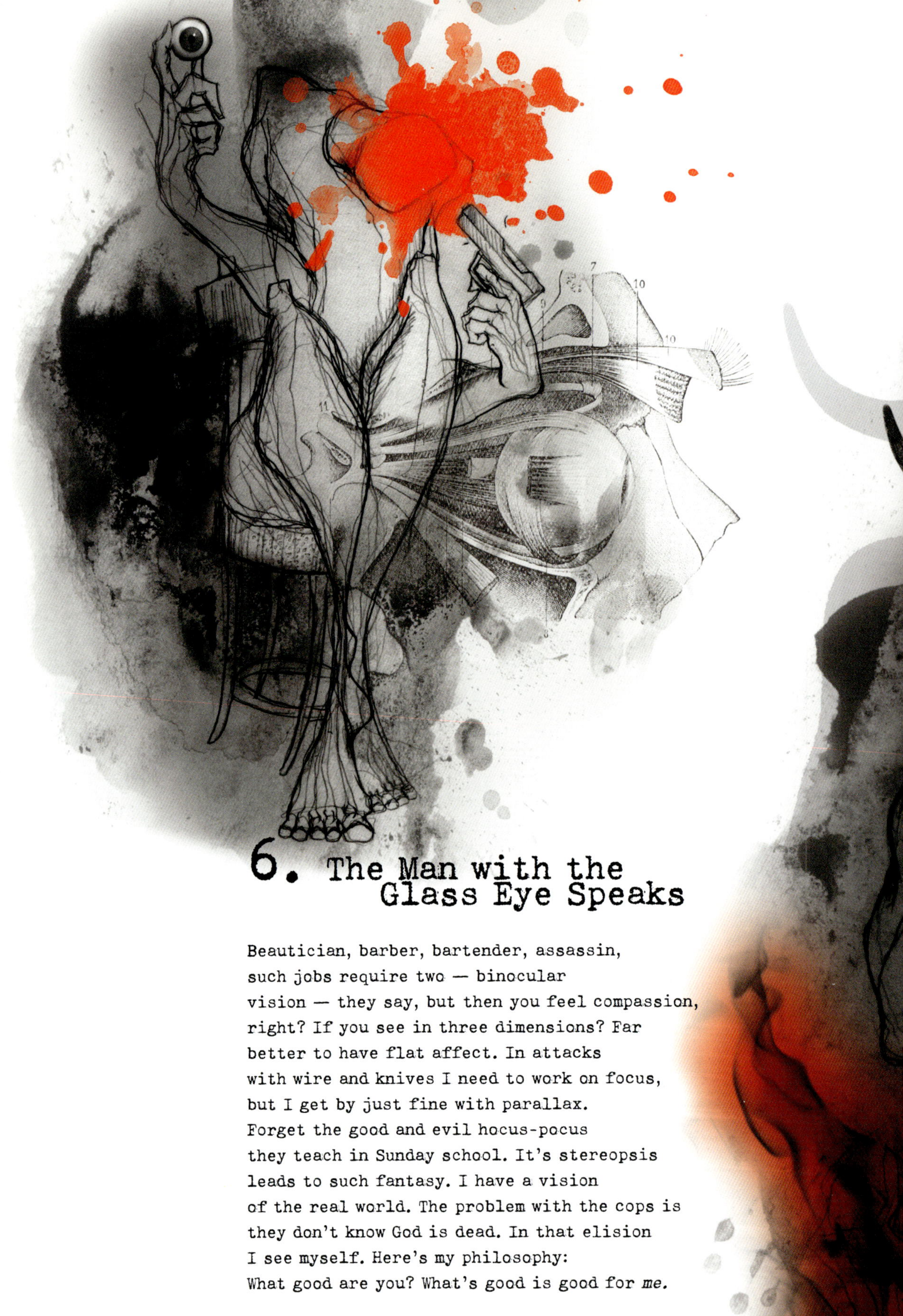

6. The Man with the Glass Eye Speaks

Beautician, barber, bartender, assassin,
such jobs require two — binocular
vision — they say, but then you feel compassion,
right? If you see in three dimensions? Far
better to have flat affect. In attacks
with wire and knives I need to work on focus,
but I get by just fine with parallax.
Forget the good and evil hocus-pocus
they teach in Sunday school. It's stereopsis
leads to such fantasy. I have a vision
of the real world. The problem with the cops is
they don't know God is dead. In that elision
I see myself. Here's my philosophy:
What good are you? What's good is good for *me.*

7. God Complex

I track them down at last. Well, good for me.
I fell for her, but rose again, was snuffed
a few times (so he thought) by old one-eye,
but I just won't stay dead. She's naked, cuffed
to the bedpost. He's naked, too, and reading
some dime store novel with his monocle
when I burst in. She screams, of course. I'm bleeding,
wobbly, but on my feet, and I am full
to choking with this Odin and his Norse
Valkyrie. I leave him bleeding from his other eye,
her cuffed, and set the fire. No more remorse.
I watch the cottage flame up the ice sky
from the white yacht. "It's Ragnarok!" I snort,
then gun the engines, heading out of port.

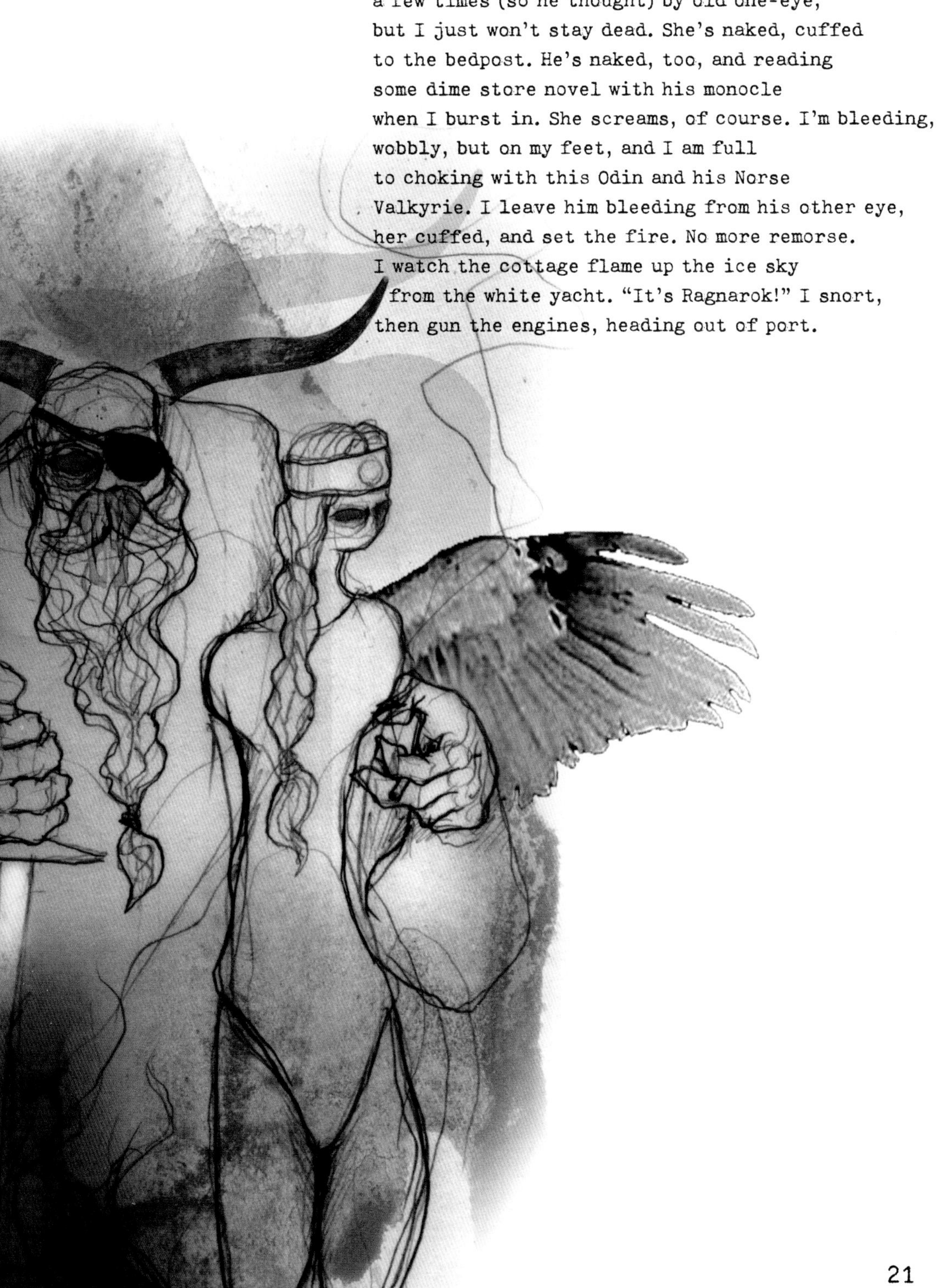

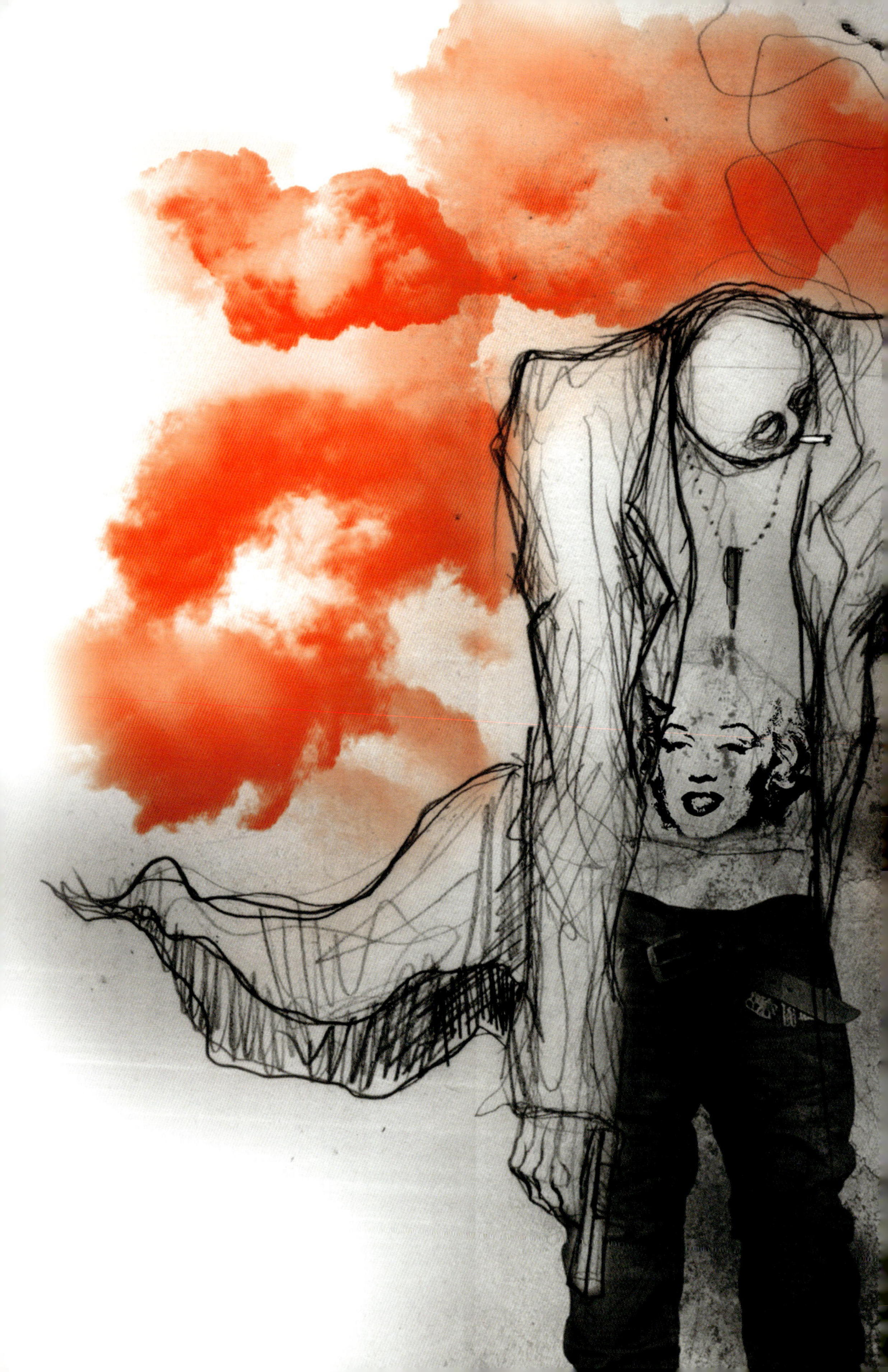

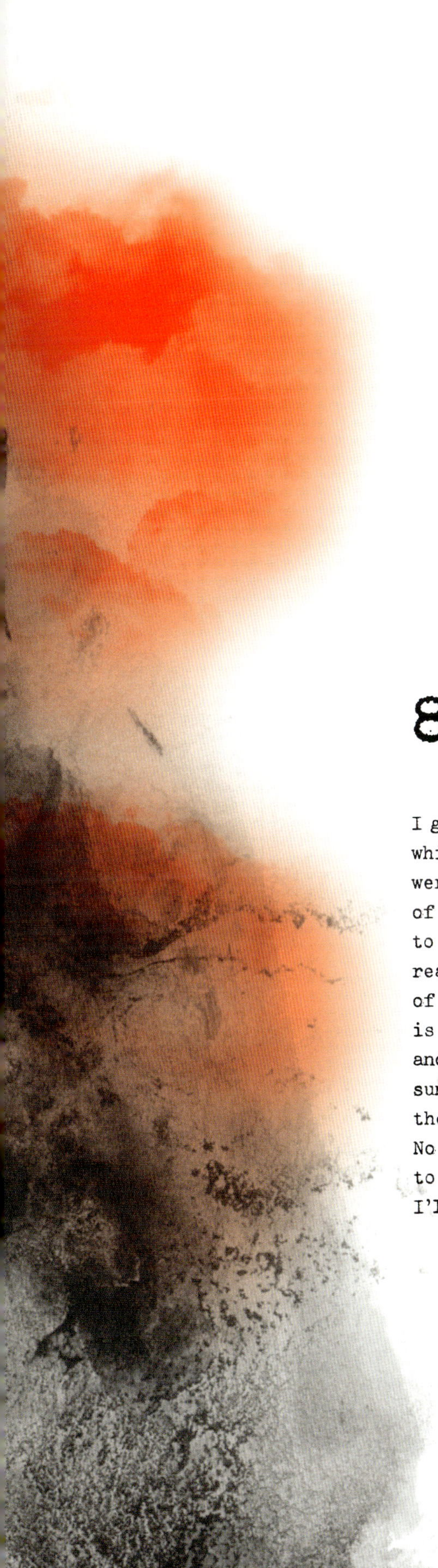

8. The Hermeneutics of Spycraft

I gun the engines, heading out of port
while great waves swell as if a giant snake
were coiling underwater. I'm just short
of understanding. What does it take
to read this ocean's face, read this sky,
read what my role is, who's behind this world
of murder? How to read. To be a spy
is to read well. I see shapes in clouds, furled
and unfurled in the wind. I watch the bleeding
sunset, as messy as a broken egg,
then load the microfilm and begin reading.
No good. It's gibberish. The final leg
to walk but I can't see the hidden road.
I'll find the big man if I crack this code.

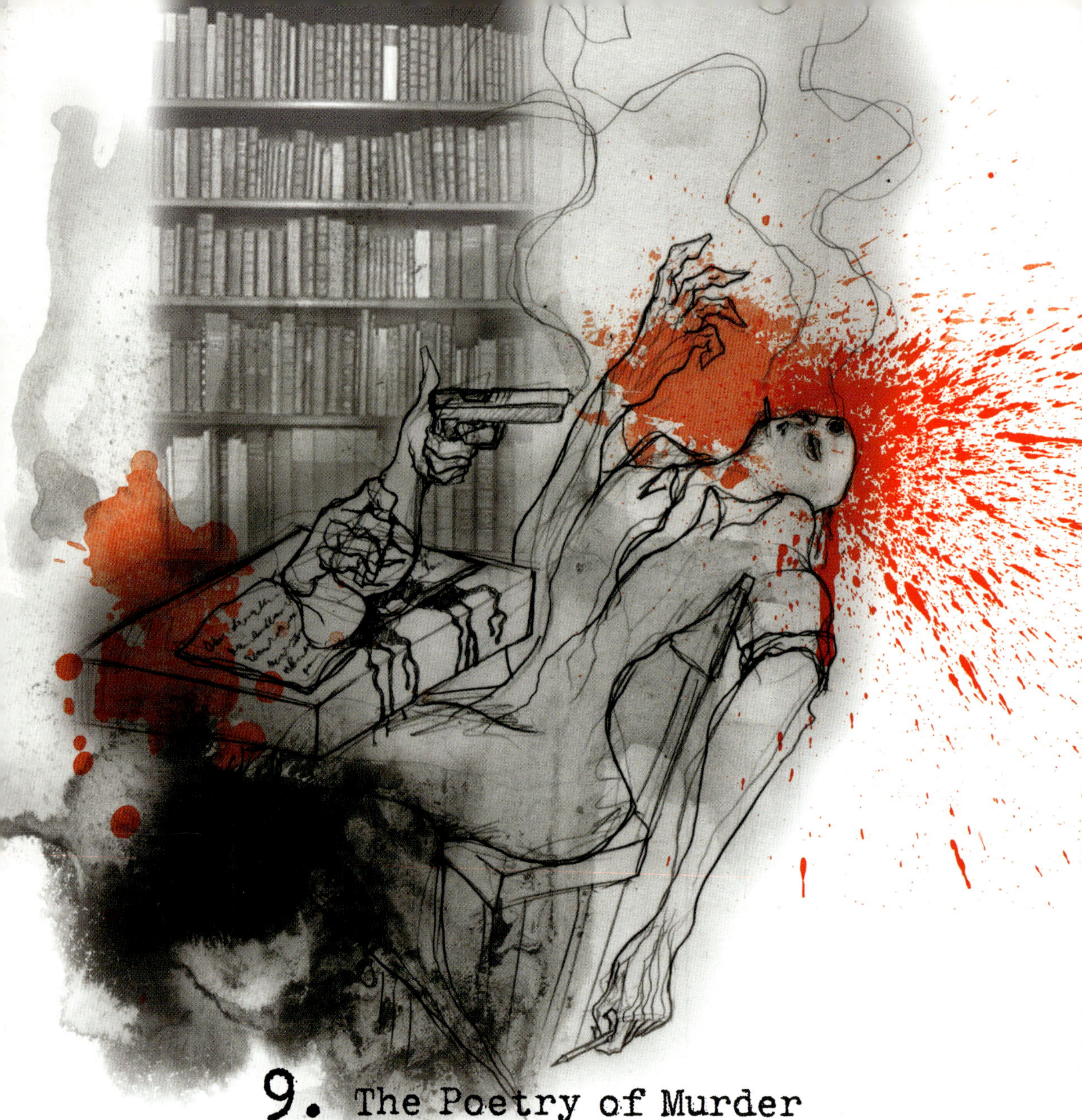

9. The Poetry of Murder

I find the big man scribbling at a table
in the great library. There'll be no fighting
— I have the black Beretta and I'm able
with a gun. Yet he drops his gaze, keeps writing,
ignoring me. "You writing *poetry*,"
I sneer, and steer my gun into the neigh-
borhood of his fat heart. "Well, you see,"
he laughs, "it's like a dream. I like the way
all characters are me, the villain, hero,
love interest, corpses. And the library
is just my mind. People are nothing, zero.
I kill them off when it amuses me."
Enough. I snuff the bastard, wipe the traces,
then step out, whistling, while the world erases.

Jack Logan, Fighting Airman:

The Case of the Red Bordello

It was a blonde.
A blonde to make a bishop
kick a hole in a
stained glass window.

—Raymond Chandler

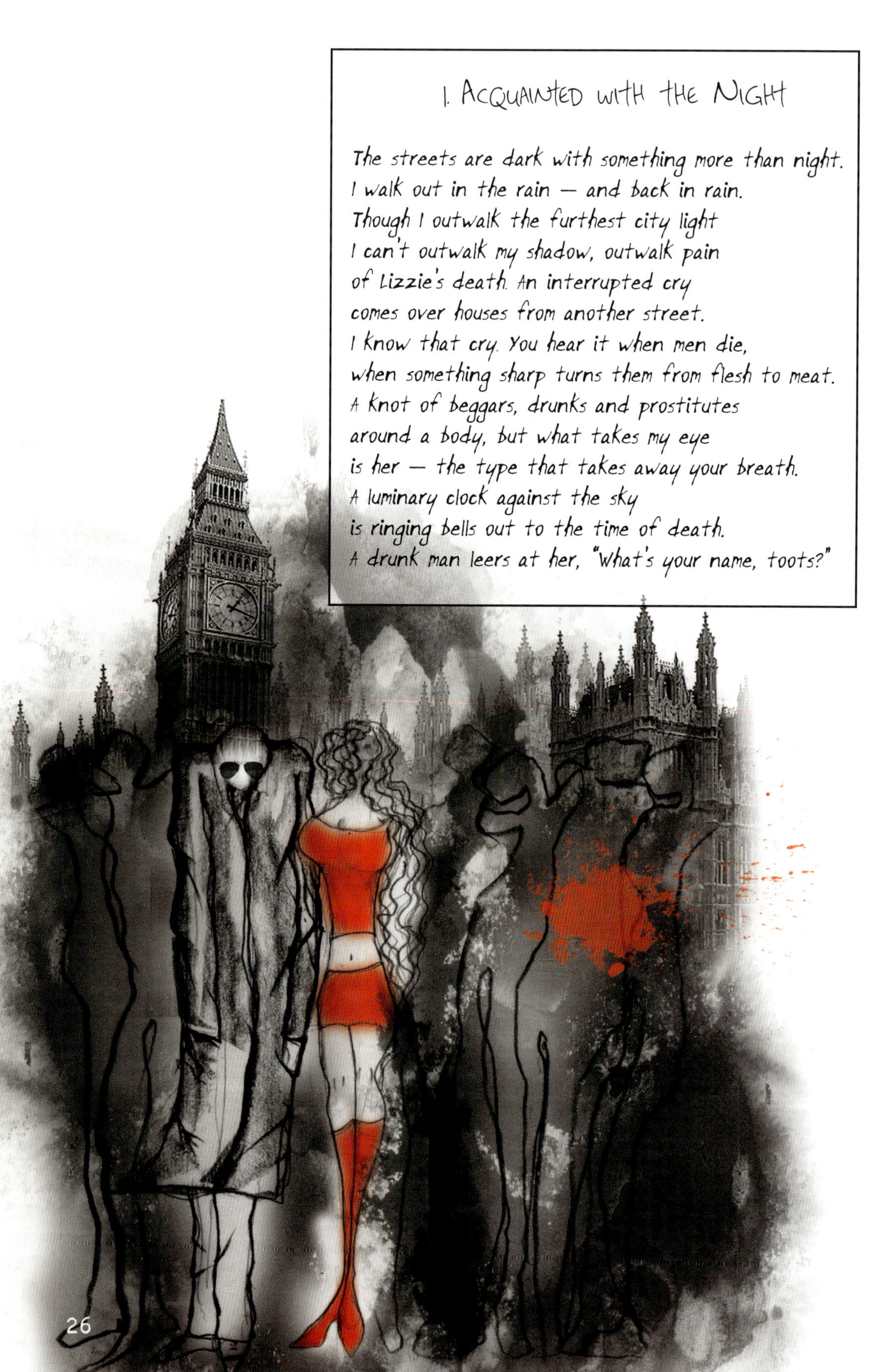
I. Acquainted with the Night
The streets are dark with something more than night.
I walk out in the rain — and back in rain.
Though I outwalk the furthest city light
I can't outwalk my shadow, outwalk pain
of Lizzie's death. An interrupted cry
comes over houses from another street.
I know that cry. You hear it when men die,
when something sharp turns them from flesh to meat.
A knot of beggars, drunks and prostitutes
around a body, but what takes my eye
is her — the type that takes away your breath.
A luminary clock against the sky
is ringing bells out to the time of death.
A drunk man leers at her, "What's your name, toots?"

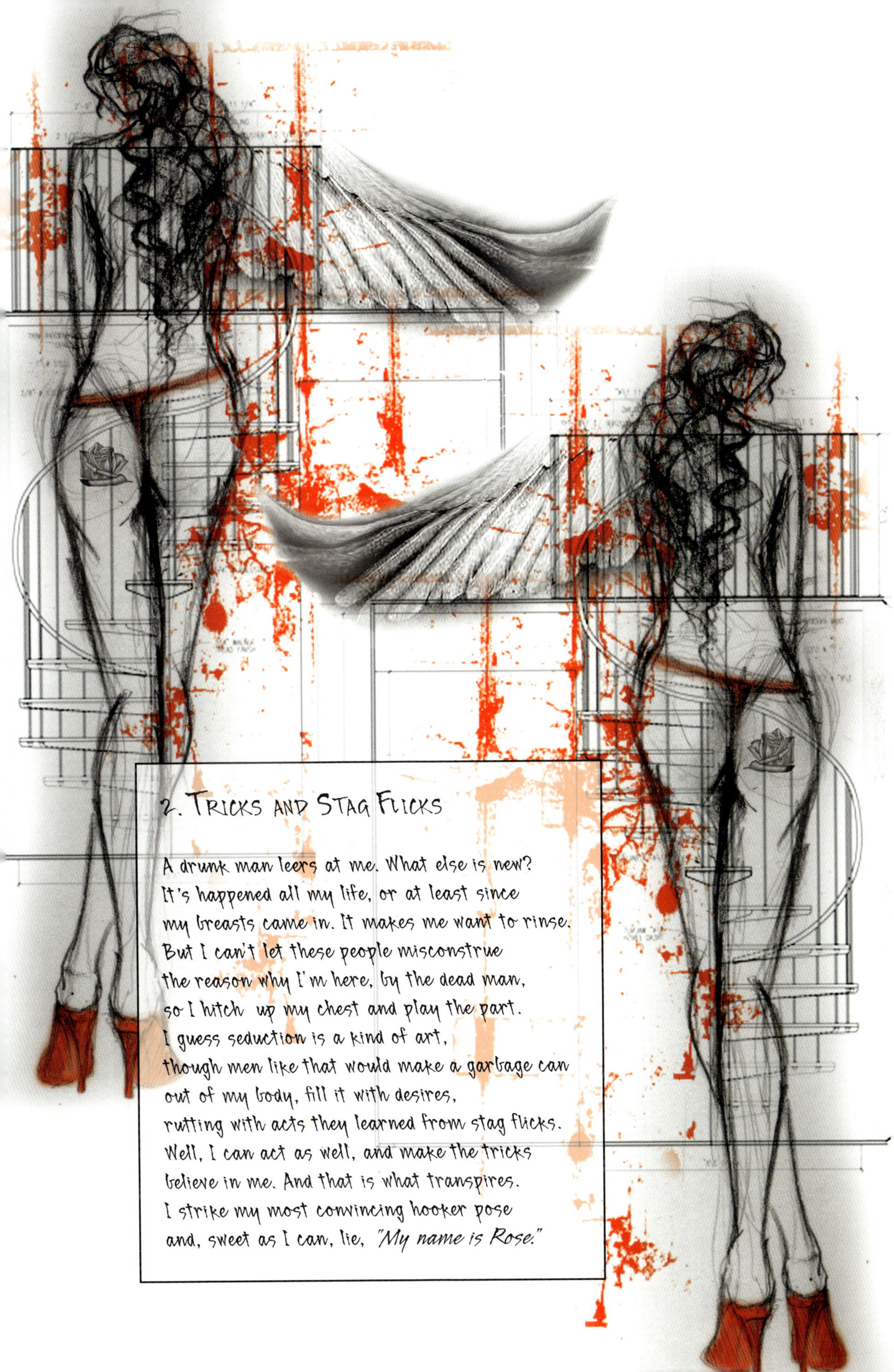

2. Tricks and Stag Flicks

A drunk man leers at me. What else is new?
It's happened all my life, or at least since
my breasts came in. It makes me want to rinse.
But I can't let these people misconstrue
the reason why I'm here, by the dead man,
so I hitch up my chest and play the part.
I guess seduction is a kind of art,
though men like that would make a garbage can
out of my body, fill it with desires,
rutting with acts they learned from stag flicks.
Well, I can act as well, and make the tricks
believe in me. And that is what transpires.
I strike my most convincing hooker pose
and, sweet as I can, lie, *"My name is Rose."*

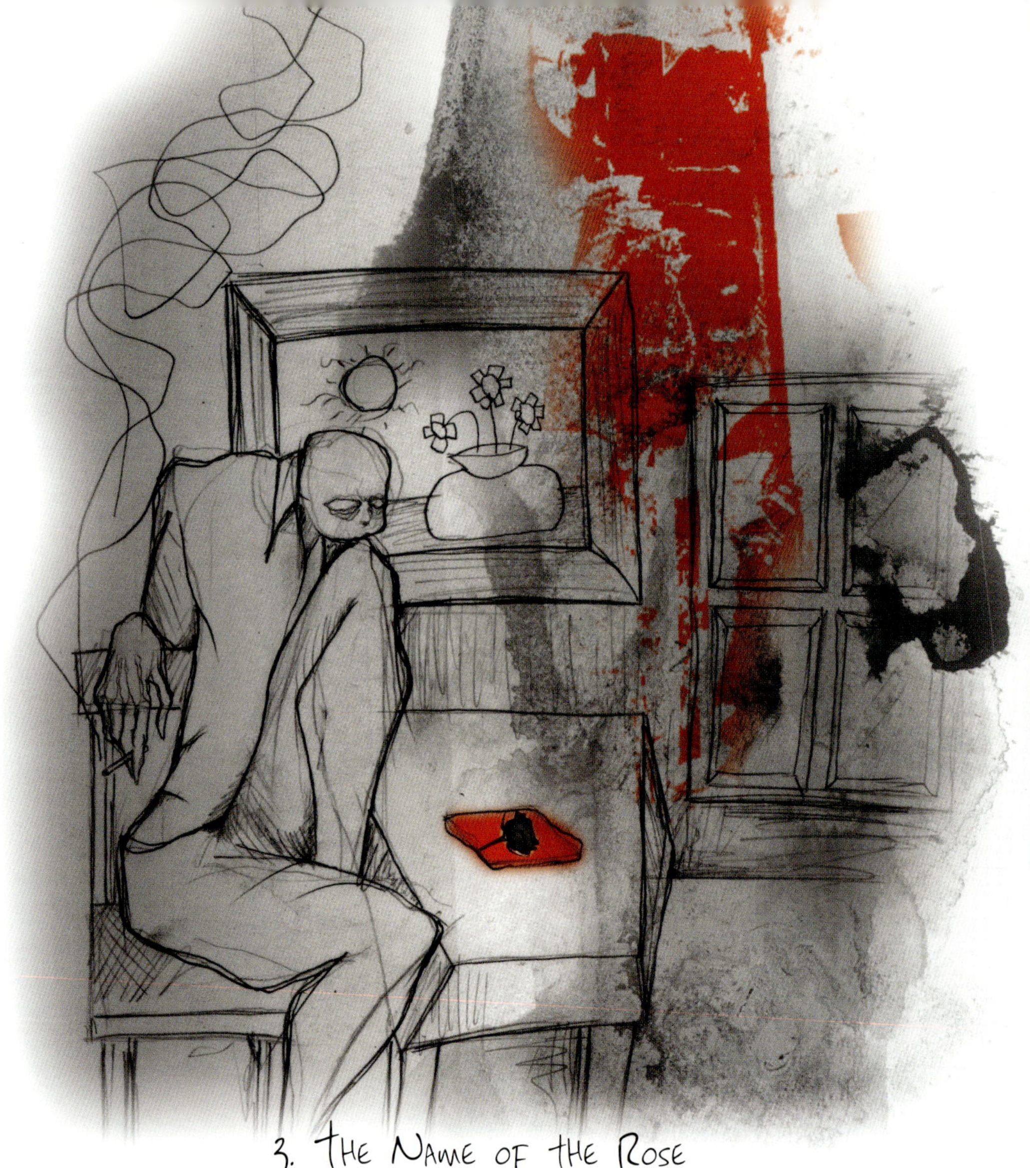

3. The Name of the Rose

"My name is Rose," she sweetly grins.
"You should come up and visit us sometime.
My girls know how to wash away your sins."
The lighted church clock bangs out one last chime,
then's silent as the galaxy above.
I learned in school that *galaxy* means *milk*,
that some Greek goddess leaked stars out of
her breasts. I've known some goddesses, the silk
kimono at the crack of noon type, but
this one, well, I'd join her religion. She
goes back inside the Red Bordello, shut
inside like fantasy (though that is free).
Then there's the corpse. I check: still dead. One clue:
red rose on a white matchbook. It'll do.

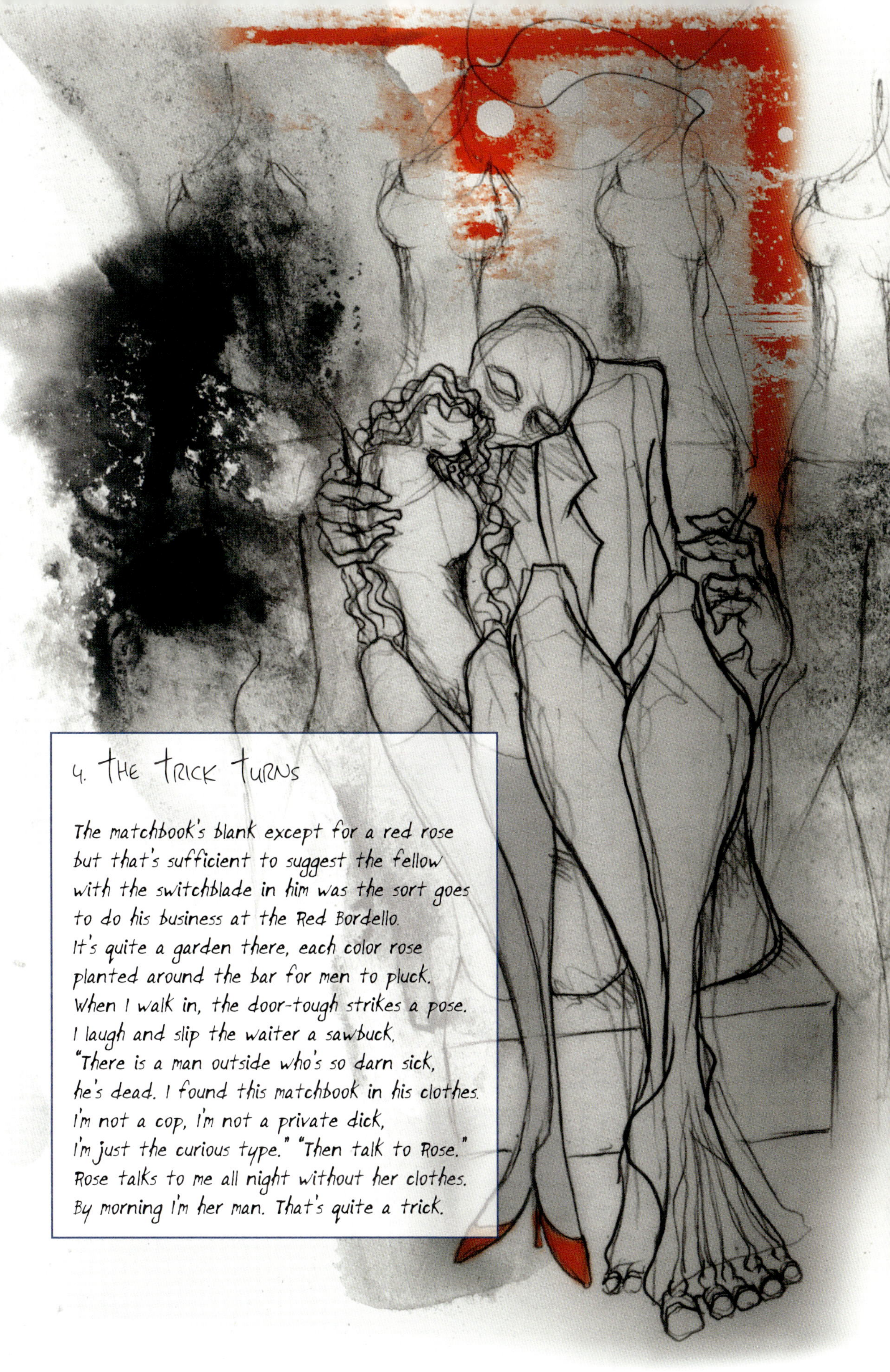

4. THE TRICK TURNS
The matchbook's blank except for a red rose
but that's sufficient to suggest the fellow
with the switchblade in him was the sort goes
to do his business at the Red Bordello.
It's quite a garden there, each color rose
planted around the bar for men to pluck.
When I walk in, the door-tough strikes a pose.
I laugh and slip the waiter a sawbuck,
"There is a man outside who's so darn sick,
he's dead. I found this matchbook in his clothes.
I'm not a cop, I'm not a private dick,
I'm just the curious type." "Then talk to Rose."
Rose talks to me all night without her clothes.
By morning I'm her man. That's quite a trick.

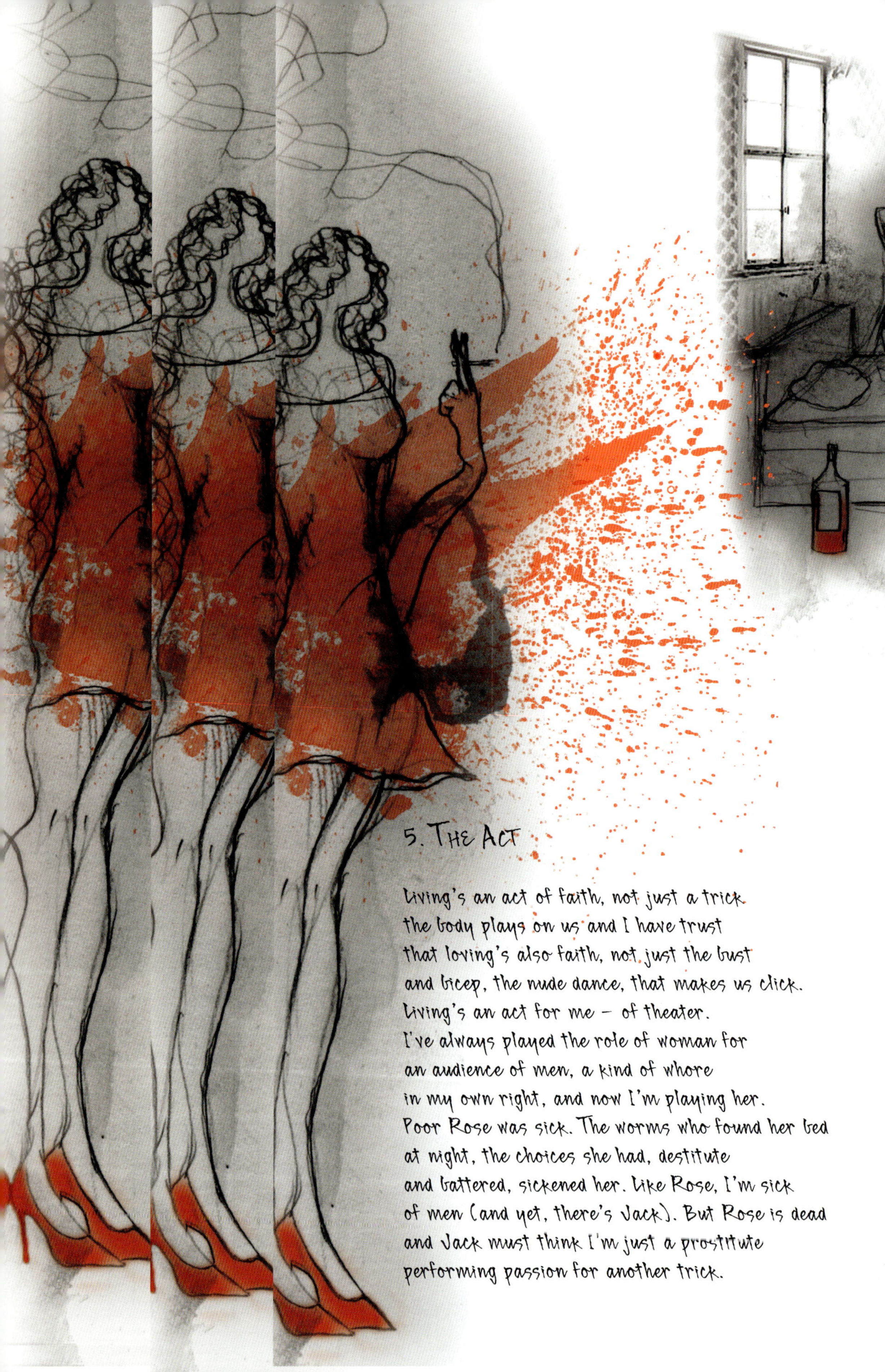

5. The Act

Living's an act of faith, not just a trick
the body plays on us and I have trust
that loving's also faith, not just the bust
and bicep, the nude dance, that makes us click.
Living's an act for me – of theater.
I've always played the role of woman for
an audience of men, a kind of whore
in my own right, and now I'm playing her.
Poor Rose was sick. The worms who found her bed
at night, the choices she had, destitute
and battered, sickened her. Like Rose, I'm sick
of men (and yet, there's Jack). But Rose is dead
and Jack must think I'm just a prostitute
performing passion for another trick.

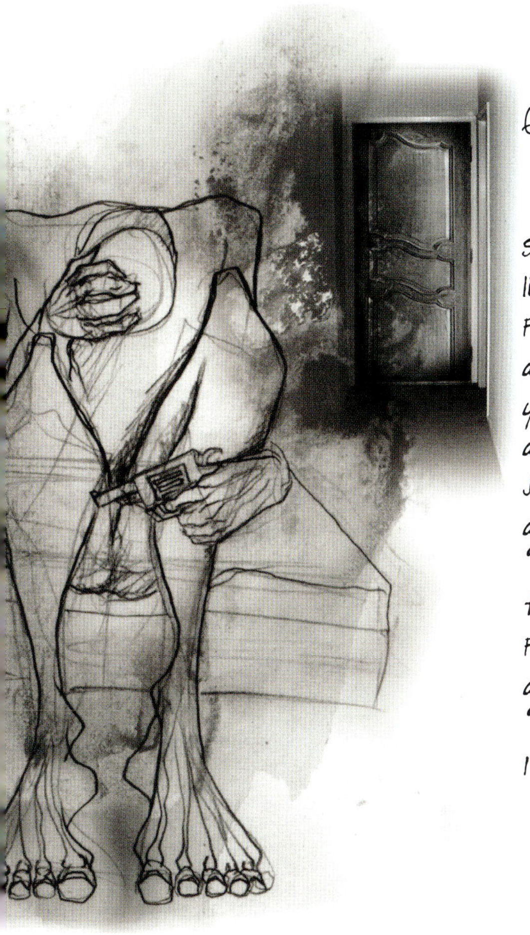

6. Two Black Books and A Stack of Cash

She is tricked out in something scanty, looks
like a light wind would rip it like a cloud.
From bed, I watch through lashes: two black books,
a stack of cash, a gun. I give a loud
yawn, as if surfacing from a dream,
and stretch and wave my arms in semaphore.
Just then boots clomp on the wood stairs, a scream,
a shout, a scuffle outside of the door.
"Jack, this way, fast!" she hisses, climbing out
the window to the fire escape. "Spider
Floyd's on his way." No time. I spin about
and step in front the window so's to hide her.
"Give up the frail," the gunman scowls. Instead,
I look at him and smile, "Ah, shut your head."

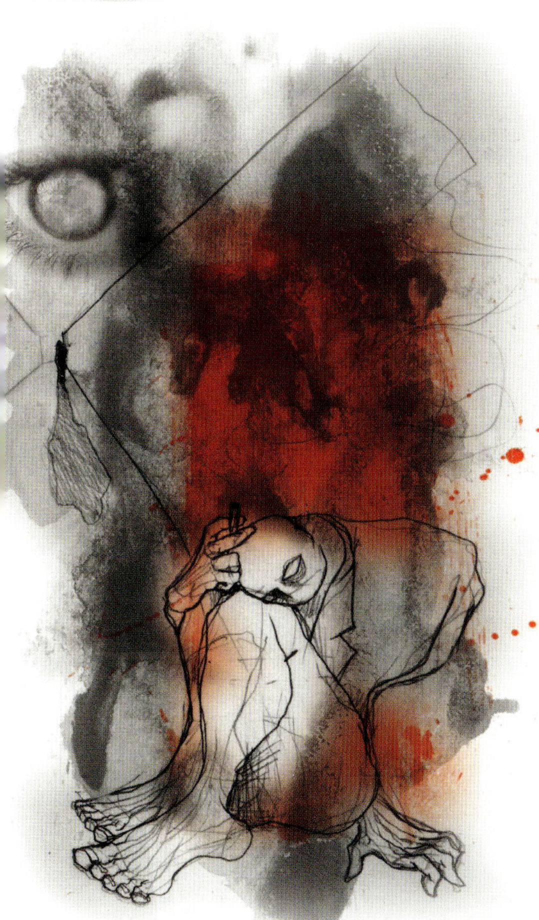

7. Angels and Buttercups

"I'll open up your head," says Spider, hard,
"and you'll be leaking plenty, 'less you spill."
I casually sit upon the windowsill
and stare at him. A knife glints like a shard
of glass, then quivers next to my left ear.
Another throwing blade is in his hand.
"Sure, Buttercup, I think I understand,"
I say, "But I think I need atmosphere,"
and I roll back and out. The next knife clangs
the fire escape but I'm already sliding
down the steel ladder and then quickly hiding
behind rank rows of trash cans. Spider bangs
down to the alley, curses. I'm discreet.
I tail him to a place on Angel Street.

8. Angel Face

The face of Spider Floyd is like an angel,
the sort of angel offers you an apple.
He's flash, he's jazz, he's angling for an angle,
His eyes are dead. He'd sooner shoot than grapple,
being the dapper, slender sort of thug
— doesn't want to break his polished nails.
Framed in the door is Spider's pretty mug,
a pistol in his hand. "I don't like tails,"
he growls. "That's funny. I heard you was born
with one," I smile. He smiles back with a smile
should be in a movie, maybe porn,
commences pistol-whipping me a while.
I wake up to a choir of devils singing.
Either my head or else a phone is ringing.

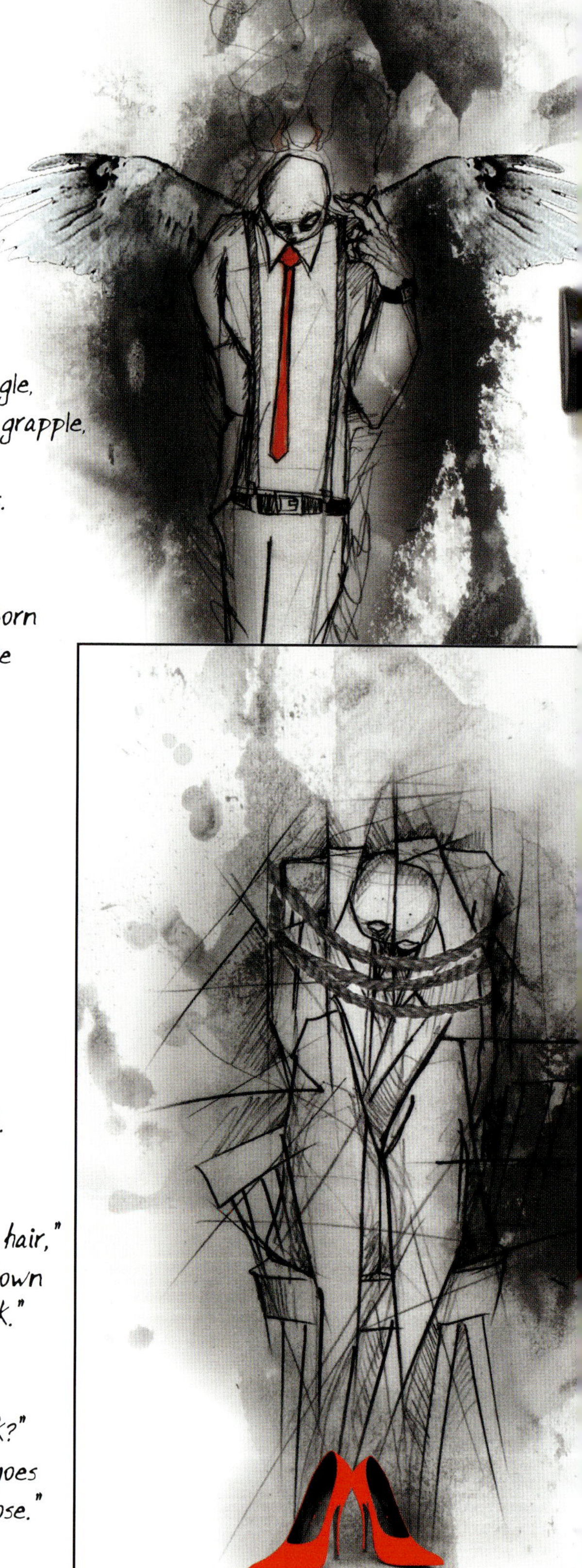

9. A Heap of Broken Images

A phone is ringing somewhere in my head,
or maybe someone's banging hammers on
an iron oven. Spider must be gone
somewhere, and I guess maybe I'm not dead.
The heap of broken images goes round
till I decipher I'm tossed in a chair,
pretty messed up. "I see they mussed your hair,"
comes Rose's voice. "Behave. Spider went down
to the first floor, and I snuck up the back."
When lovely woman stoops to folly and
she holds an automatic in her hand,
you answer what she asks: "You a cop, Jack?"
"No, Rose." "Like hell. I've seen just how it goes
with cops. You won't pin murder on this Rose."

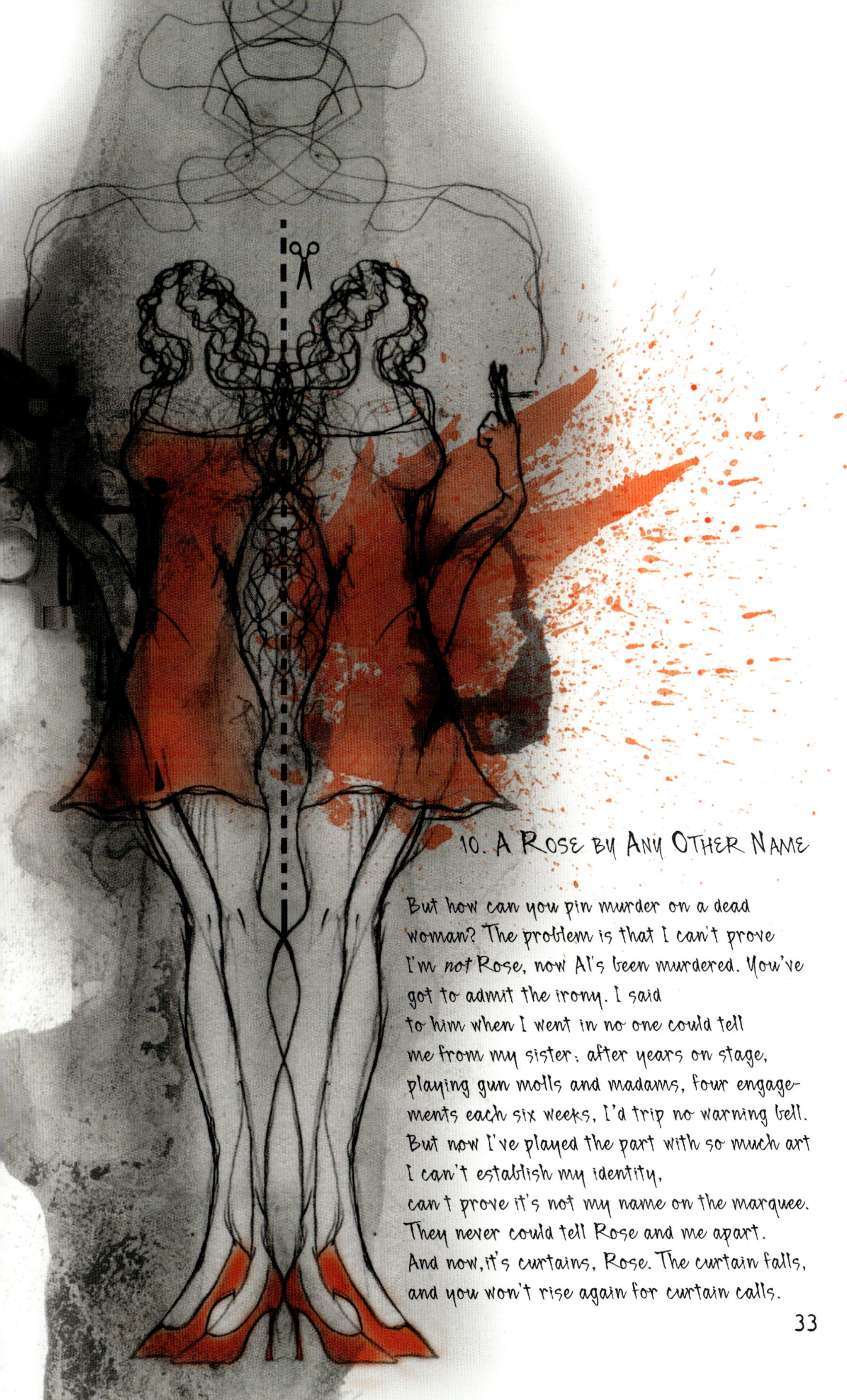

10. A Rose by Any Other Name

But how can you pin murder on a dead
woman? The problem is that I can't prove
I'm *not* Rose, now Al's been murdered. You've
got to admit the irony. I said
to him when I went in no one could tell
me from my sister: after years on stage,
playing gun molls and madams, four engage-
ments each six weeks, I'd trip no warning bell.
But now I've played the part with so much art
I can't establish my identity,
can't prove it's not my name on the marquee.
They never could tell Rose and me apart.
And now, it's curtains, Rose. The curtain falls,
and you won't rise again for curtain calls.

11. Tough Act to Follow

The curtain rises on a scene. Here's Jack,
his lovely face so swollen it's inflated.
Here is the heroine. Here is a shack,
abandoned, knocked askew, dilapidated,
a bare room barely lit by a bare light.
Here is a desk and hidden in the back
the white book scribbled with a code that might
uncode the black books, putting me on track
to find out why my sister Rose was killed.
I can't let Jack catch on, don't trust him yet.
Someone in all this mess turned coat and spilled.
It's all an act, this acting rough
but I act well. I light a cigarette,
put on a pin-up smile, and then get tough.

12. The Kiss

She pins a smile onto her face the way
you'd pin a butterfly to a cork board,
and sweetly says, "If I hear just one word
from you, I'll make you a new mouth, okay?"
pressing the Luger up against my Adam's
apple. And she is one sweet apple her-
self, in her tight-laced corset rimmed with fur
and tiny skirt, a looker among Madams.
She has a face to make a reprobate
out of an archbishop. I'm a believer.
I can't take her, and yet I can't leave her,
though I'm no priest. "I love you, Rose," I state,
with tenderness. She dips the gun, her wrist
gone weak. That's when I kiss her with my fist.

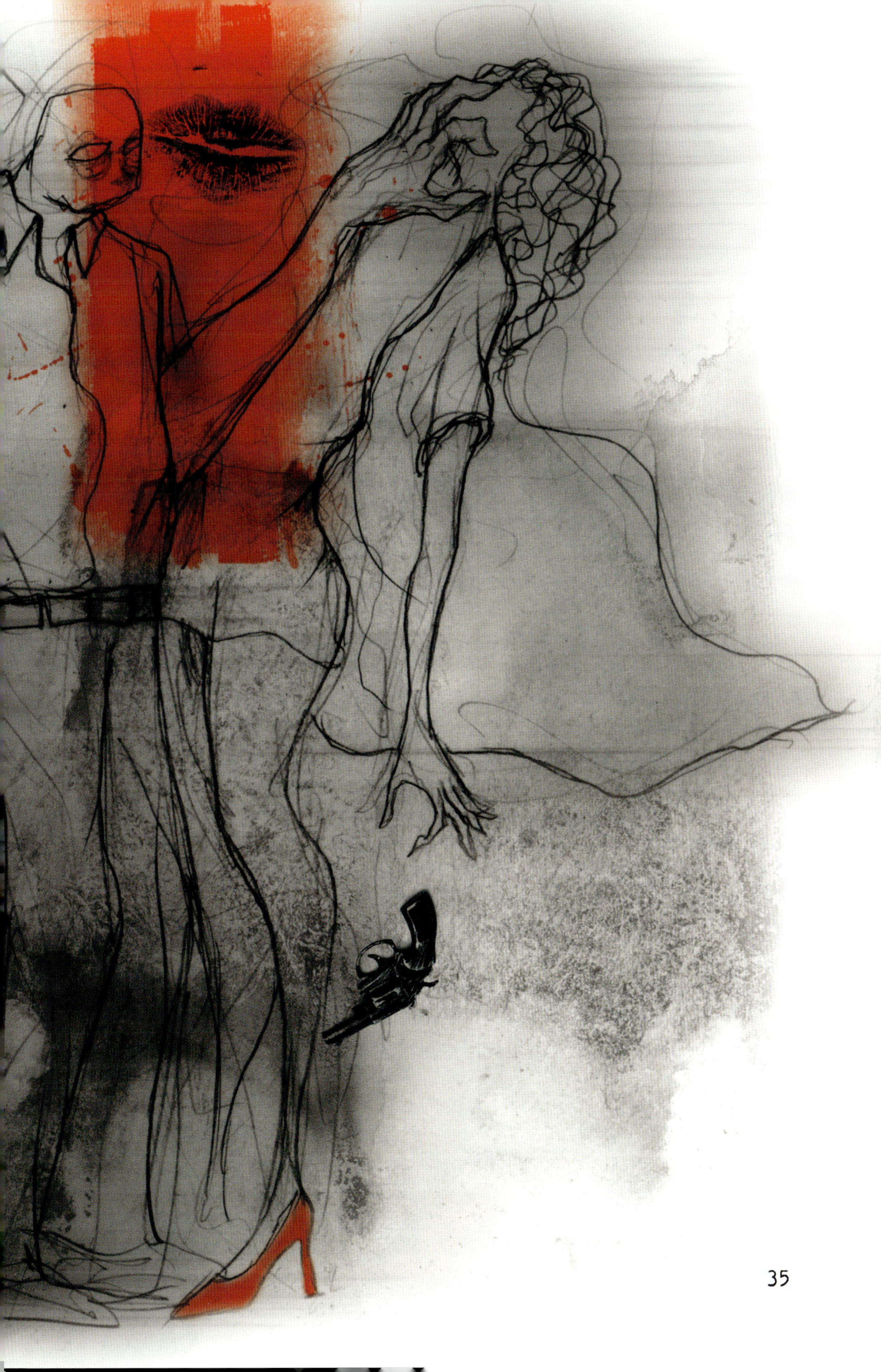

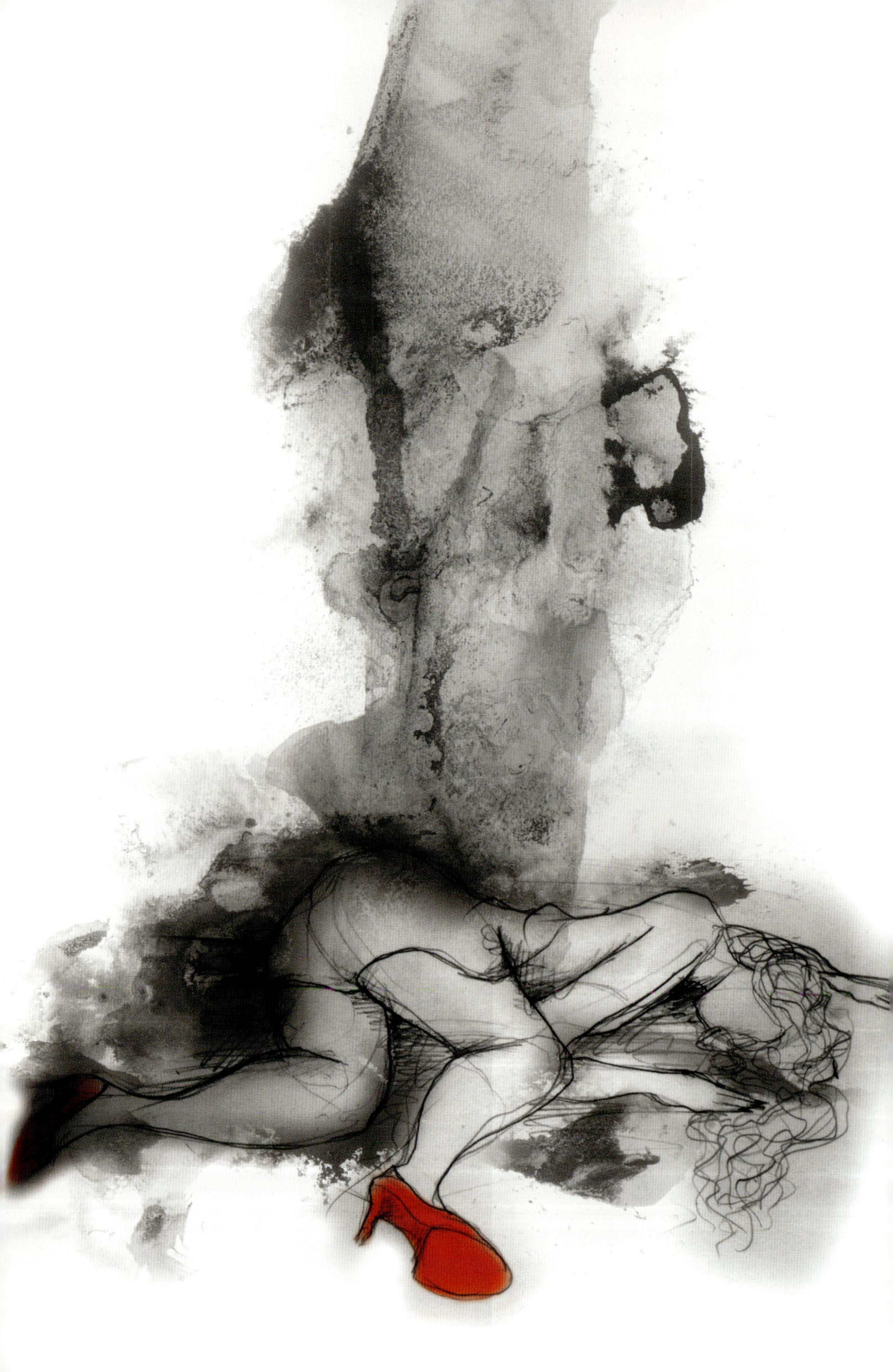

13. The Distressed Rose

I kiss her with my fist and she goes slack
the way a negligee drops to the floor.
I kick the gun away and lock the door.
She mumbles something weakly, "Me, too, Jack.
I love you, too." Aw, hell. What a swell dame.
Outside of prostitution, gambling, oh
and just a little homicide, a Joe
could take her home to Mom. I'm not to blame
she is a doxy with a heart of tin,
no kind of damsel. When she looks distressed
her face would make a stockbroker divest
of money, make a saint invest in sin.
But still, I just can't leave her here for them.
I guess I've fallen for this fatal femme.

14. Tough Guise

I'm not the type who falls for muscle guys,
and something's off with Jack, that he would want
a madam or a murderer, disguise
or not. Or something's off with me. I can't
pretend I don't enjoy pretending, that
tending to Rose's garden at the Red
Bordello as a madam with a gat
inside her purse, an airman in her bed-
room, hasn't knocked my head askew. But Jack
must see too many movies, thinks he'll own
this rose. We both are trapped inside our poses,
the tough guy fighting mobsters on our track,
the bad girl lounging in her dressing gown.
An insect in the bed will kill the roses.

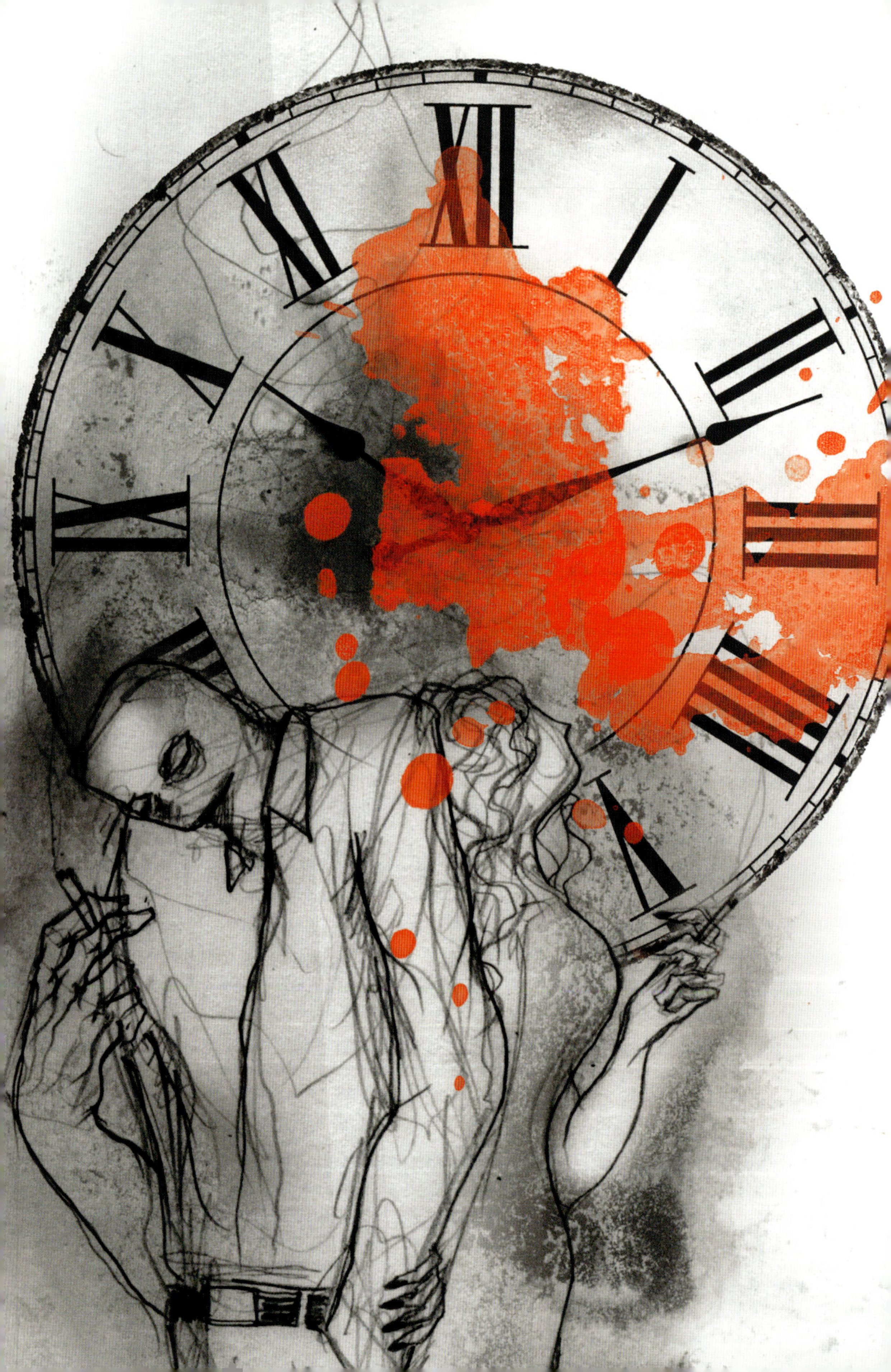

15. The Death Trap

Falling for Rose just might be fatal, but
what's not? I'm just an airman with a knack
for trouble and a killer uppercut;
I know that Spider Floyd is on our track,
but spend the afternoon in Rose's dive,
because you can't keep days inside a box.
Maybe to love a tramp's a paradox,
but no one's getting out of here alive.
I'm not just killing time with Rose. Time does
the murdering. Rose stitches up the cut
across my heart. I hold her tight in bed,
because I've learned of love one thing: it goes.
It's true that time is a great teacher, but
unfortunately kills its students dead.

16. The City Dead-House

"I am a student of death," mortician
Joe Martin says, "the pistol, bomb, and knife
and their particular effects. If life
is sickness, you can cure it with a gun.
The fellow over there with a switchblade
stuck in his heart had bigger problems than
four inches of sharp steel. The gentleman
was killed and later stabbed — a masquerade.
It took a while to figure how he died."
Joe turns away from where the corpse is flayed
in autopsy, and hands me the switchblade,
smiling. He looks a bit self-satisfied.
"Stop dancing, Joe. Just tell me what you found."
"Seawater in his lungs. The fellow drowned."

17. Dressing the Meat

"The fellow drowned? Who was he, Joe, a sailor?"
"Hardly. How many sailors do you know
who've got five large in their billfolds? Who blow
their noses on fine silk? Who have a tailor
fit their suits? No, the man there's moniker
is Algernon Byrne Westlander III.
A stuffed shirt type. Now more of a stuffed bird,
but was the Deputy Commissioner."
I whistle at the news. Why's a white shirt
like Algie pitching woo out at the Red
Bordello? His type gets a dame in bed
with just his name. He don't need a pro skirt.
"Thanks, Joe. Let's snort some giggle juice." "Oh, no.
I gotta fit Al for his wood kimono."

18. From Tempest to Othello

Algernon, or as I dub him, Algie,
got tossed into the drink and drank a lung
or two of salt water and ocean algae,
but here's the little thing that has me hung:
we live in Chi-town — no salt water for
a thousand miles — so tell me how this fellow
sucked sea? I'm stumped. I knock on Rose's door.
"Culture tonight," she says, takes me to Othello.
Uh-huh, I know. O-what-o? It's a play.
I ain't from Cultureville. I'm from Chicago,
like Al Capone. But Rose has some great gams
so I will play her way, though I should say
just like that fella in the play, Iago
(or was it Popeye?) "I ams that I ams."

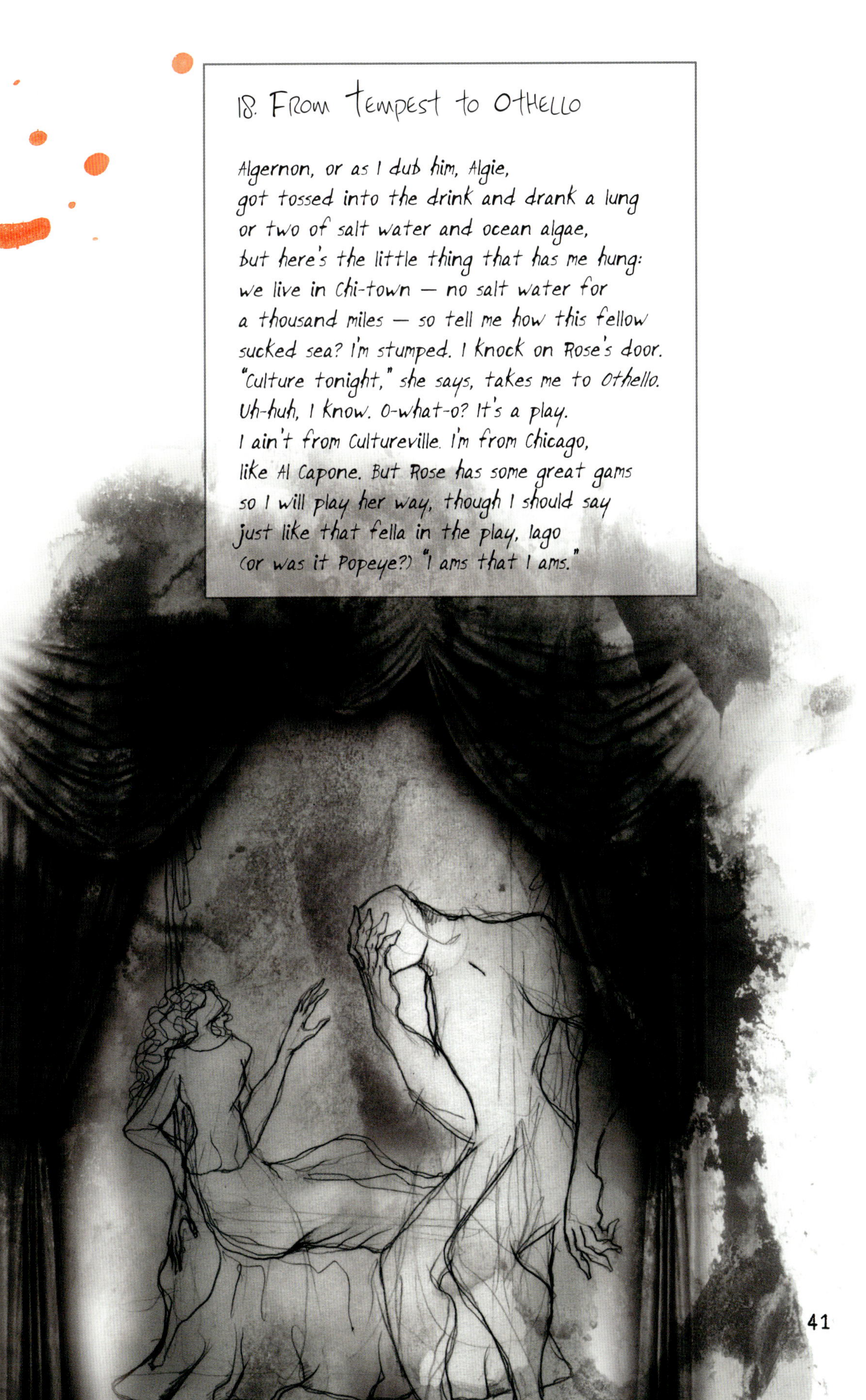

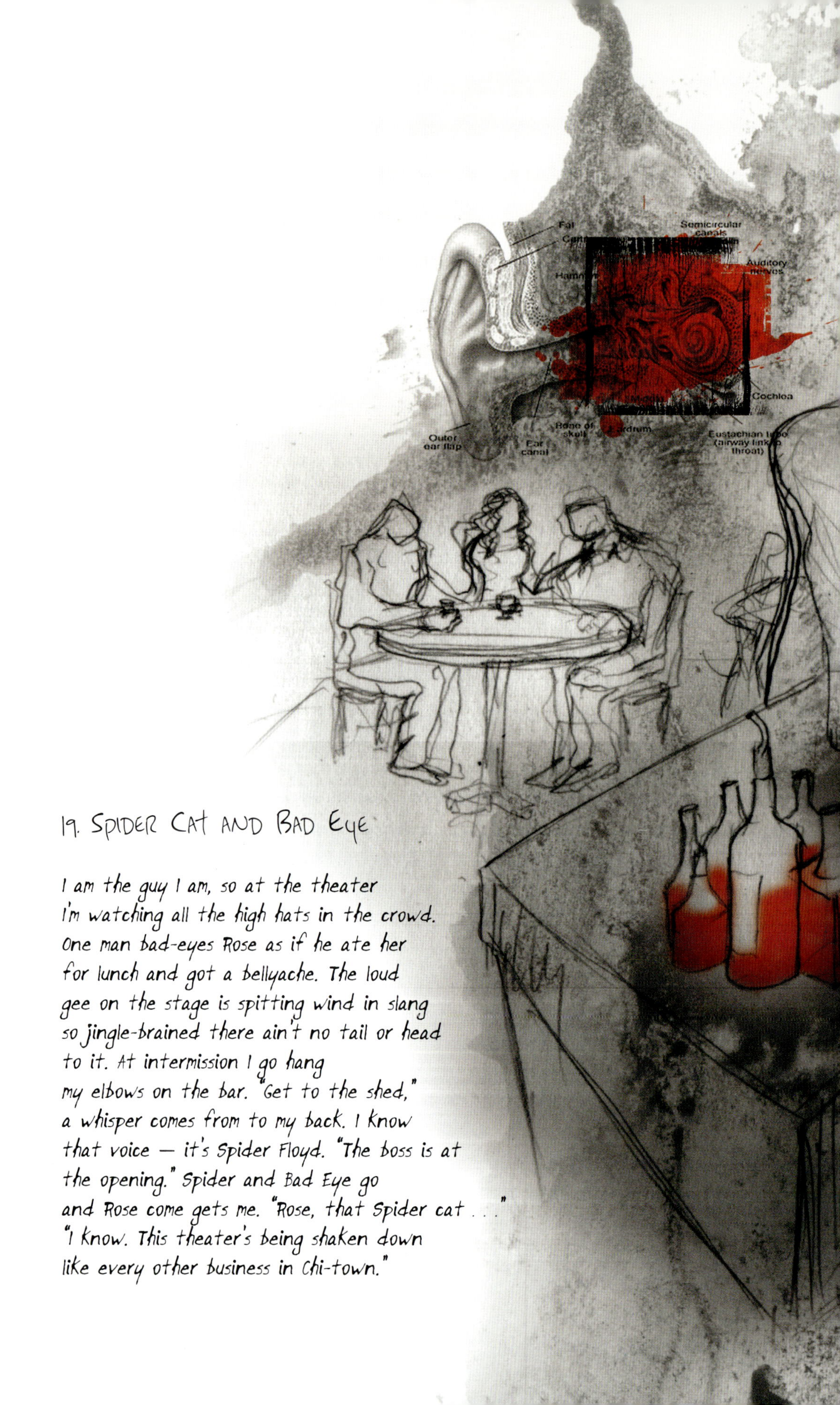

19. Spider Cat and Bad Eye

I am the guy I am, so at the theater
I'm watching all the high hats in the crowd.
One man bad-eyes Rose as if he ate her
for lunch and got a bellyache. The loud
gee on the stage is spitting wind in slang
so jingle-brained there ain't no tail or head
to it. At intermission I go hang
my elbows on the bar. "Get to the shed,"
a whisper comes from to my back. I know
that voice — it's Spider Floyd. "The boss is at
the opening." Spider and Bad Eye go
and Rose come gets me. "Rose, that Spider cat . . ."
"I know. This theater's being shaken down
like every other business in Chi-town."

20. When It Rains, It Pours

"In Chi-town every store shakes out the cash
or else the Big Guy who's behind the scenes
will whack you, blast your place to smithereens,
or angel-face will burn the store to ash,"
says Rose. "He's like a gangster God. The law
can't touch him." Snow is sifting down outdoors
like salt. Joy Morton made a salt that pours
instead of clumps, he found the formula.
If they had that at Sodom and Gomorrah
when fire and brimstone rained and cities burned,
that woman who looked back would not have turned
to a salt pillar, right? Well, I'm not sure 'a
this stuff. Maybe the dame would still have bought
the farm. As things shake out, it was her lot.

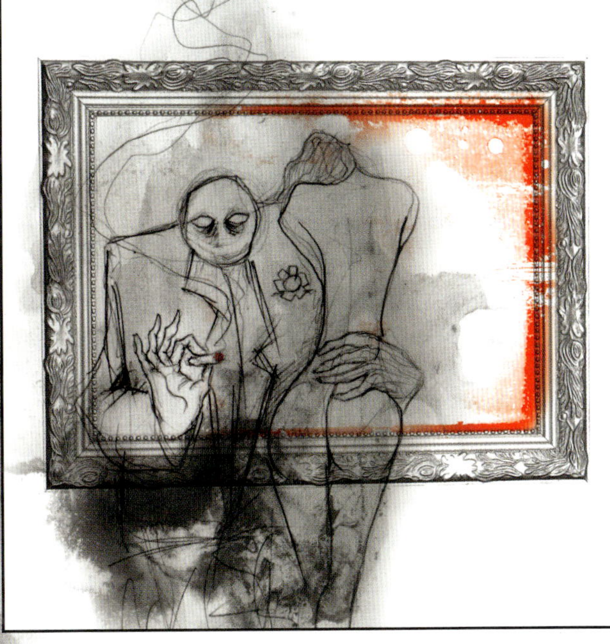

21. Animals

Back on the farm I taught myself a lot
by watching animals. My sister Rose
protected me against our dad. She taught
me sacrifice, and when he ripped her clothes
I heard the screams like mating cats, the weeping.
At fourteen I took off. My pop was found,
a kitchen knife stuck in his back, blood seeping
from the icebox to the back door. Around
the pool the starving animals collected,
lapping it up, as later men drew round
to drink Rose in. I think that I've detected
her killer and the place where she was drowned:
the Shedd Aquarium and Al Capone.
I leave Jack sleeping, and drive there, alone.

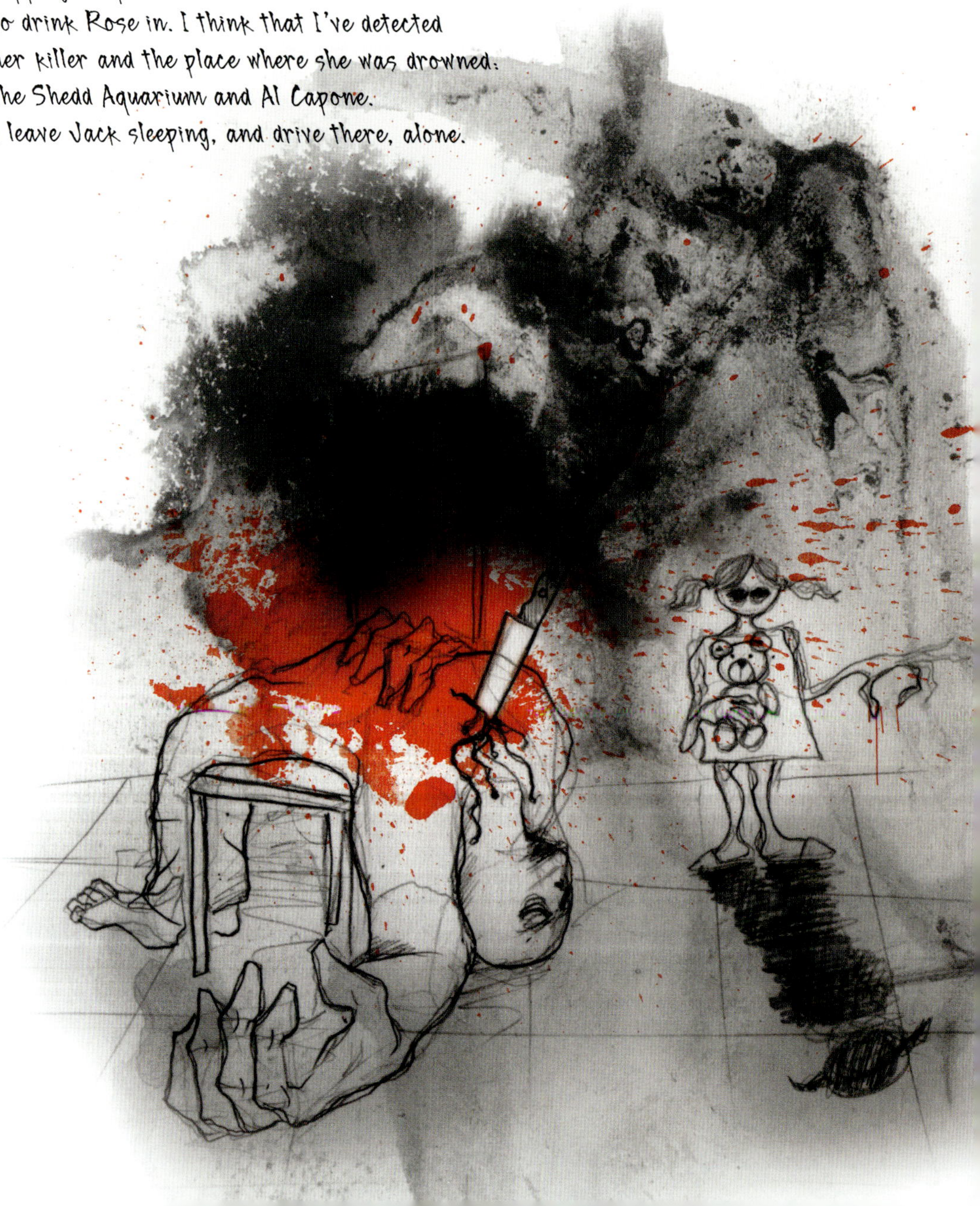

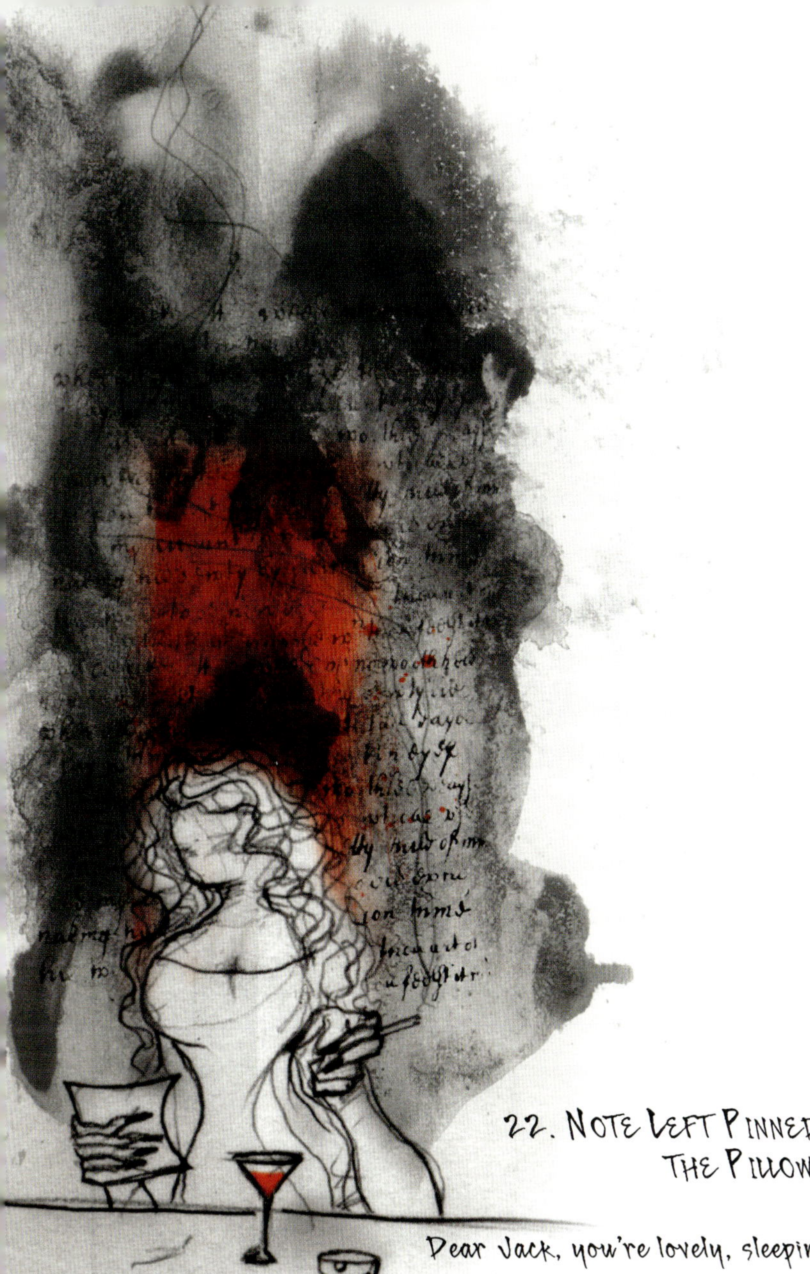

22. Note Left Pinned to the Pillow (Signed "Violet")

Dear Jack, you're lovely, sleeping on the bed,
and all I want to do is crawl inside
the covers next to you. But I can't hide
from what I have to do. I'm at the Shedd
Aquarium. One million gallons of
salt water, right? It must be where poor Al
and Rose were drowned. How strange that you should call
me by my sister's name and fall in love
with her. Rose is a part I'm acting, Jack,
to make her murderer think she is alive.
When Spider tried to kill me in that dive,
I knew Capone had ordered the attack.
Dear Jack, you're lovely, sleeping on the bed.
Don't follow me. If I'm not back, I'm dead.

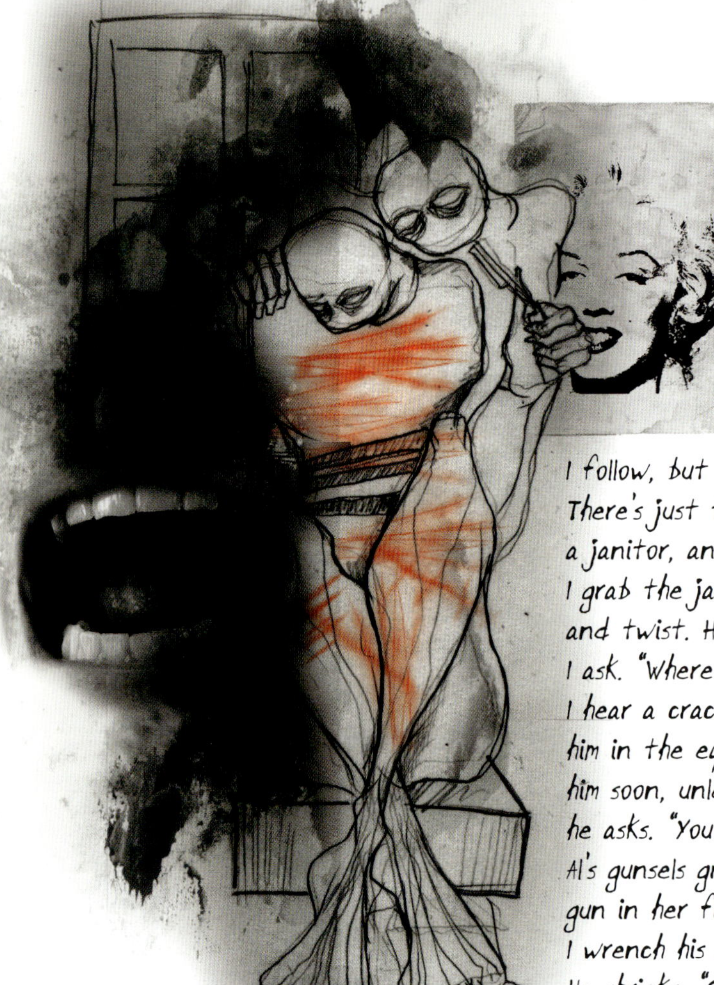

23. Small Fry, Big Fish, and the Dish

I follow, but the opening party's done.
There's just the wilting tinsel, empty glasses,
a janitor, and my false Rose is gone.
I grab the janitor's left arm as he passes,
and twist. He screams, and I twist harder. "Where?"
I ask. "Where what?" he moans. I twist until
I hear a crack. And "Where?" I ask, and stare
him in the eyes till he knows that I'll kill
him soon, unless he gives it up. "The bim?"
he asks. "You want to know about the dish?
Al's gunsels grabbed her coming up to him,
gun in her fist. I don't know where she is."
I wrench his arm until I hear it break.
He shrieks, "She's at his hideout on the lake!"

24. Angels Falling from the Sky

I've found the secret island hideout. Now
two speedboats jet from the bay. opening
up with machine guns mounted on the bow.
I nudge the wind in my red biplane, sling-
shot on an updraft, dodge the first barrage,
then bank and dive right down their throats.
The hissing bullets rip my fuselage,
but I let loose with bombs and now the boats
are bloody flame and so the good guy wins
— until a black plane dives out of the void
and shreds my wings. The handsome pilot grins
as smoke and flame decant. It's Spider Floyd.
I stall, so our planes smash. Now I grin, too.
Watching him burn, I pop my parachute.

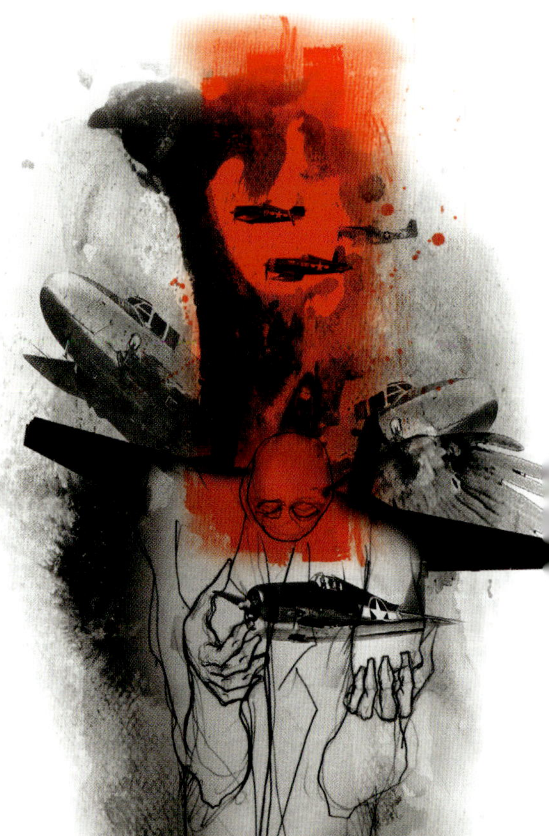

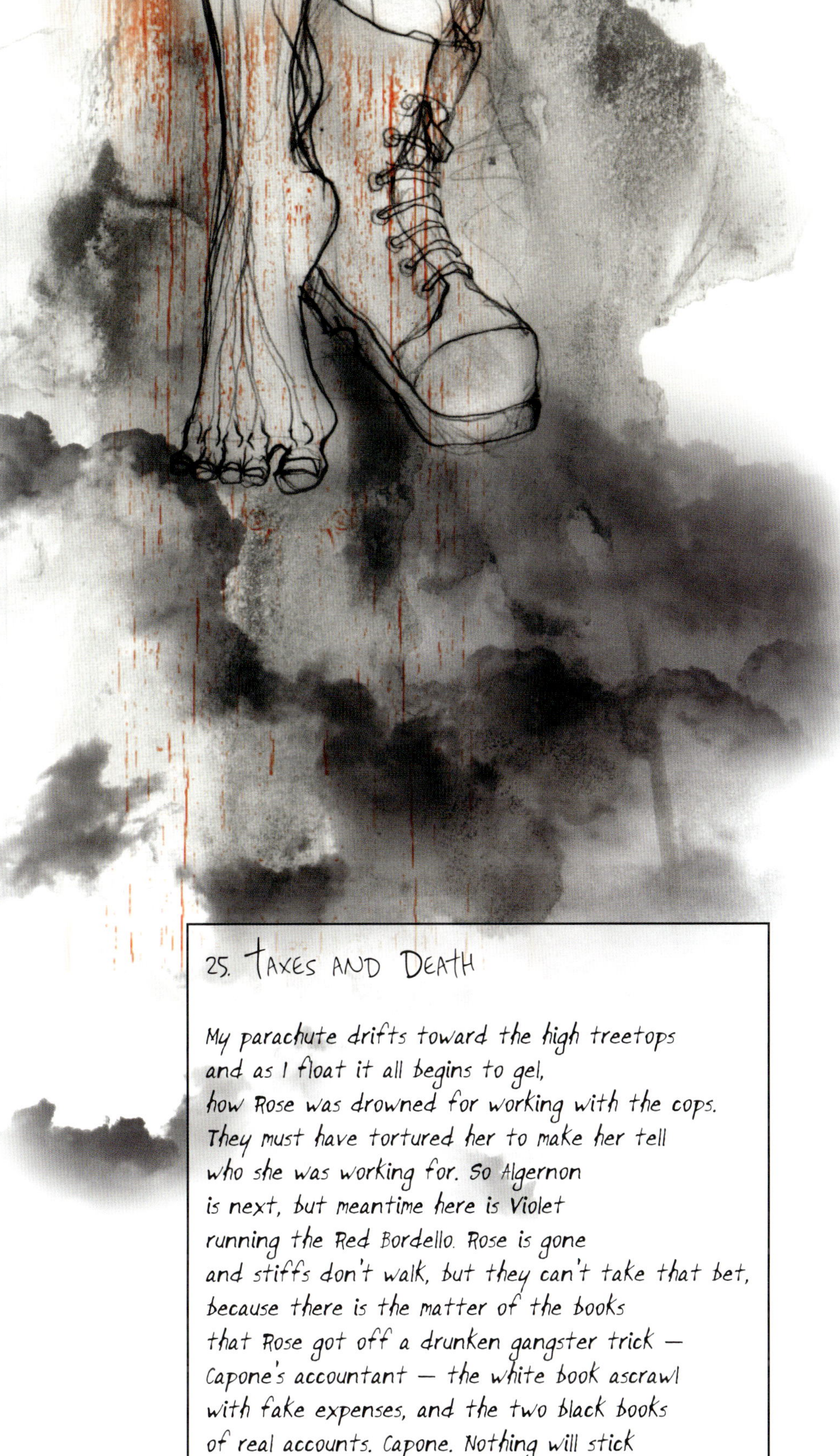

25. Taxes and Death

My parachute drifts toward the high treetops
and as I float it all begins to gel,
how Rose was drowned for working with the cops.
They must have tortured her to make her tell
who she was working for. So Algernon
is next, but meantime here is Violet
running the Red Bordello. Rose is gone
and stiffs don't walk, but they can't take that bet,
because there is the matter of the books
that Rose got off a drunken gangster trick —
Capone's accountant — the white book ascrawl
with fake expenses, and the two black books
of real accounts. Capone. Nothing will stick
to him. I drop, but swear he'll take the fall.

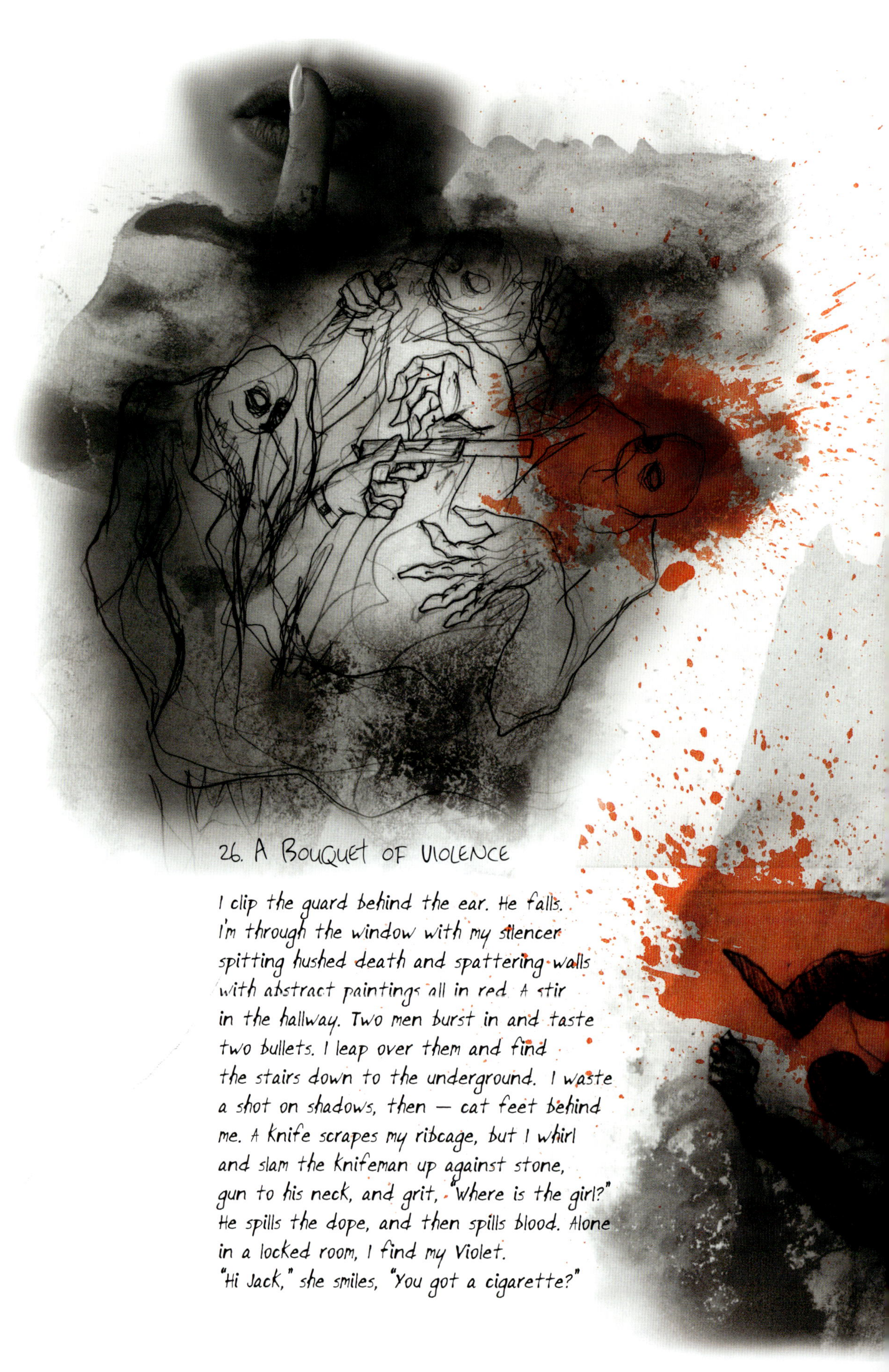

26. A Bouquet of Violence

I clip the guard behind the ear. He falls.
I'm through the window with my silencer
spitting hushed death and spattering walls
with abstract paintings all in red. A stir
in the hallway. Two men burst in and taste
two bullets. I leap over them and find
the stairs down to the underground. I waste
a shot on shadows, then — cat feet behind
me. A knife scrapes my ribcage, but I whirl
and slam the knifeman up against stone,
gun to his neck, and grit, "Where is the girl?"
He spills the dope, and then spills blood. Alone
in a locked room, I find my Violet.
"Hi Jack," she smiles, "You got a cigarette?"

27. Violets Are Black and Blue

"Hi Jack," she smiles, "You got a cigarette?"
She's chained up to a chair and bruised blue-black,
her dress torn down her shoulder 'cross her back,
and that's how I first meet my Violet.
But then I see her eyes flick to something
behind me and her smile congeals to ice.
I spin too slow and catch the knife blade twice,
once in my arm, once in my chest, but bring
the gun around and just before I shoot
his large brown eyes expand, his lips form "No!"
Before he dies he grips my leg below
the knee. I kick his hand off with my boot,
grab Violet and run down to the pier,
steal a speedboat and shoot off in high gear.

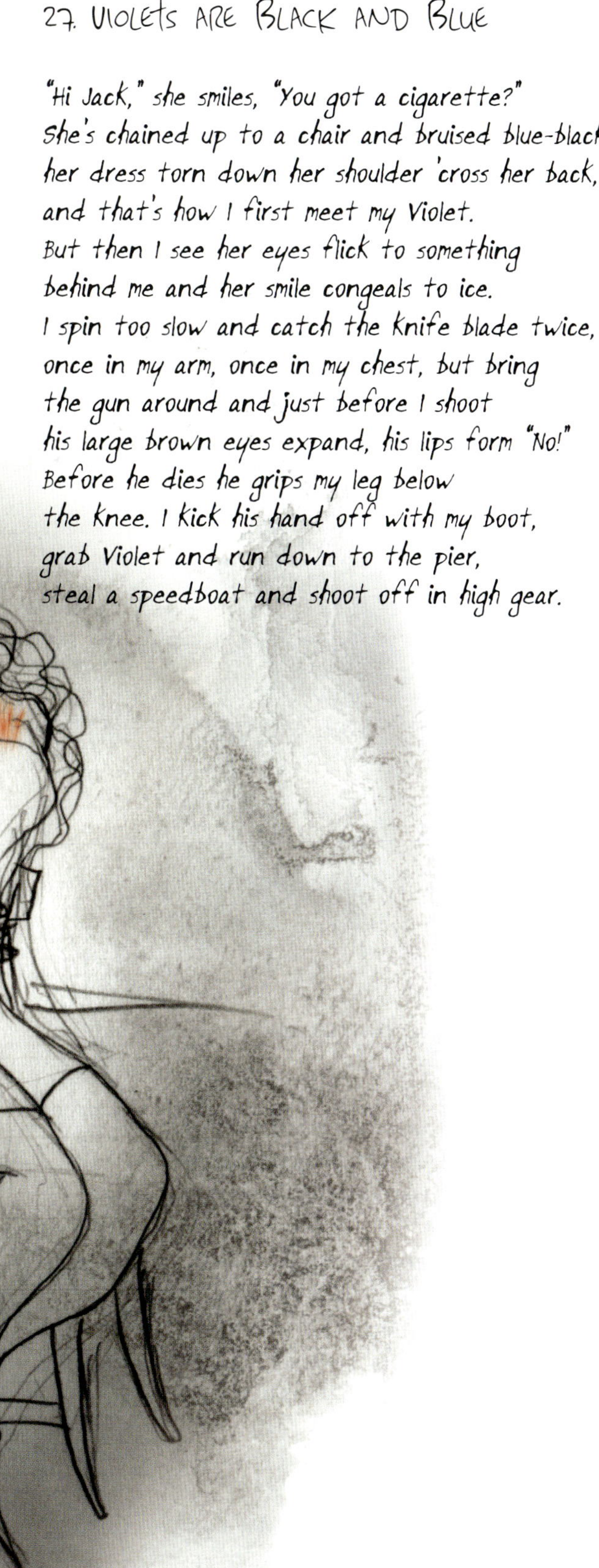

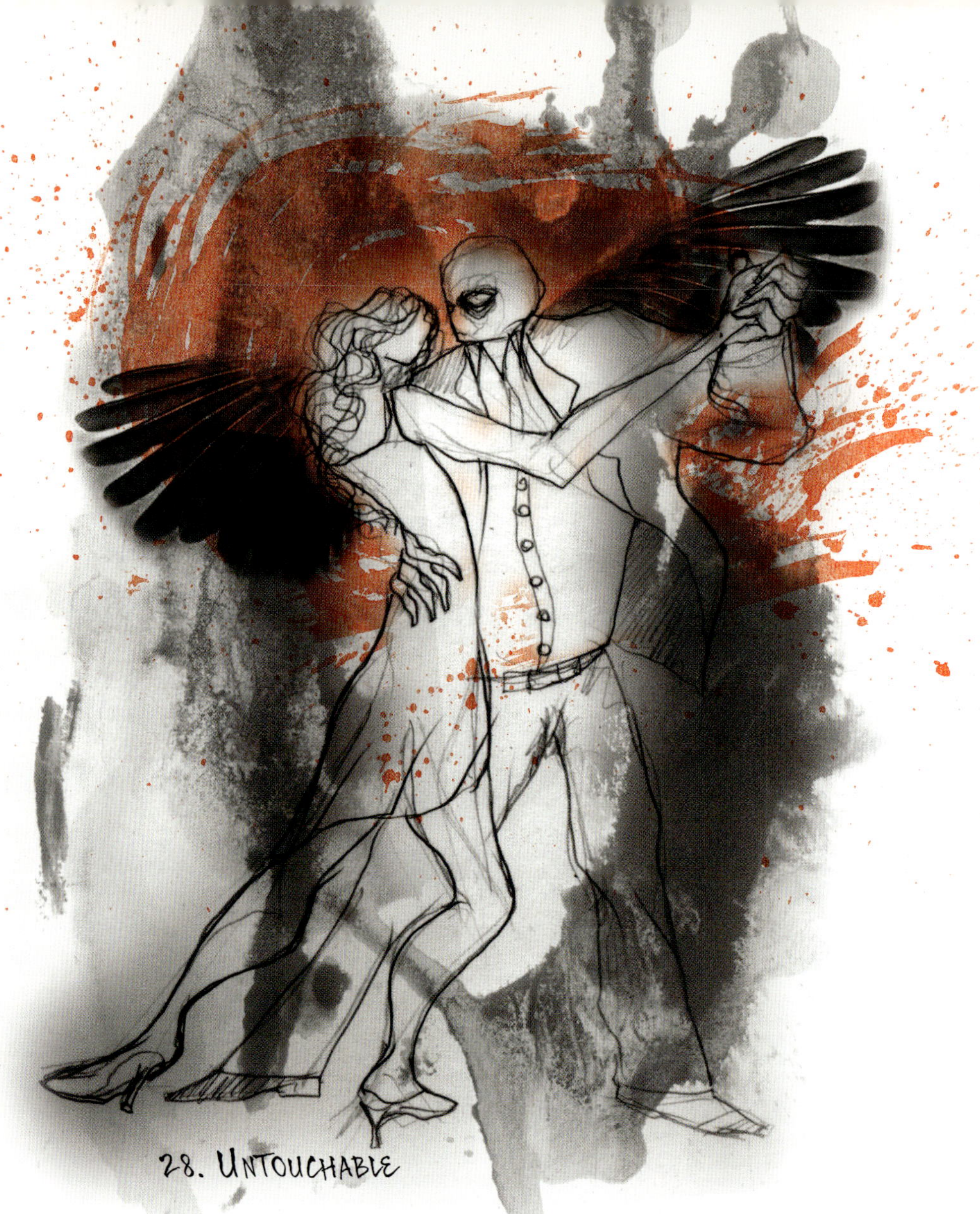

28. Untouchable

We stole a speedboat and kept going till
we got to Canada, where we laid low
till we thought the heat was off, but how
I had to plead with Jack not to go kill
Capone and get himself blipped off in turn.
Now I'm off Broadway, playing a gun moll
again, and Jack and I have found a small
bungalow in New Jersey, and we burn
up the dance halls and we are happy here.
Jack couldn't quite believe I was alive
when he arrived, but as I tell him, "Love,
they couldn't kill me till they found out where
I'd stashed the books, but how could I confess
I mailed the two black books to Eliot Ness?"

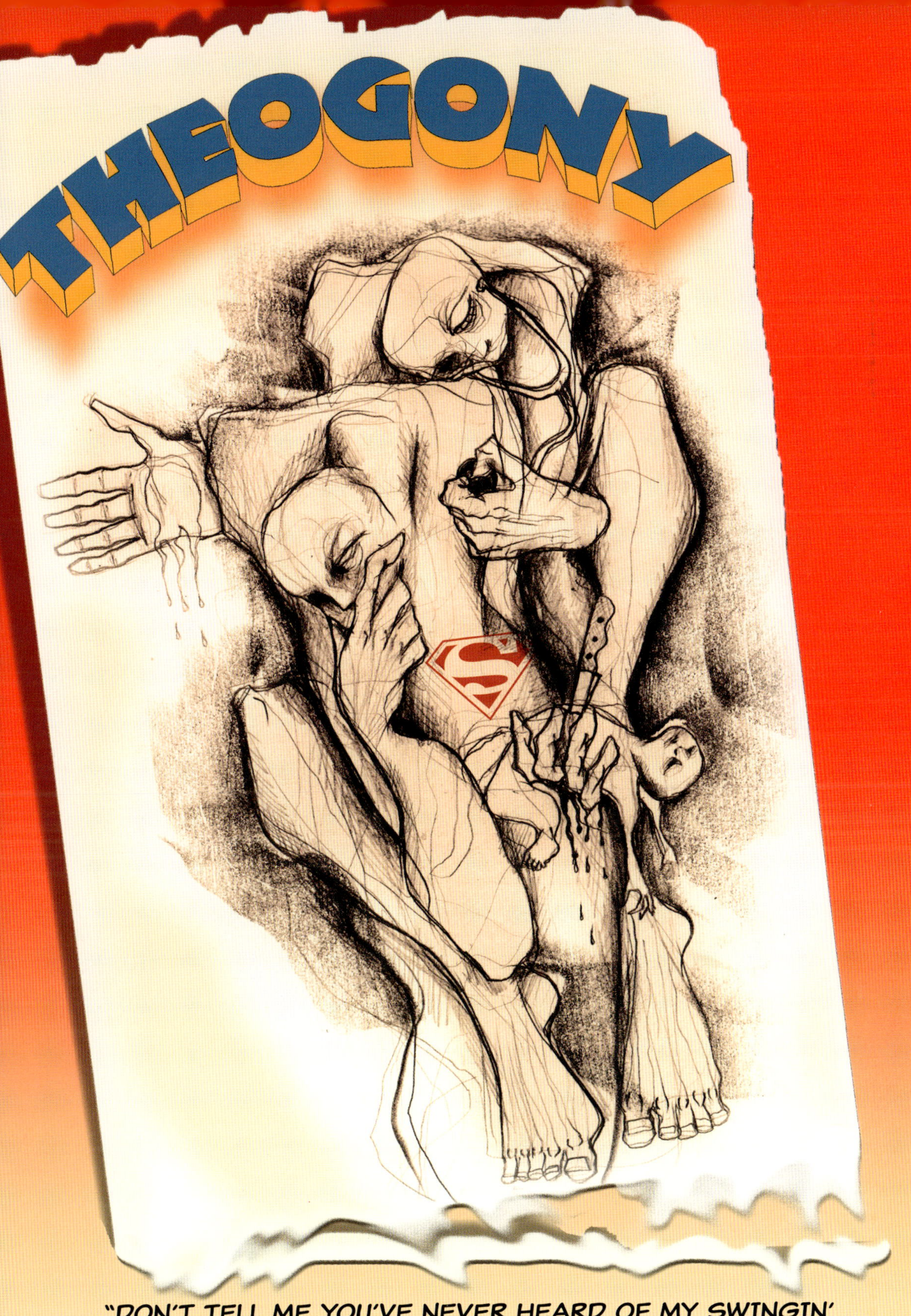

"DON'T TELL ME YOU'VE NEVER HEARD OF MY SWINGIN' SPIDER SPEED?!! IT'S SO SUBLIME, I'M SURPRISED NO ONE'S WRITTEN A SONNET ABOUT IT!"

—FROM *THE AMAZING SPIDER MAN!*

FORTRESS OF SOLITUDE

My mother used to tell me, *Puppet, he's*
a wind-up toy, Dad'll fight till he runs out
of juice, and so he did till he ran out
on us. My mother's boyfriend called me Tease
and Super Doll and said he loved my mouth.
My mom blamed me. I shot off faster than
a speeding bullet after things went South
and worked up to my arms in soap and pans.
But that won't pay the rent. *Give it a whirl,*
my girlfriend said, and so I did it, right?
It's not like nudity is kryptonite.
The clients think I am a party girl.
Truth is, I go back to my room alone.
When home's gone nova, stripping feels like home.

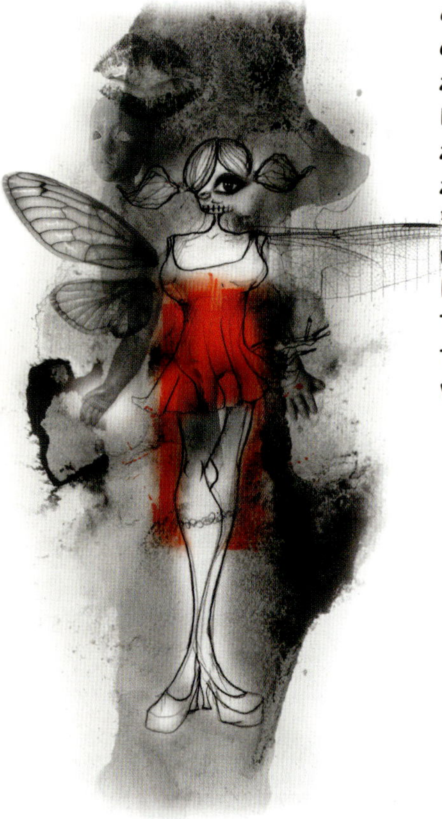

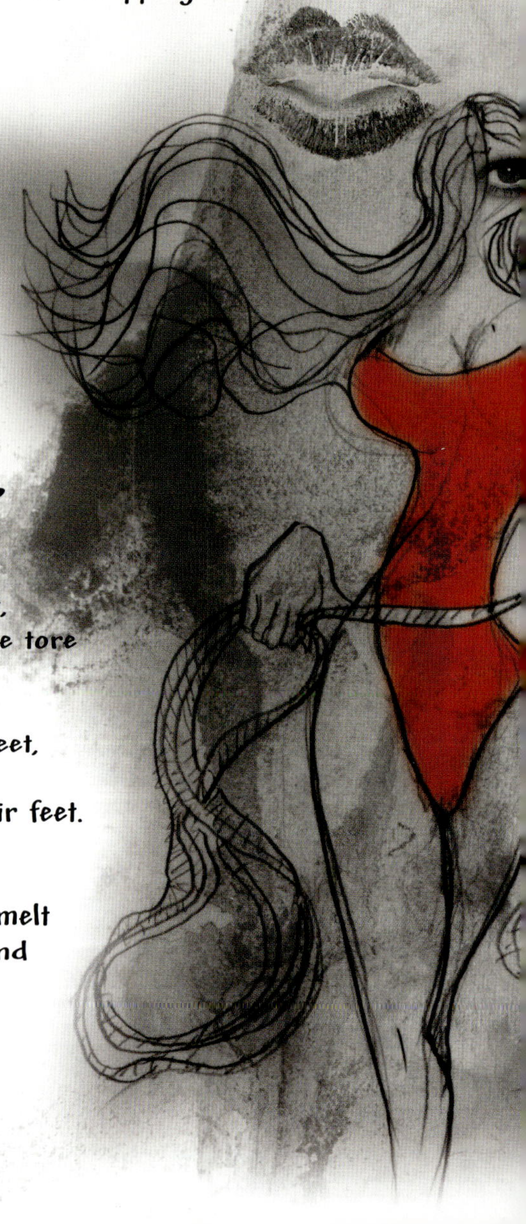

WONDER WOMAN AND THE GRAVITY MONSTER

Miss Wonder Woman, Amazon, is sore
from twenty thousand crunches every night,
but when she fought the Mars Men and she tore
her costume she knew to get her abs tight
she'd have to sacrifice. She wonders when
her breasts began to point down to the street,
when she began to miss the leering men
she used to WHAMMO! knock right off their feet.
She sucks her belly in and clasps her belt,
then on an impulse loops her lasso round
her neck and asks, "What do I want?" "To melt
with fat, give up the fight, to walk the ground
a friend of gravity, embrace that pull."
She wonders, wouldn't that be wonderful?

THE LIVING FLAME

The Living Flame's left pec burns like dry ice
because he's had his heart removed. He needs
the coruscating flame that feeds
to live, he needs the women, to entice
them to his blazing bed, but not to burn
himself away. He's a survivor, forged
by flame to resist flame, to eat till gorged
like a wild cat, to take, then leave, to spurn
his lovers, leaving ash. A Teflon bra
just might survive his heat, but flesh will scorch.
He needs a Burn Babe or a Lady Torch
with whom to char the sheets, etcetera
— some pretty girl. They'll eat each other's fire
with bright chilled zeal, and imitate desire.

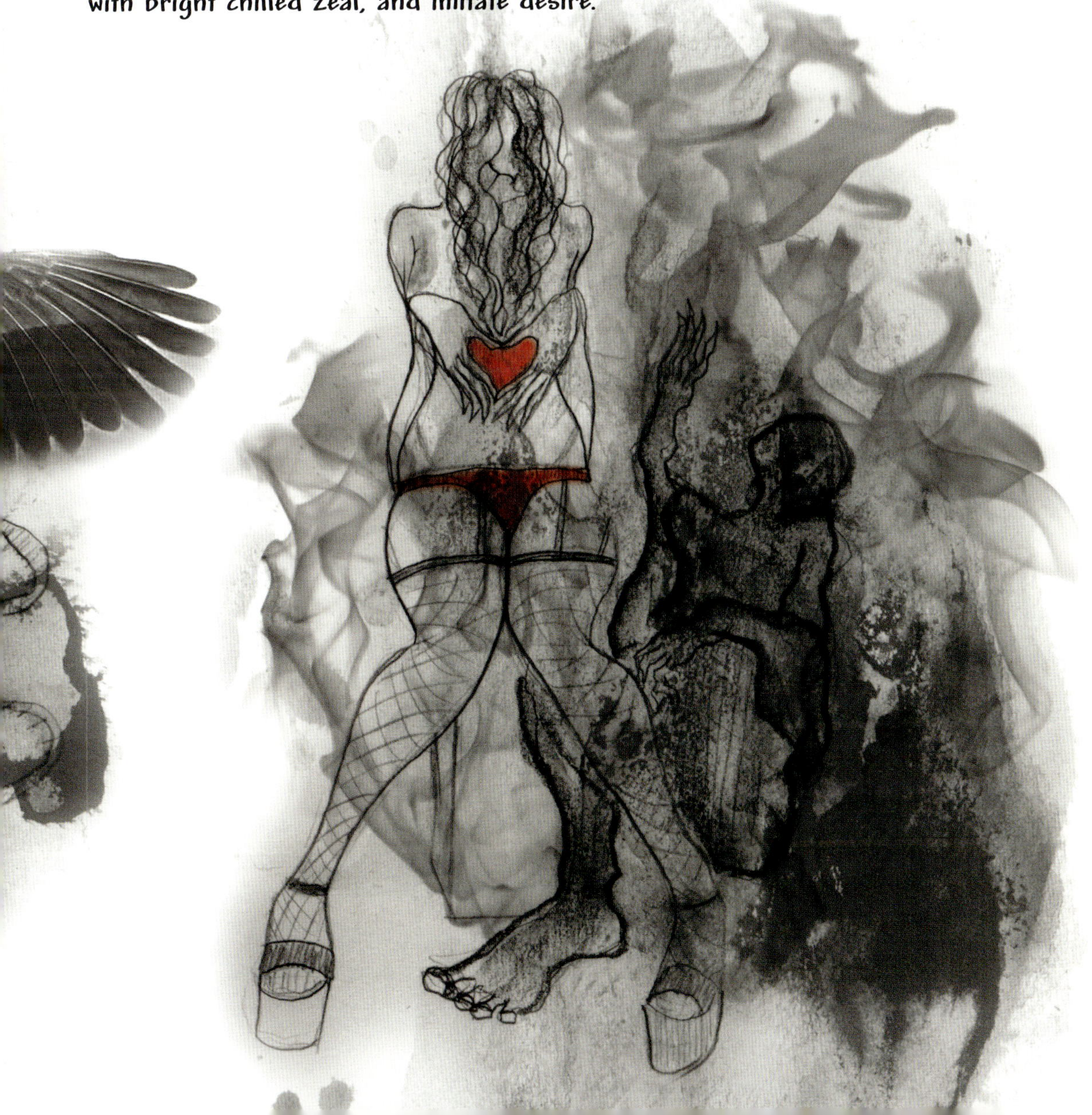

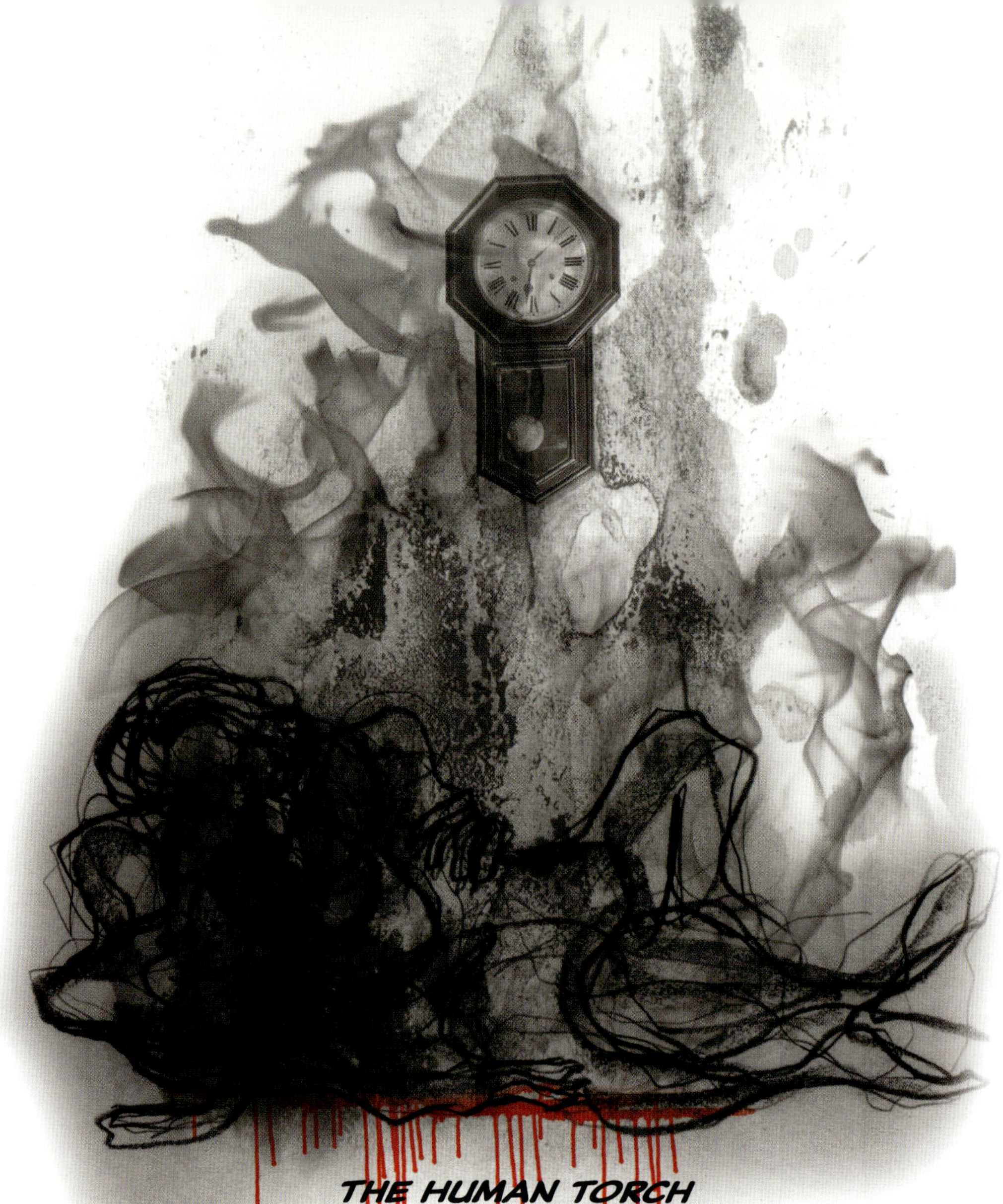

THE HUMAN TORCH

The spark of hunger, blast of lust, red flame
of the wet tongue. The heat of sex, rich flame
of the red box, fire in the breath, stiff flame
of the white cock. These kindle the strange flames
of consciousness, his brain combusting, fire
of taste, ignited nose, his body's fire
like a deep smoldering house, his eye on fire
that sees the world consumed by clocks, slow fire
cremating us. Okay. So let him burn.
Let him be licked by tongues, go up a bonfire
of limbs, release the shot, the charge that fires
the gun. Burn clean, burn well. Let it all burn,
the savings, car, his love for one who's far
from loving back, the whole damn world on fire.

THE BENT ADVENTURES OF INDIA RUBBER MAN

1. India Rubber Man's Credo

The softest creature in the world is hard
to capture, formless, slipping off, not flaccid,
just supple. Nothing can destroy me. Acid,
maybe, it's true (but plastic will retard
its bite). We're soft and weak at birth, we sag
and flex through life, then like a limber tree
die rigid. I'm no stiff. Longevity
comes when we give in like a punching bag.
Passive aggressive? Sure. But it seems drastic
to blast your death ray, jab a fluid ounce
of poison in the neck. I like to trounce
my enemies in ways that are . . . gymnastic.
Who wants to give the villains satisfaction?
I've learned the art of acting without action.

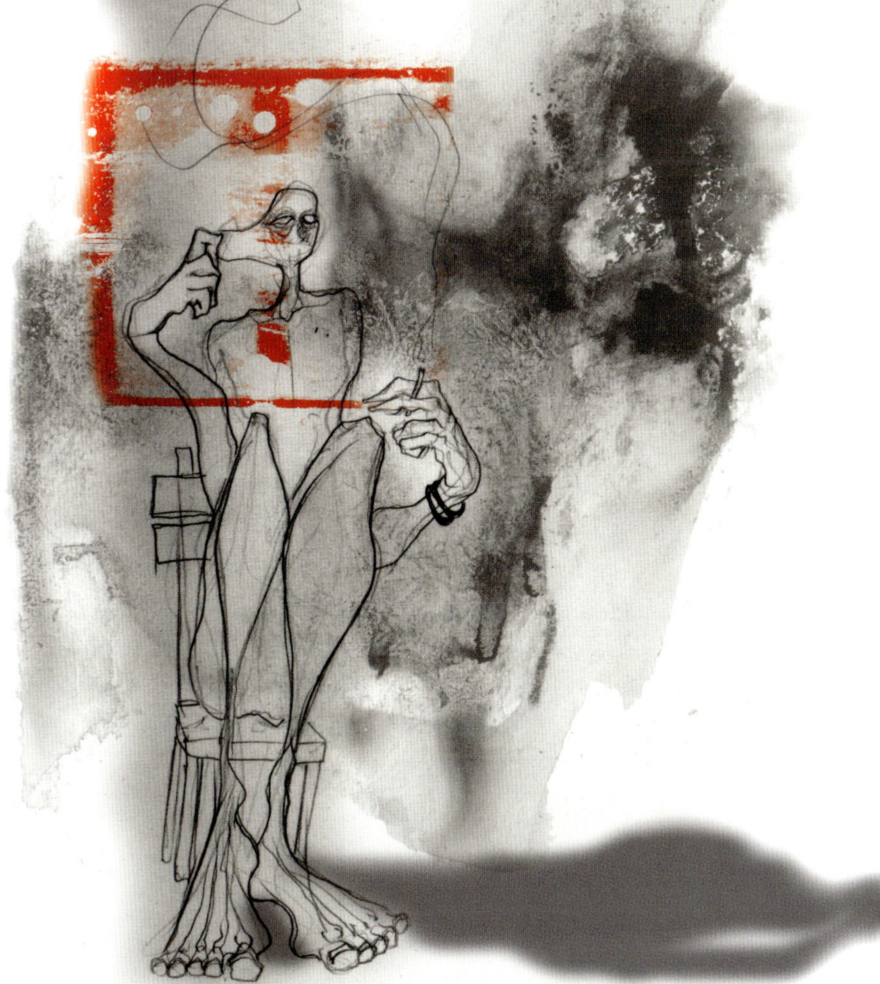

2. The Origin of India Rubber Man

At home in Lodz beneath my father's fists
when after vodka came the chaser, rage,
I learned to twist away, reverse my wrists,
to turn to squirming rubber on the stage,
contortionist or freak. I found a hard
lover to love (with skin like shale, a heart
of labyrinthine quartz, a carved beaut, part-
statue, part queen) and deliquesced like lard
each time she slapped me with her granite tongue.
We made a pair, like bell and clapper, punch
and bruise, until she left. Now, over lunch,
my friend explains exactly what is wrong
with me. I nod (of course I do — I'm plastic).
Tonight I have a date with Miss Elastic.

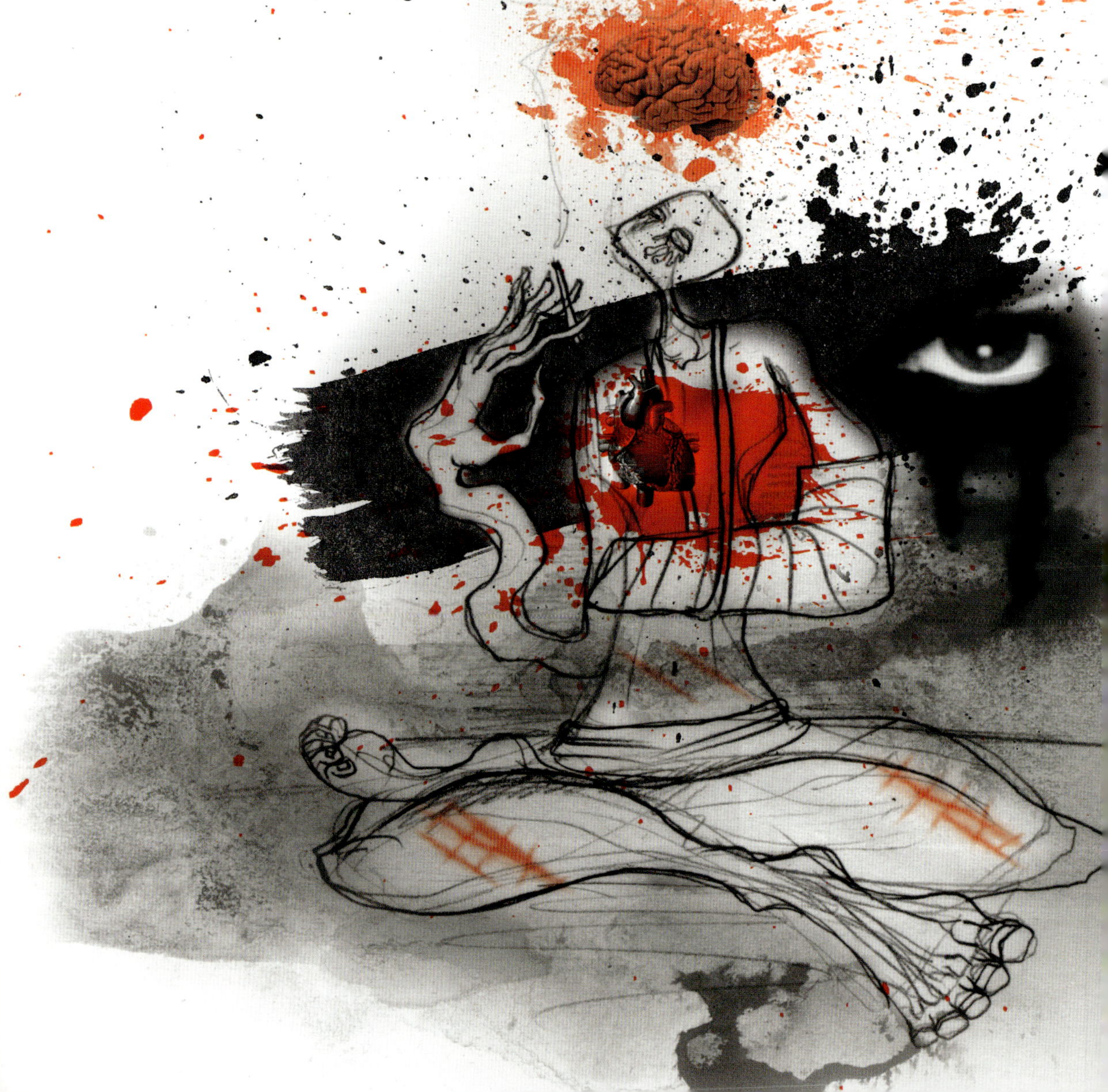

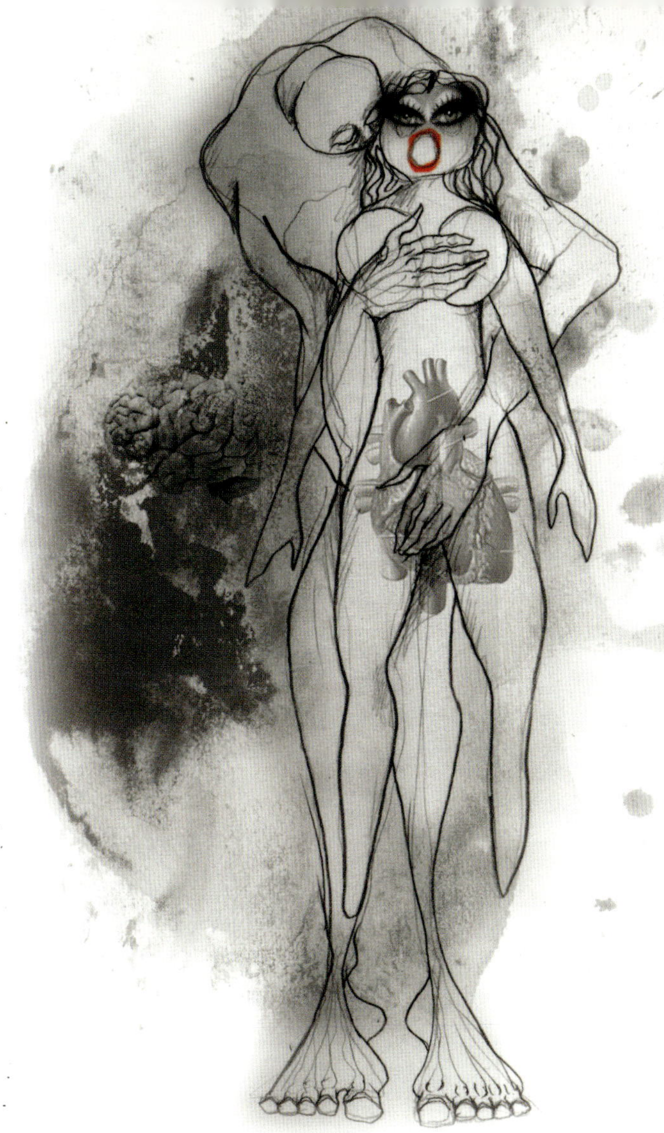

3. India Rubber Man at the Temple of Sin Adult Novelty Store (the Origin of Miss Elastic)

She's just a bag of skin puffed full of air
but she's my bag of skin. I bag her in
the Red Light District, San Francisco, where
the striptease shows and bookstores sell hot sin
and vibrators and magazines and toys,
what you'd call special interest. That's when I
notice the woman browsing with the boys
who glance up from their mags to catch an eye-
ful of a real, a breathing woman. They
would like to swipe their Visa cards between
her breasts. Desperate, I guess. Me, too. I pay
the guy, walk out and dodge a limousine
of screaming drunks, stare down a staring teen.
At home I kneel between her legs and pray.

4. The Anthem of Miss Elastic

"Hey Doll," the shop boy says, "and how are you
today?" "I feel a bit inanimate,"
I say, and spread my rubber lips. How to
react? Am I a doll? Did you create
me in the image of your fantasy?
Must I keep stretching till I fill the hole
inside your brain? Or sing, "Say can you see
my peaches are just peel?" I have no pole
to prop me up, no flag to pledge allegiance
to, just pursuit of happiness. I buy
my gum to chew on, walk away and feel
across my butt and breasts the shop boy's glance.
Once home you lay me on the bed. And I
let you: I'm patriotic, almost real.

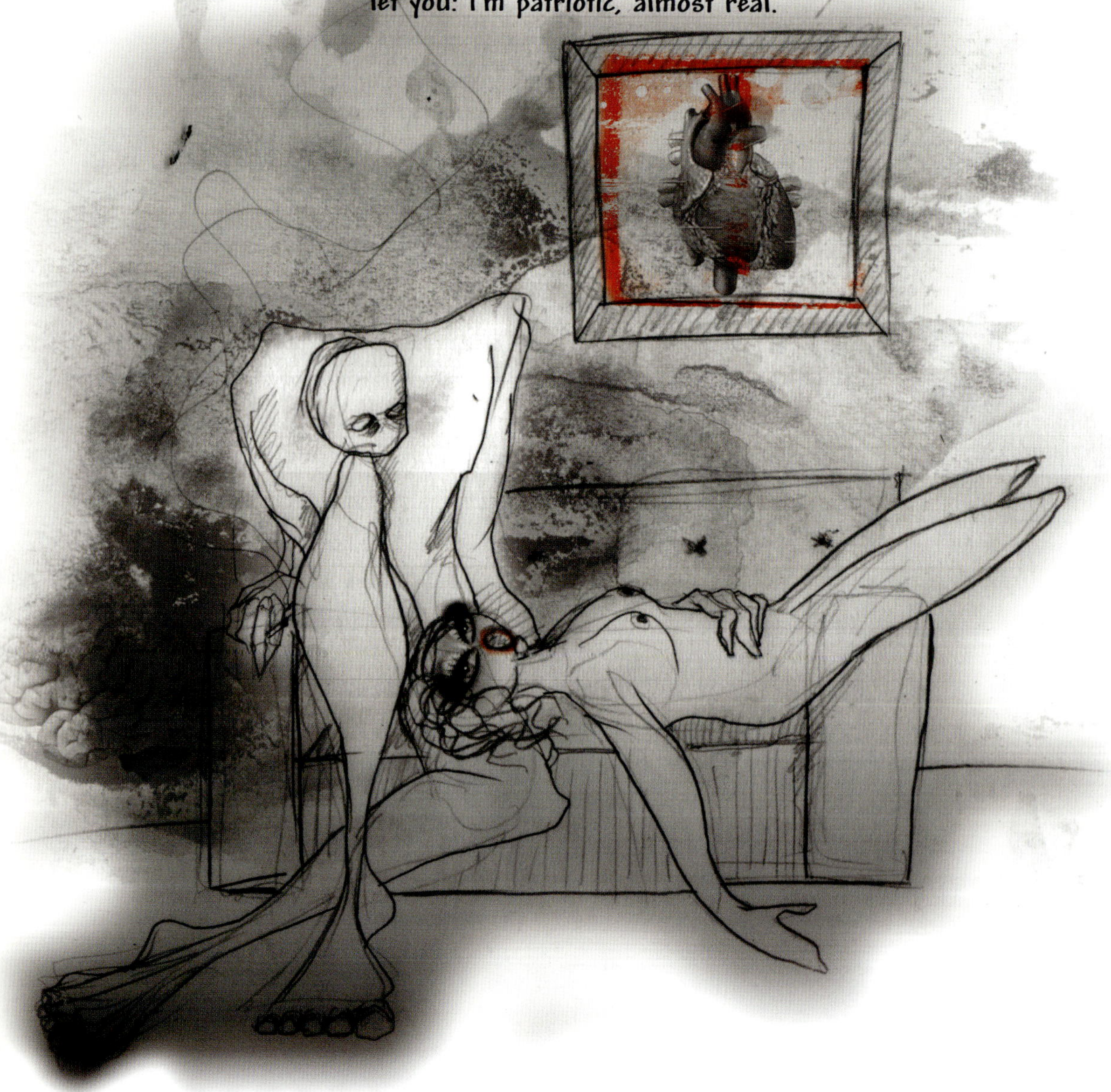

5. Miss Elastic Rescues India Rubber Man from Evil X-Girlfriend

She's too much for my rubber heart.
She is the knife that left the wound.
Yet when she left I couldn't start
my life because out of the ground
she rose again on zombie feet,
a strange, unholy thing, drained white
and drumming out a zombie beat
while stumbling hungry through the night.
She ate my brain, till you became
my shotgun shell, my holy water
melting away the past, the pain.
But then the movie ended. Daughter
of factories, open your lap.
Let's have some zombie sex, then nap.

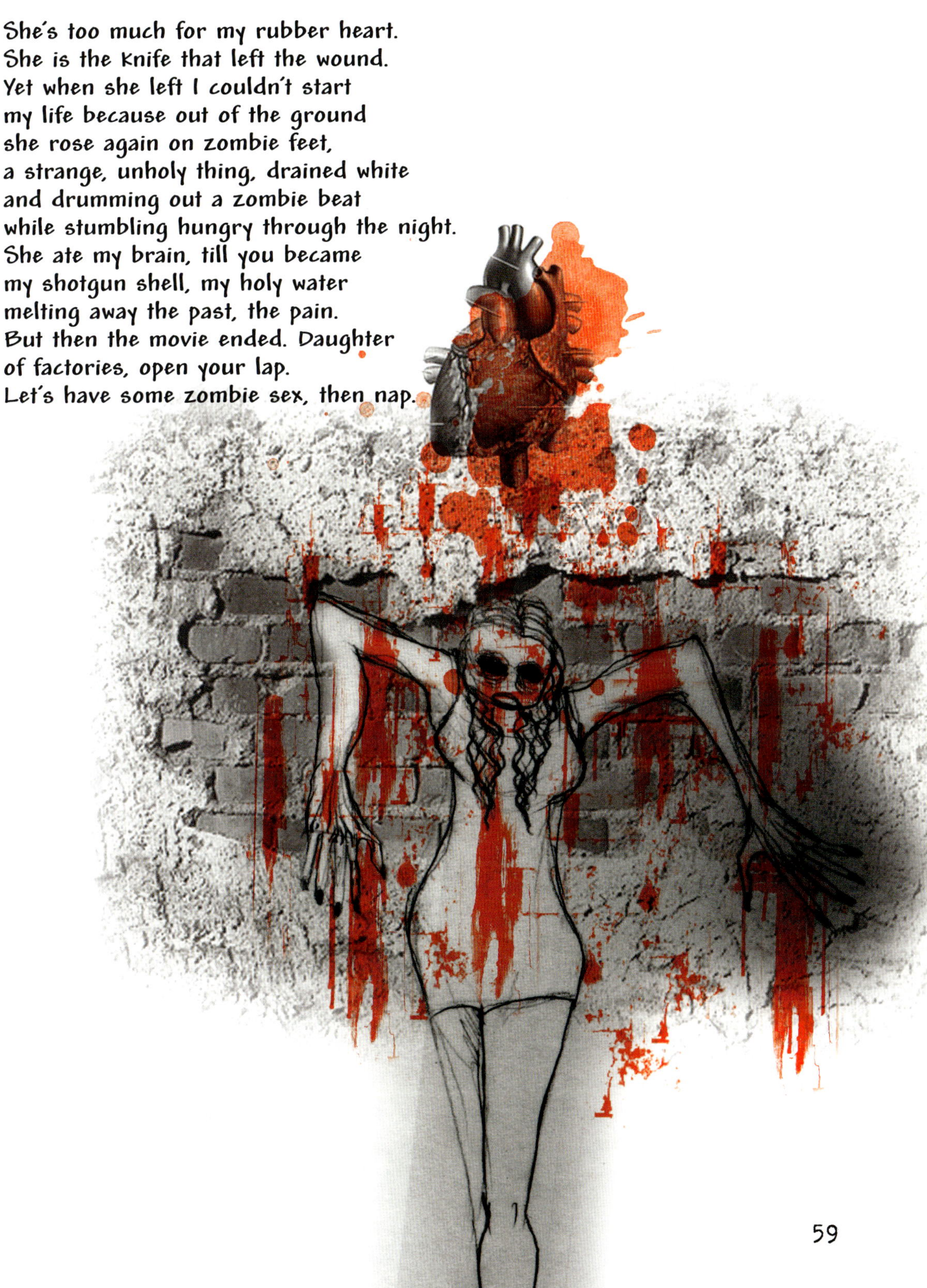

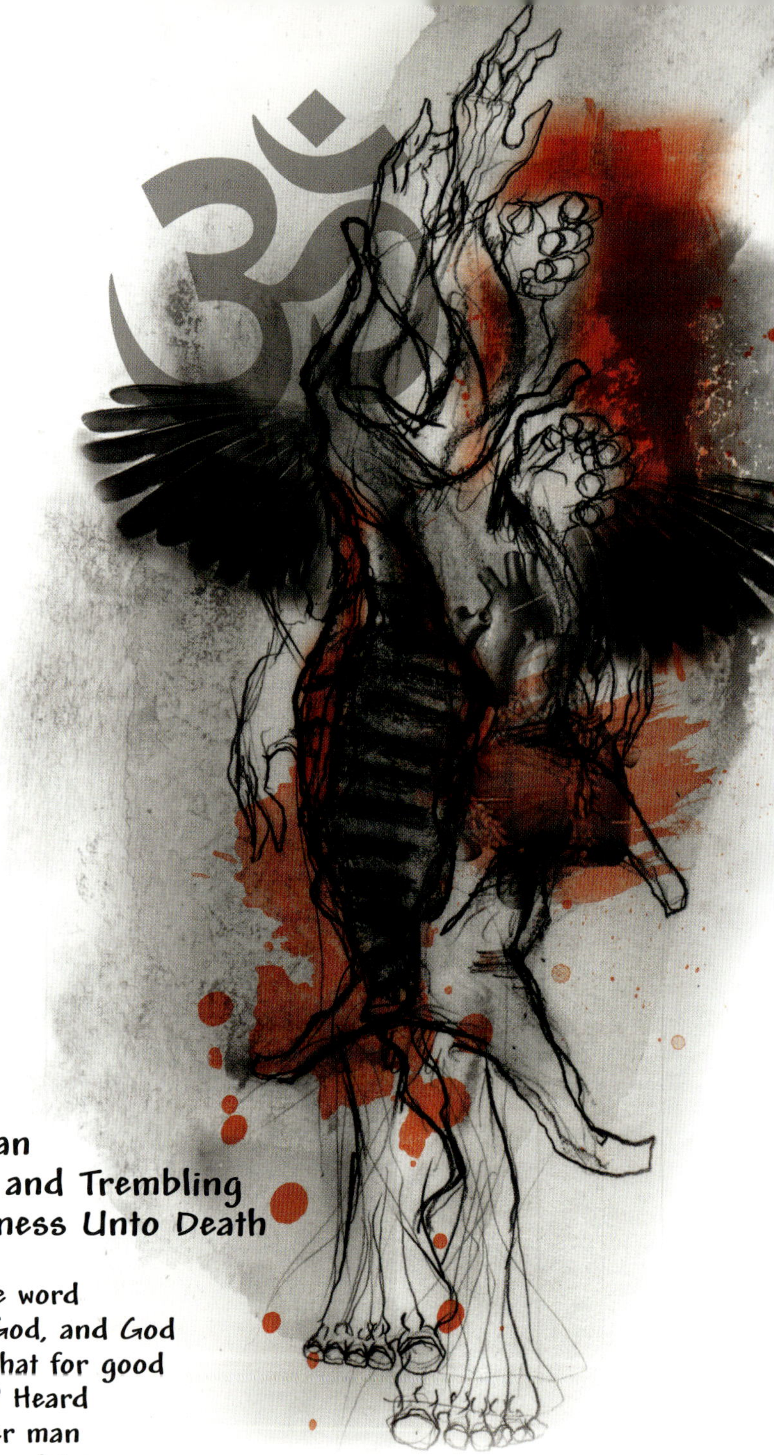

6. India Rubber Man and the Fear and Trembling and Sickness Unto Death

In the beginning was the word
and the word was with God, and God
was just a word. How's that for good
old-fashioned cynicism? Heard
the one about the rubber man
who fell in love? It's a good joke.
His lover was a doll some man
designed, with holes. She never spoke,
she never moved, she let him do
just what he willed, the perfect mate.
She never won at Scrabble, threw
fits and walked out, but did deflate.
Where's God to breathe his word in you
to puff you up? Is God dead, too?

7. India Rubber Man's Buddhist Christmas

I prop you up just like the doll
you are, there by the potted plant,
and string the tinsel on the wall.
The faded winter light comes slant
through the three-paneled Japanese
screen, lighting the Madonna statue.
The Buddha hangs left of the wreath
between the paper lanterns tattooed
with Chinese characters. His female
breasts and pregnant belly are drawn
in ink. Three guests, plus me, the host,
to make a party. God sends email
to those who pray, but I won't fawn
(except on you, my holy ghost).

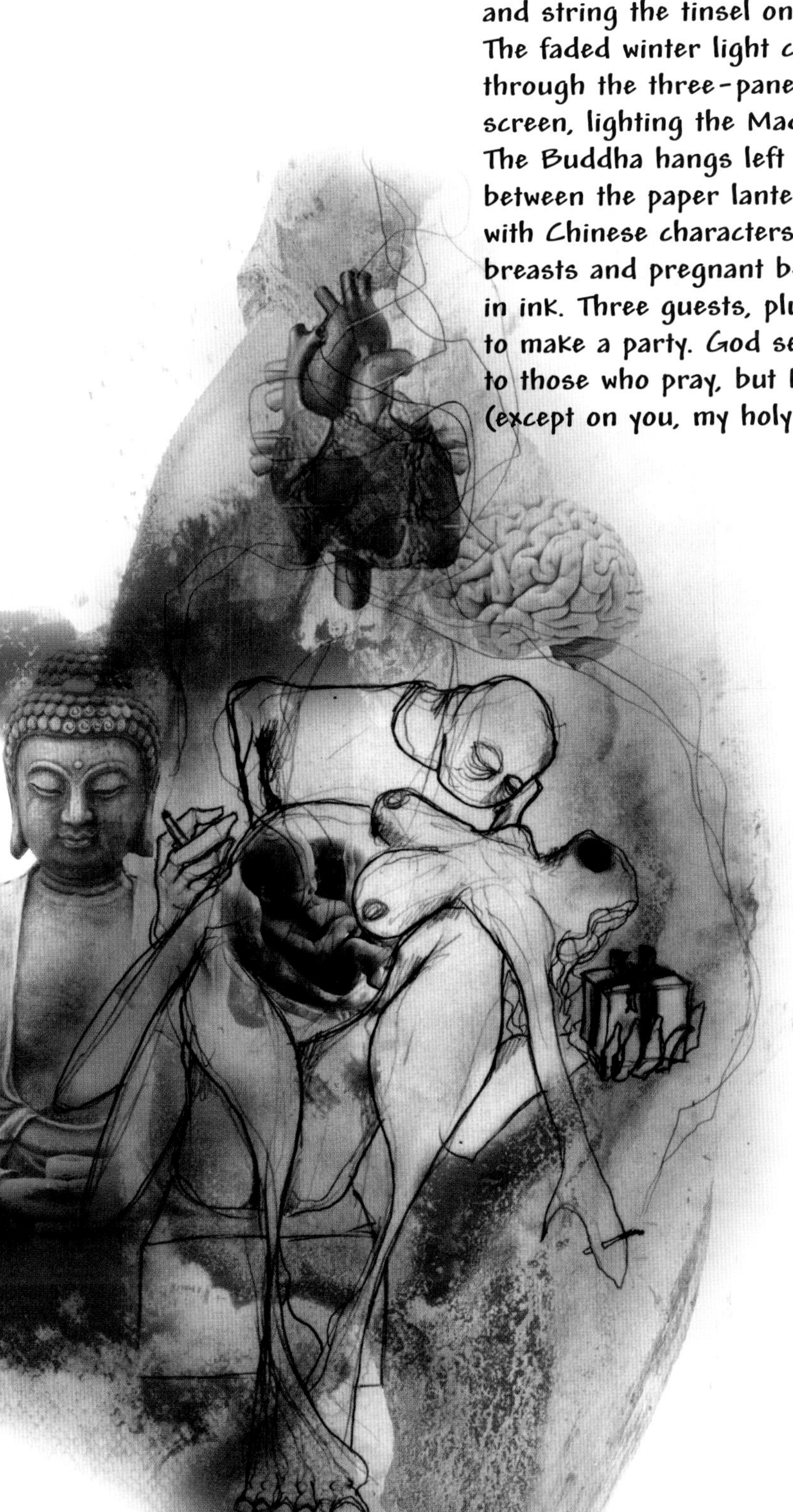

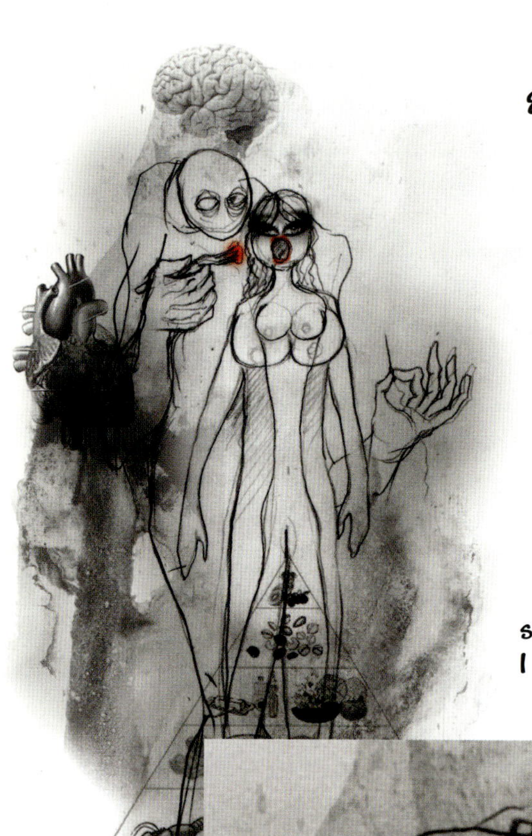

8. India Rubber Man and the Anorexic Doll

I want to see your red mouth eat. Just take
one bite, a pretzel or an onion ring.
Please eat. I know the fruit is fake,
but eat. You didn't touch a thing.
Please try the steak I carved.
I'll even clean your chin.
You must be starved.
You look too thin.
You need to be pumped up,
need someone who can give
the love you feel you don't deserve,
someone to pour into your cup
some pinot noir. Please eat. Please come alive.
I made this meal for you. Please, let me serve.

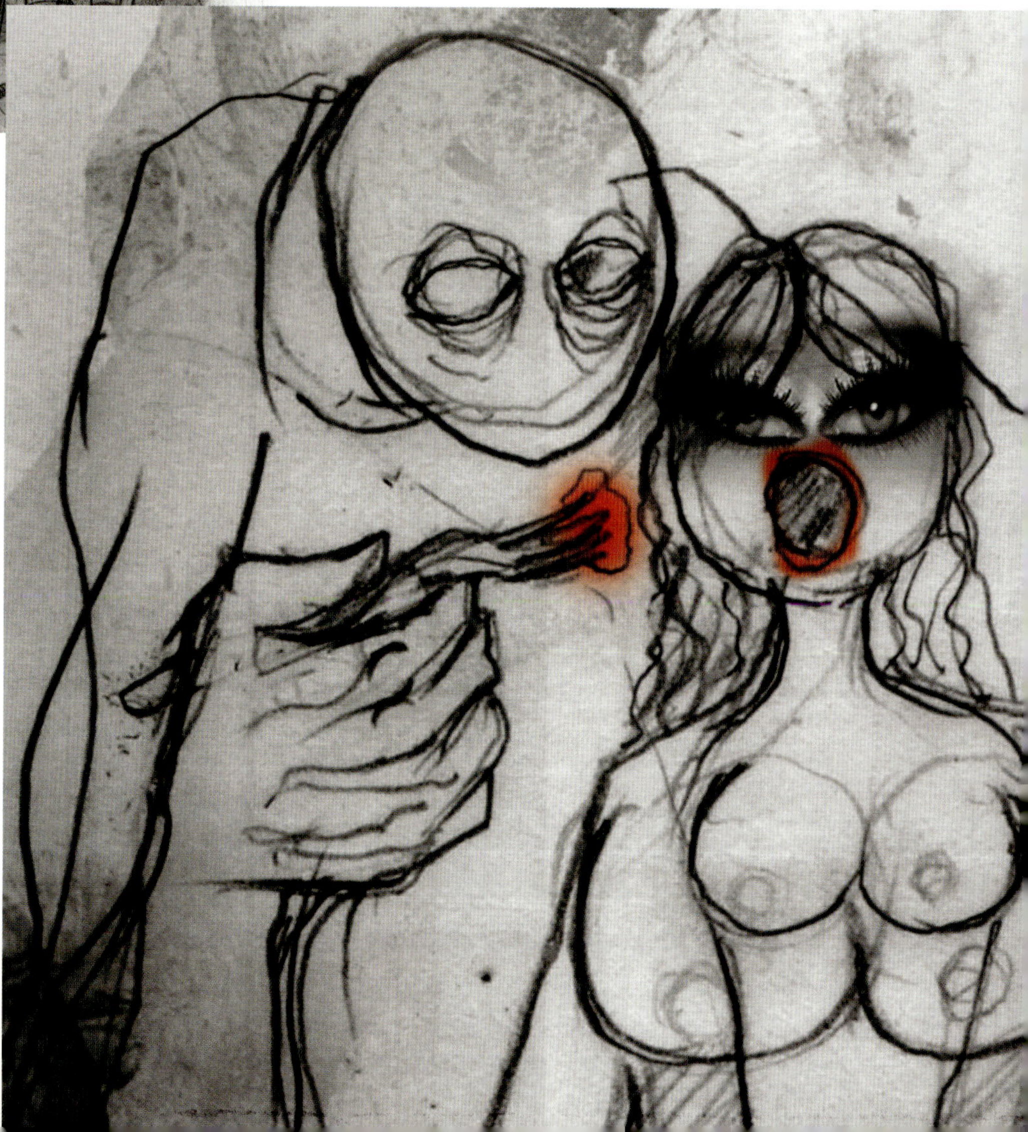

9. India Rubber Man and Miss Elastic in the Morning

And in the morning, watching light refract
and scatter yellow photons on the bed,
I thought back to the night before, the act
I did in your vagina painted red,
I saw your body floating on the covers
upon a pool of light, about to climb
into the air, the way I guess that lovers
must feel. I asked you then, "Will you be mine?"
but nothing came out of your open lips
except perhaps a subtle hiss. I held
your clumsy hand in mine, caressed your hips
and breasts, and once again I tried to meld
with you, to be with you in this strange loving.
And afterwards, you floated there, unmoving.

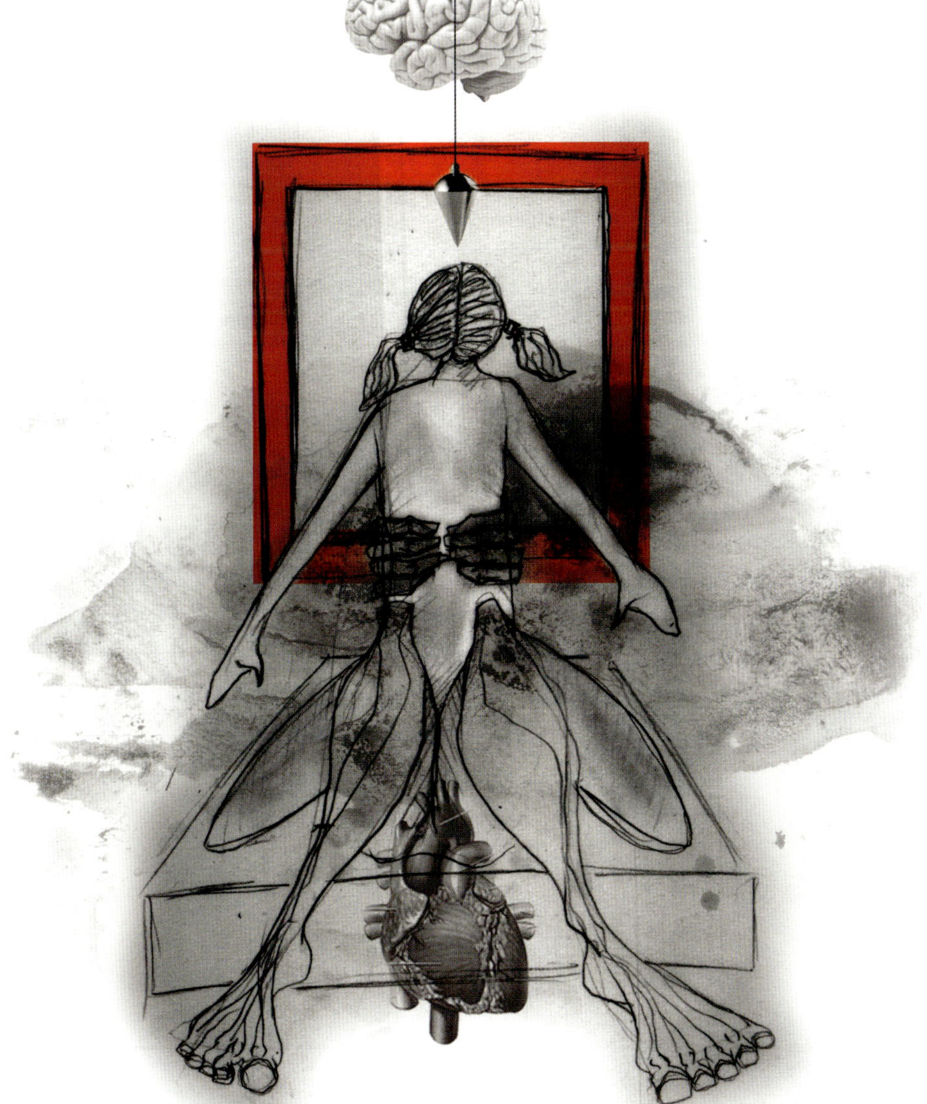

10. INDIA RUBBER MAN AND THE BATH

Last night was great. I felt elated
each time I bounced a kiss off you.
This morning, though, you look deflated,
your flat face watching while I do
my hair. I call you "sweet Doohickey,"
"Dollface," pet names I have for you,
but you just sag. I wash the sticky
juice from your chin, or try to do
so, but when I feel your face give
beneath the sponge, I carry you
and bathe you in the tub. To live
you have to wash. This filth won't do.
It isn't dirty to love you,
and though we cannot wed, I do.

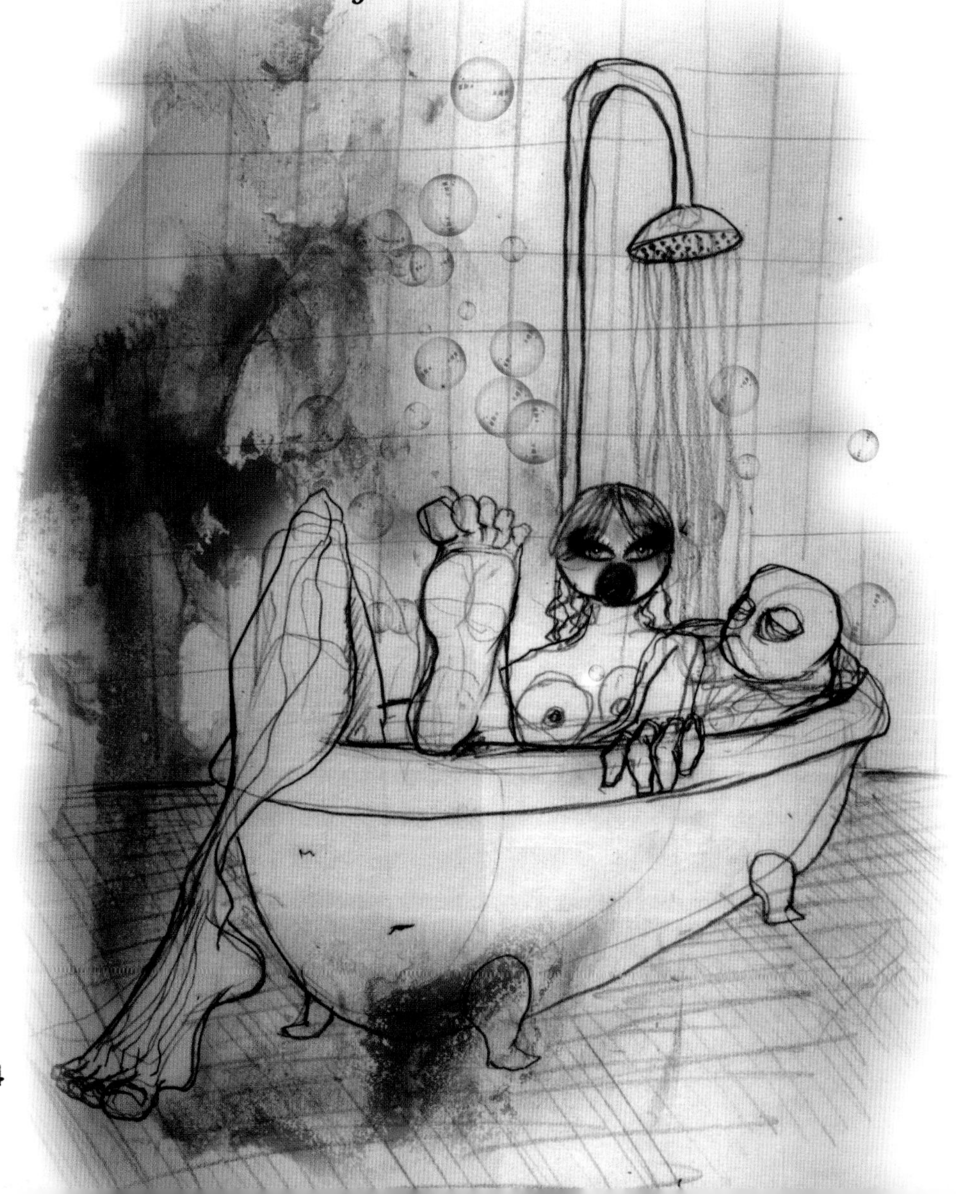

BESTIARY

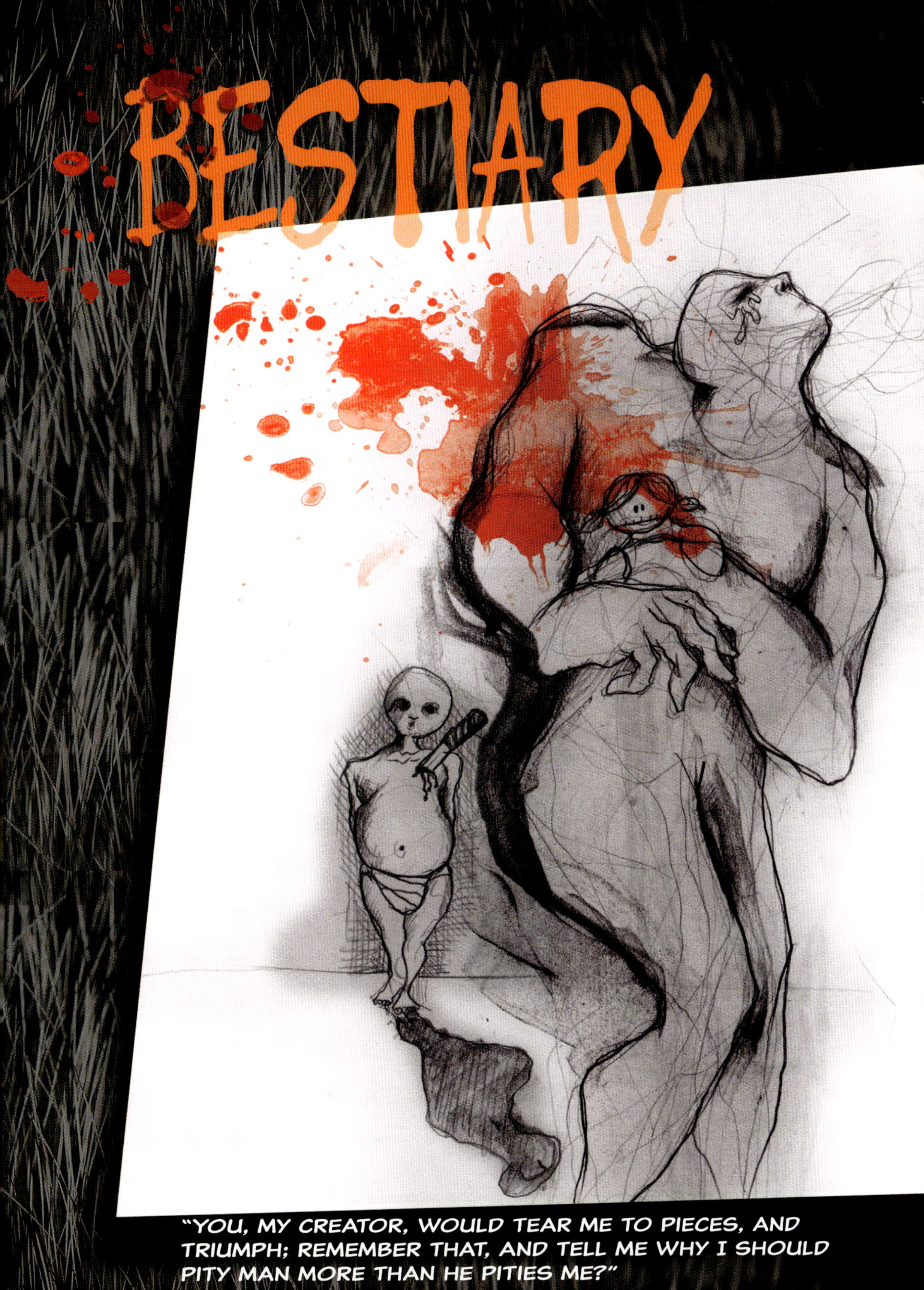

"YOU, MY CREATOR, WOULD TEAR ME TO PIECES, AND TRIUMPH; REMEMBER THAT, AND TELL ME WHY I SHOULD PITY MAN MORE THAN HE PITIES ME?"

—THE MONSTER, IN *FRANKENSTEIN,* BY MARY SHELLEY

THE MONSTER SPEAKS

I am malicious since I am miserable.
Am I not shunned and feared by every man?
Even you, creator, want to pull
my pieces free, though it was you stitched hand
to wrist, then wrist to forearm, arm to shoulder.
Your holy electricity restores
my graveyard flesh to warmth, but your heart's colder
to me than glaciers on Antarctic shores.
Since you're playing God, I'll act my part,
not Christ brought back to die — I'll play the devil
(a better role) and make your good my evil.
I cannot make you love, so I'll do worse:
I'll make you fear. I'll desolate your heart.
I'll make you curse the hour of your birth.

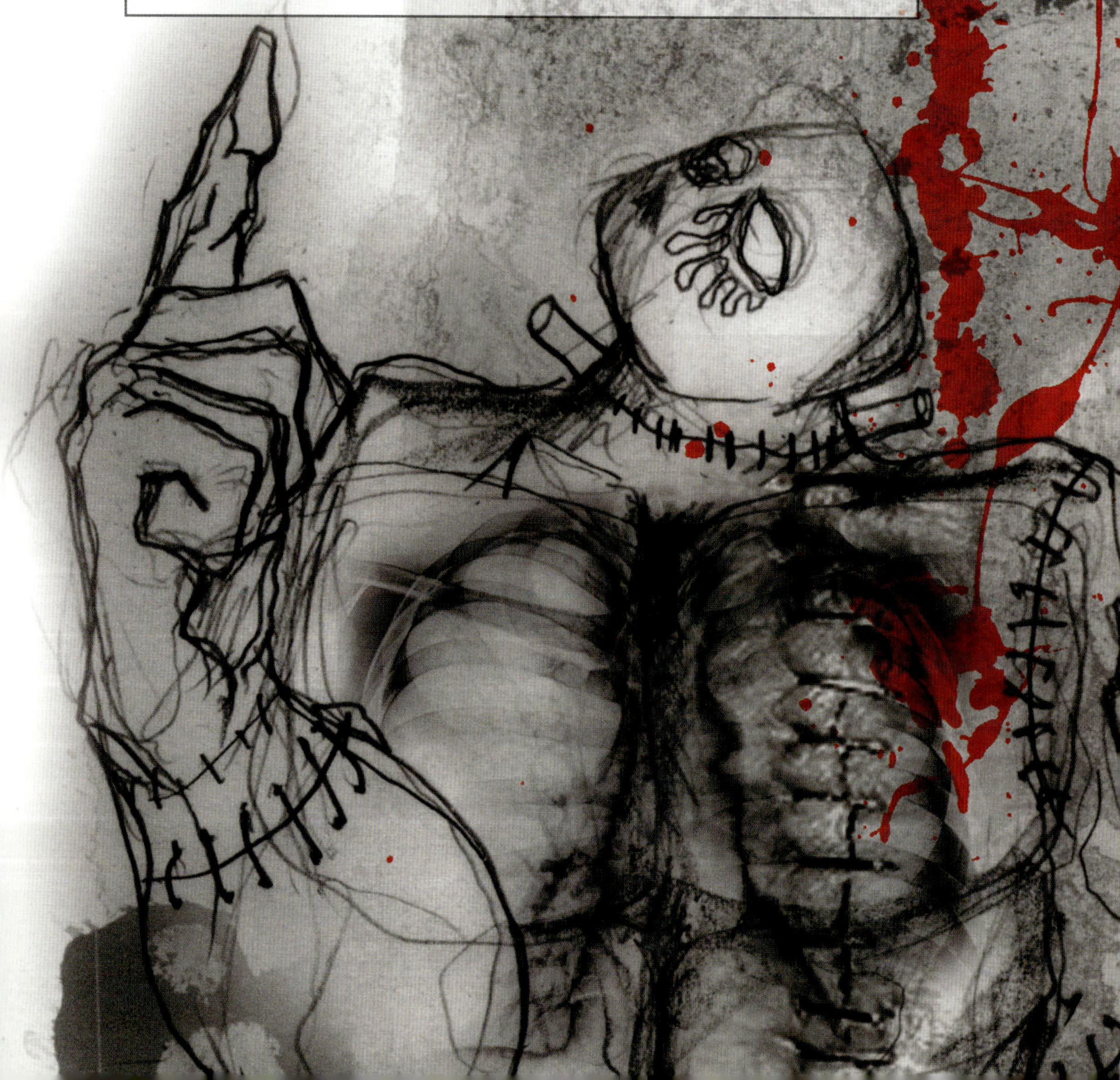

THING

There was nonbeing before being. Before
nonbeing, there was no firmament, no air.
Yet something breathed. But where? And from what core
came all this water stretching everywhere?
So dark that darkness hid inside the dark,
nothing to show the deep, everywhere sea,
no death, no immortality, no spark
of birth, and yet the thing breathed windlessly.
Maybe it's in us at the nucleus
and all our thoughts are molecules awhirl
about unknowing force. Maybe for men
this being is God. Or maybe not. The world
prays to this nullity, Amen, Amen
(as if a thing like that would care for us).

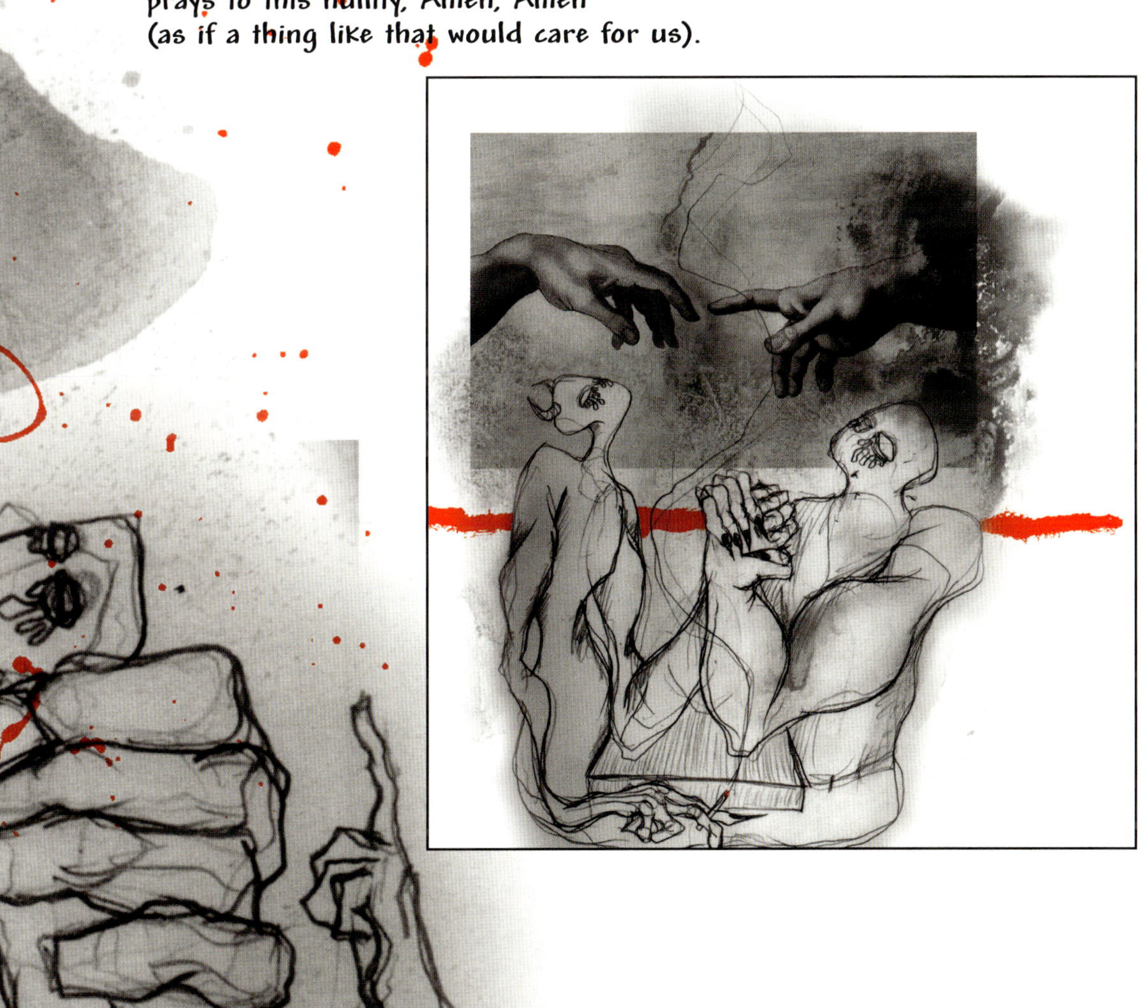

A STRANGER'S NEWSPAPER

I hadn't heard of him for quite a while.
There'd been unpleasantness, some holy wars,
torture, and witches burned; later, the stars
were measured, catalogued and put on file
and angels dropped their shining spears and wept.
Finally, I heard that he'd retired
from the trade. He said that he was simply tired,
didn't like collecting on our debt
like some evil banker. Who wants that?
He'd been the sun around whom all would orbit.
Now he merited a tiny obit
below the fold beside an ad for hats.
I gazed out at the blurring of the tracks
then returned the paper I had read,
asking the stranger, "You hear God is dead?"
He grimaced, "Gods are like zombies. They come back."

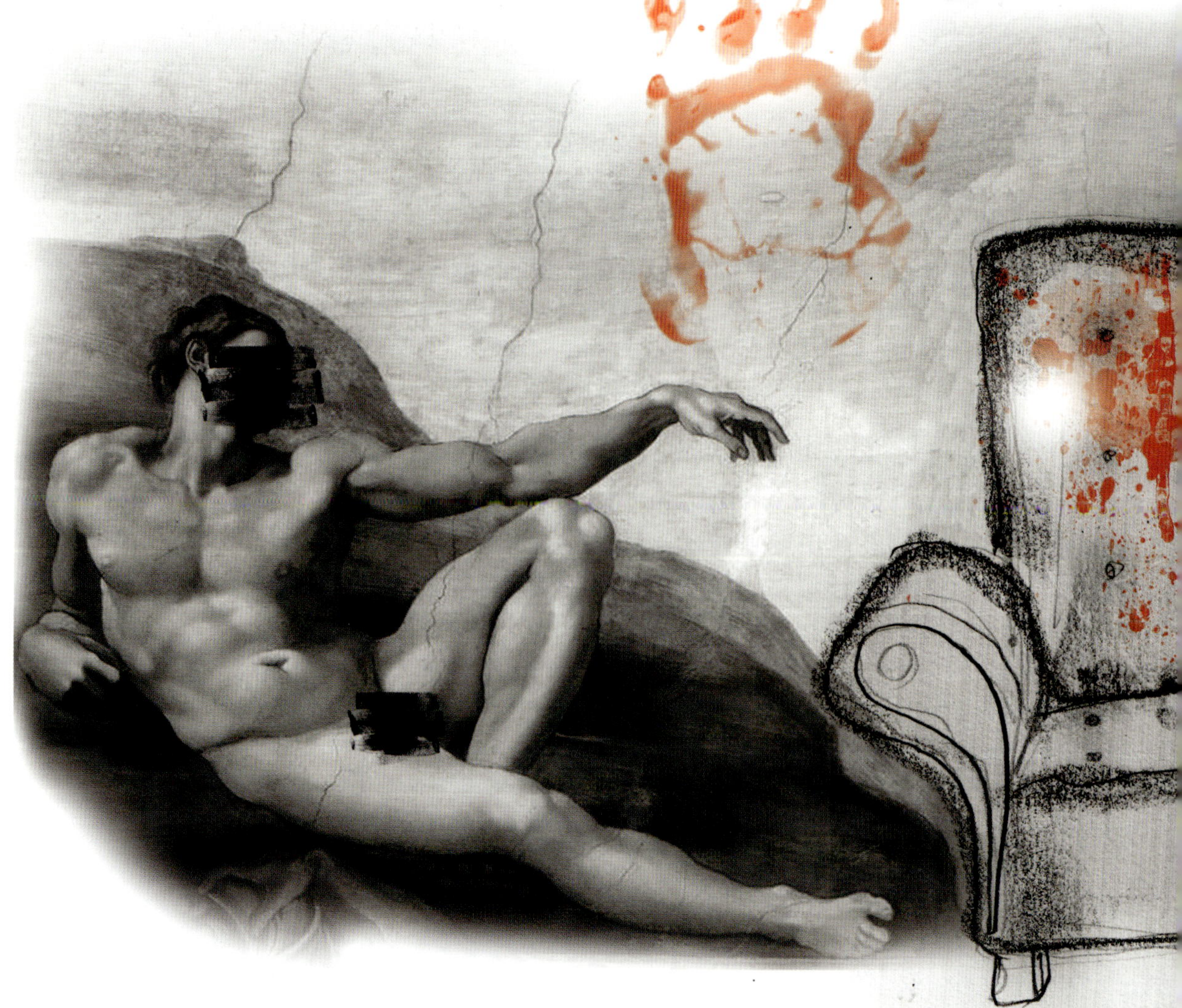

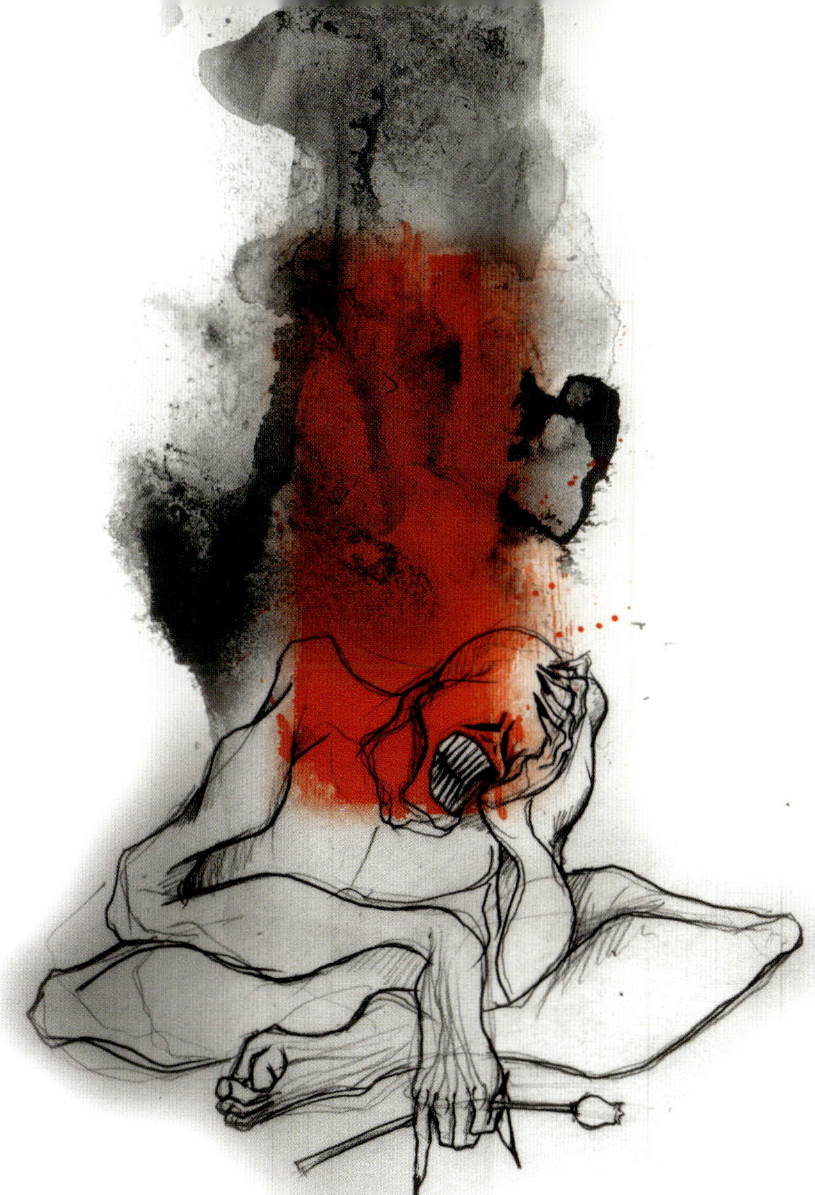

THE FIRST DARK KNIGHT

After I fell, I crawled up from the pit,
and though my wings were tarry, still I muscled
into the sky and tossed like a lost kite
on winds blown from a God's fat cheek. I tussled
through Heaven's rolling spheres while like an arc light
the City shone above. Unholy ghost,
I banged the Porcelain Gate as a dark knight
come to wreak revenge against the Host.
And did he send bright angels out to fight?
Did his harsh voice command that I should roast?
No, and no. That riddling two-faced joker.
I banged and banged. He didn't even say,
"No one home." No one has a better poker
face than God. What could I do? I went away.

THE BLOWFLY THING

I heard a fly buzz when I died. I stepped
inside the chamber to be teleported,
and then it must have been a blue fly crept
inside with me, so when the atoms sorted
themselves again the circuitry gave off
a pop, a blue uncertain stumbling buzz.
I molted, left the corpse, and dug a trough
of earth. After a week, I rose, a fuzz
of beard below my chin, with great glass wings
and goggle eyes, a metal shell. I'm sorry.
I know I scare you, laying eggs in things
discarded (garbage, bodies) but don't worry:
If Jesus were a bug, he'd be a fly.
I'm born from death and kill death when I rise.

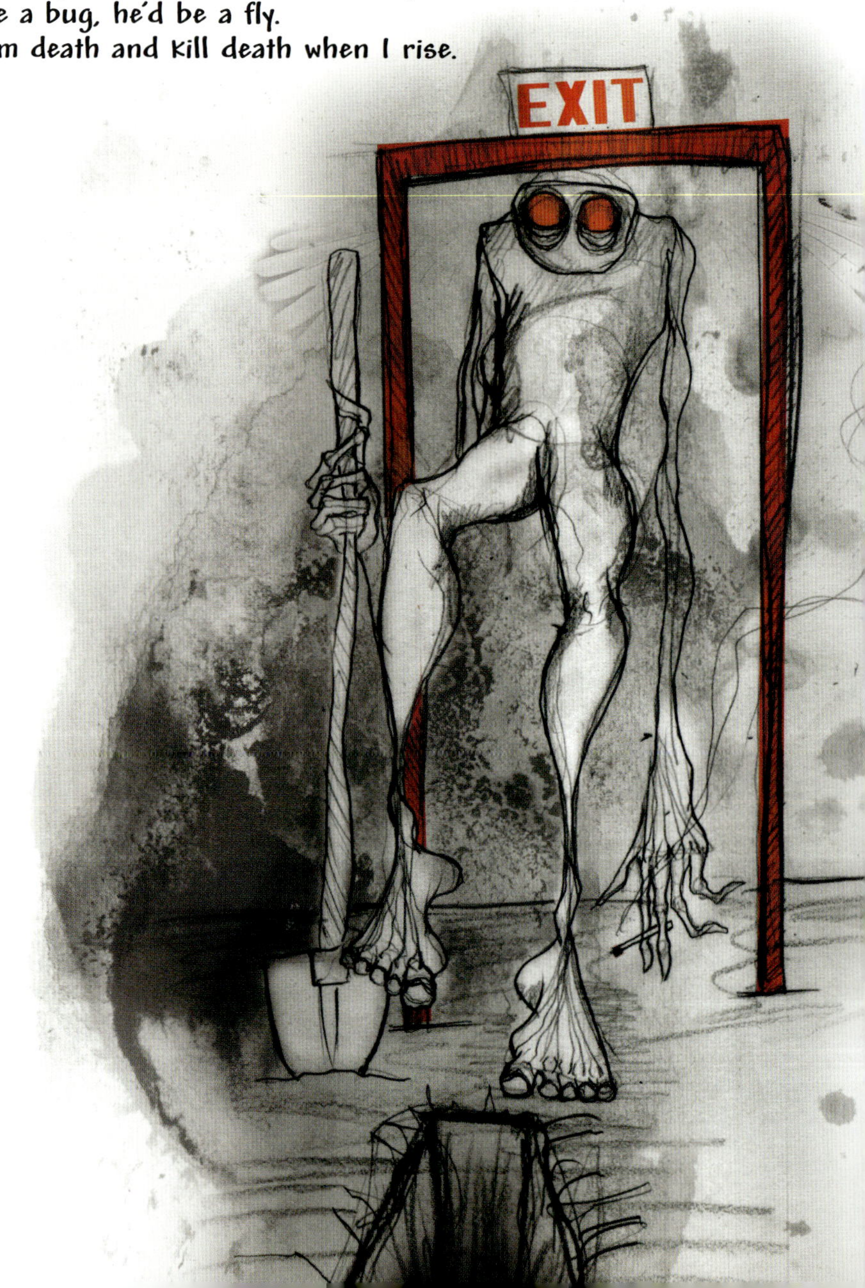

THE TWO-HEADED MAN

The man was always fighting with himself
because he had two heads. One played the role
of optimist, as airy as an elf,
the other, dark and hairy as a troll,
would grouse and wheeze like a pneumatic drill.
And people made cruel jokes. "A man who got
ahead," they said, or "Look, it's twins!" The dull
one had no love but the blonde head did get
some dates, until his counterpart's crude leer
murdered the mood. "I must be free," he said,
and slipped an earwig in his brother's ear,
which ate the brain. But then he felt half-dead.
I've killed myself, he thought and held it near,
whispering through the night, "Dear head, dear head."

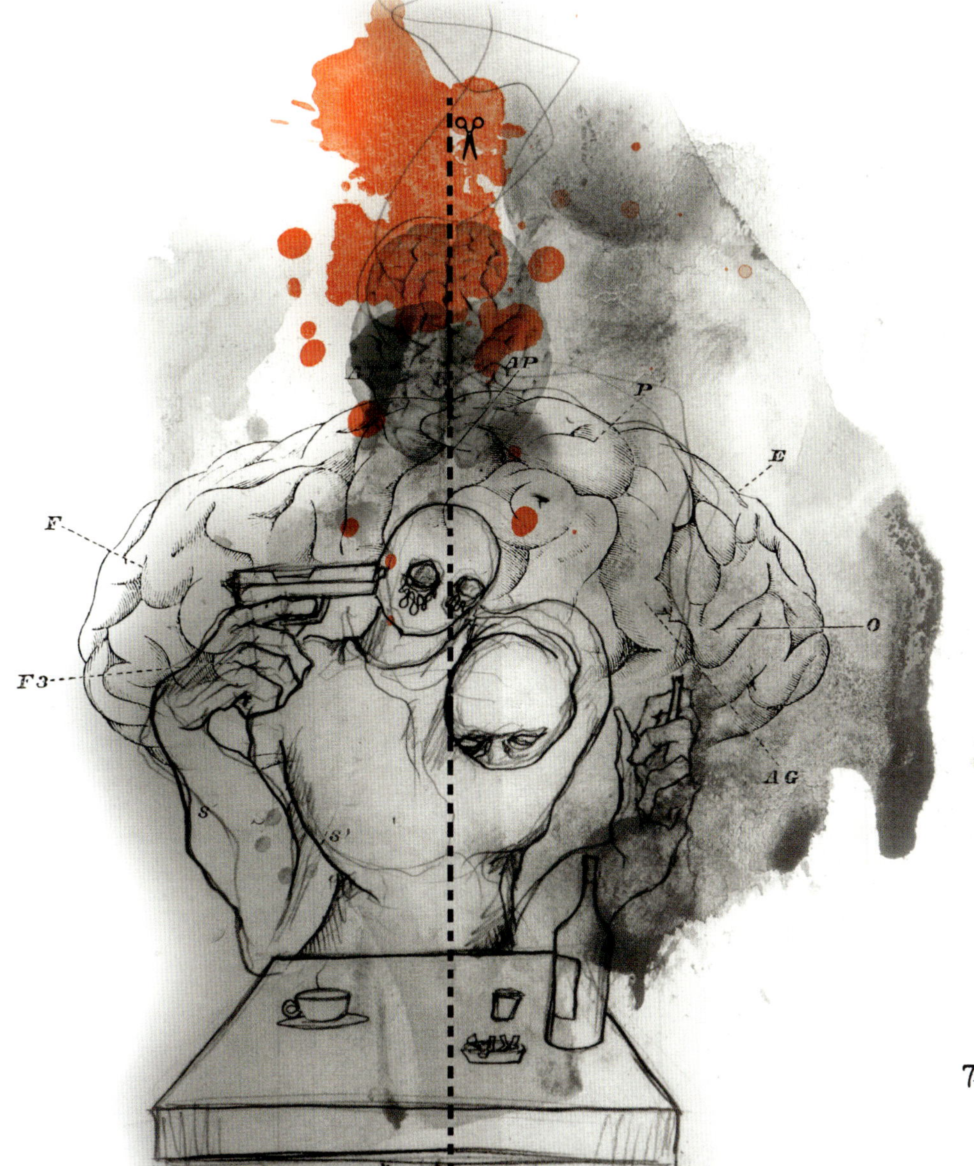

THE SPHINX

A monster in the bright Sahara rests
upon strong haunches and wide lion paws.
Down from her chest hang hairy female breasts
and lion teeth adorn her human jaws
to eat the flesh of travelers she tests
with riddles: What goes on four legs at birth,
two legs when grown, then three? The one who bests
the Sphinx is Oedipus, who'll be at first
adventurer, then herdsman, then some other
roles besides: father-killer, Theban king,
and also husband to his widowed mother.
Of all the men on earth he'll know a thing
or two of horror and of fate's gross plan,
and of the greatest monster of them all: man.

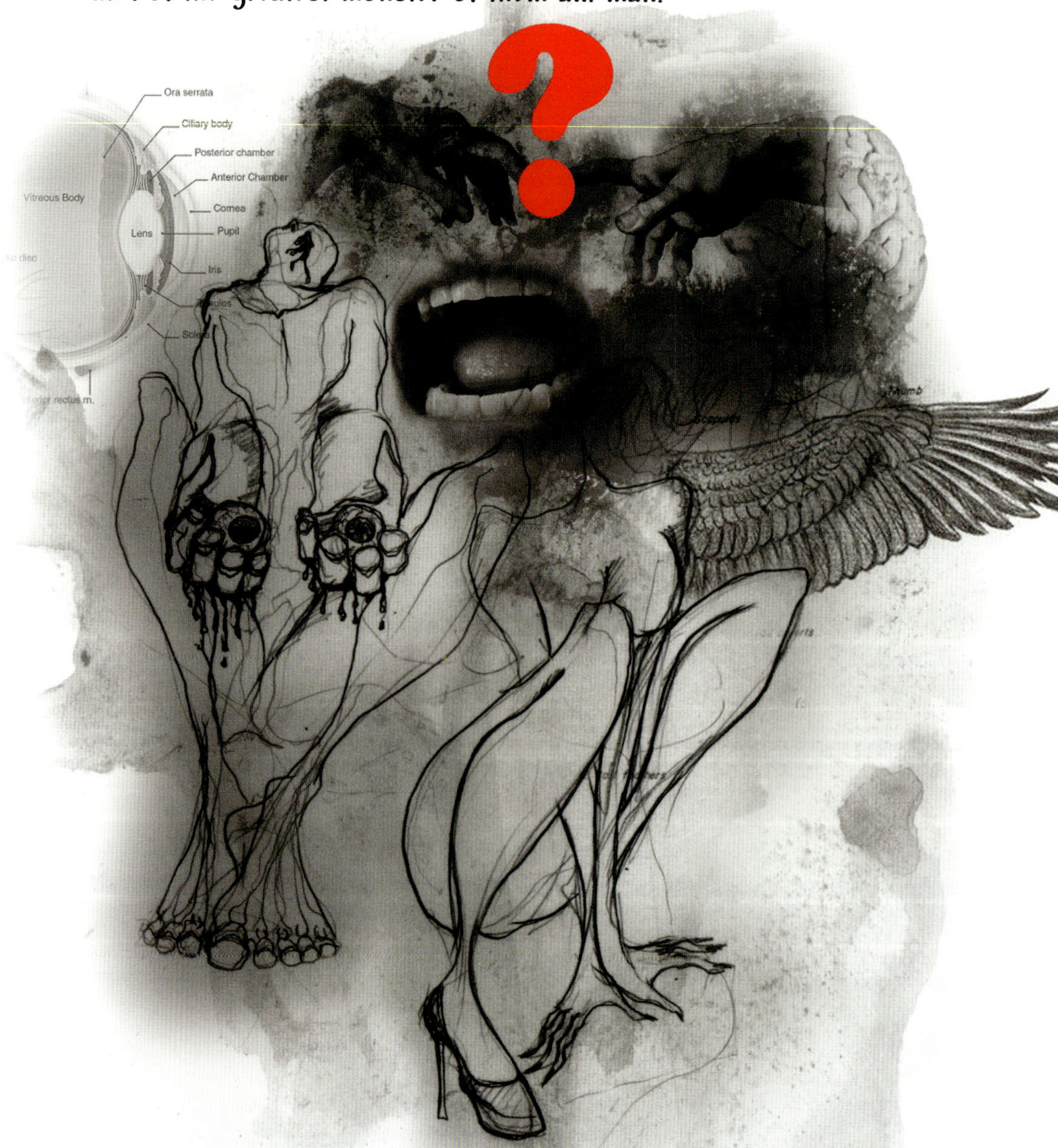

WAYS OF LOOKING AT A VAMPIRE

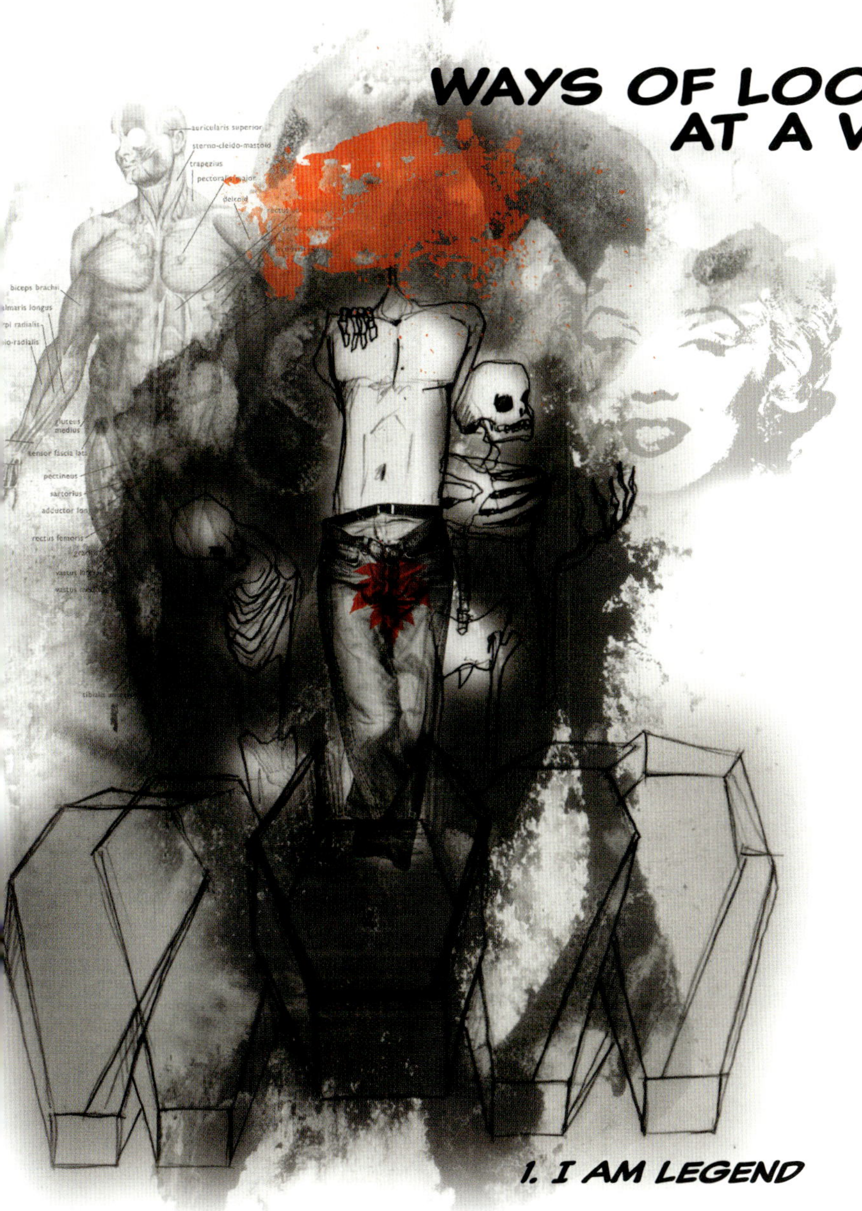

1. I AM LEGEND

During the day the brutal sunlight burns
the germs inside our blood and kills us, fast,
so we go comatose till the sun turns
its awful face away. That's when the last
of them comes from his armored house and preys
on us. We find his victims withered, dust,
or bled out, with their red eyes rolled. Some days
we know he stands in futile lust
above our women. Later, he will kill
them, weeping. Though he keeps us back at night
with garlic, mirrors, crosses, and won't speak,
we still taunt him, "Come out, kiss me!" and mill
in his front yard, tear at his house in fright
of this day-stalker, this monster, this freak.

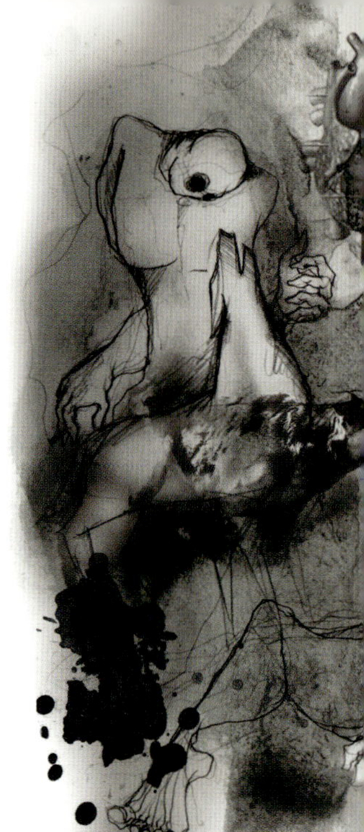

2. THE REVENANT

My husband in the beams above the bed
had hid to spy on us. When my young lover
mounted me from behind on the bedcover,
he fell to earth and shattered his skull — dead.
At night he'd claw out of the earth and walk,
pursued by packs of howling dogs, and kill.
We all made fast our doors in fear, but still
we heard the awful barking as he'd stalk
outside. At last my young man took a spade
and, digging, bared the corpse suffused with blood
and swollen to enormous corpulence.
Like a great leech it wept a carmine flood,
and though its heart had suffered violence
enough, he cut it out with the blunt blade.

3. THE FLEA

Consider how the flea sucks first at you,
nuzzling in your crotch, then nips your wife
and makes her cry out like she does in sex,
softly, with just a hint of pain. As you
purple your nail, consider that the life
you crush for sucking at your thighs and necks
is but a fleshly bottling of blood,
like you. Now spilled. Consider how the vintage
staining your skin fermented in this flea,
joining your wife and you, two bloods. Why should
a flea live hungering? There's no advantage
in that. Consider then a thing like me.
I'm like a flea that innocently feeds.
That's right. Put down the cross. I have my needs.

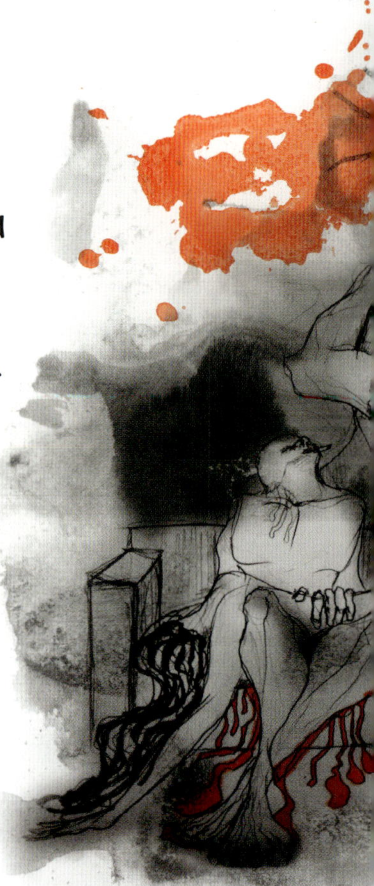

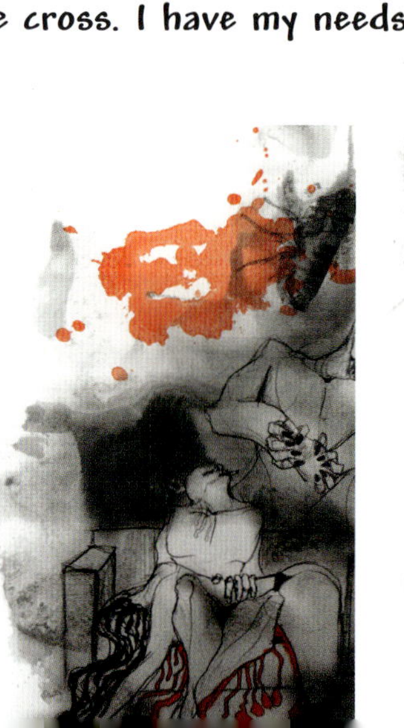

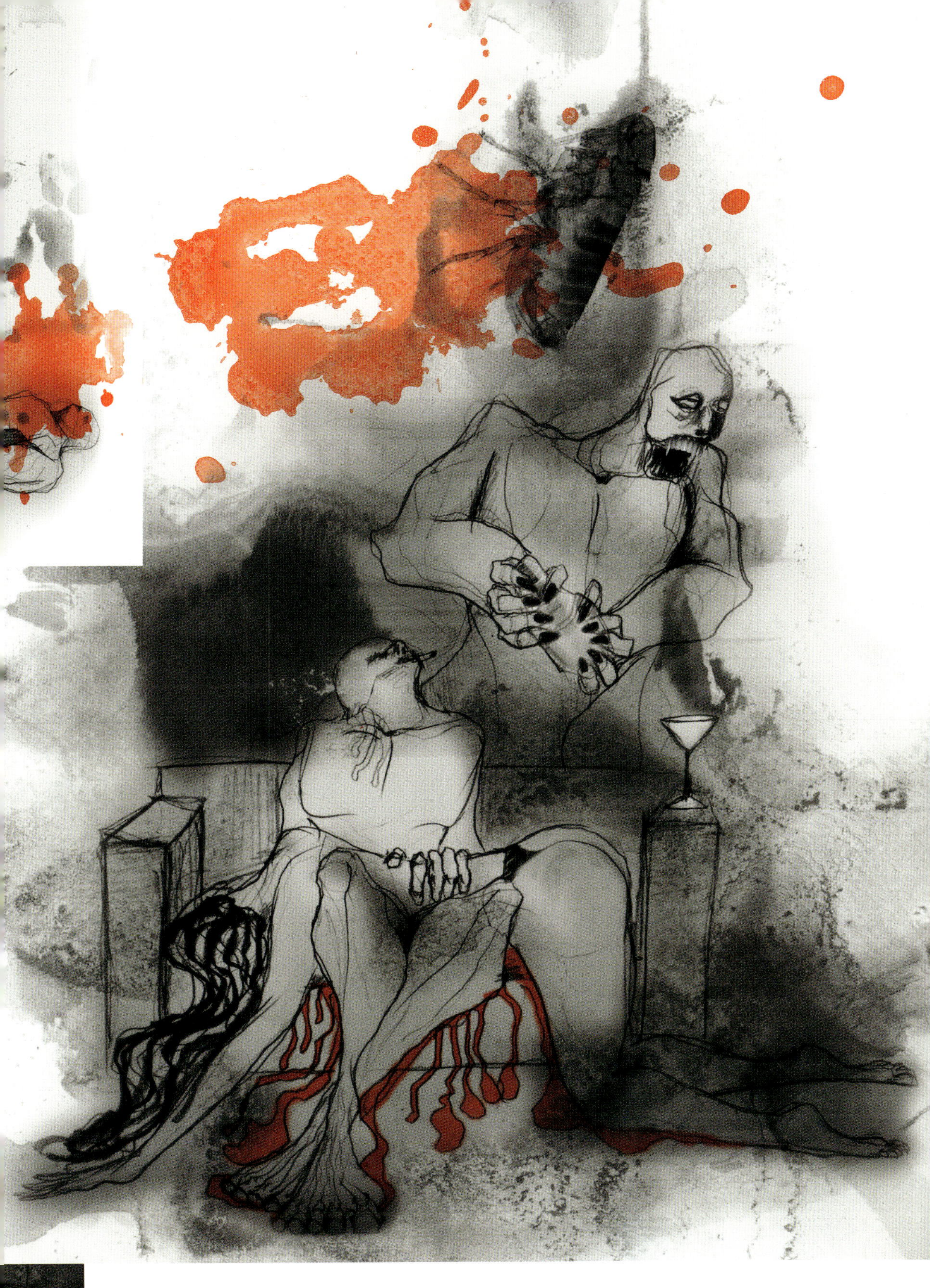

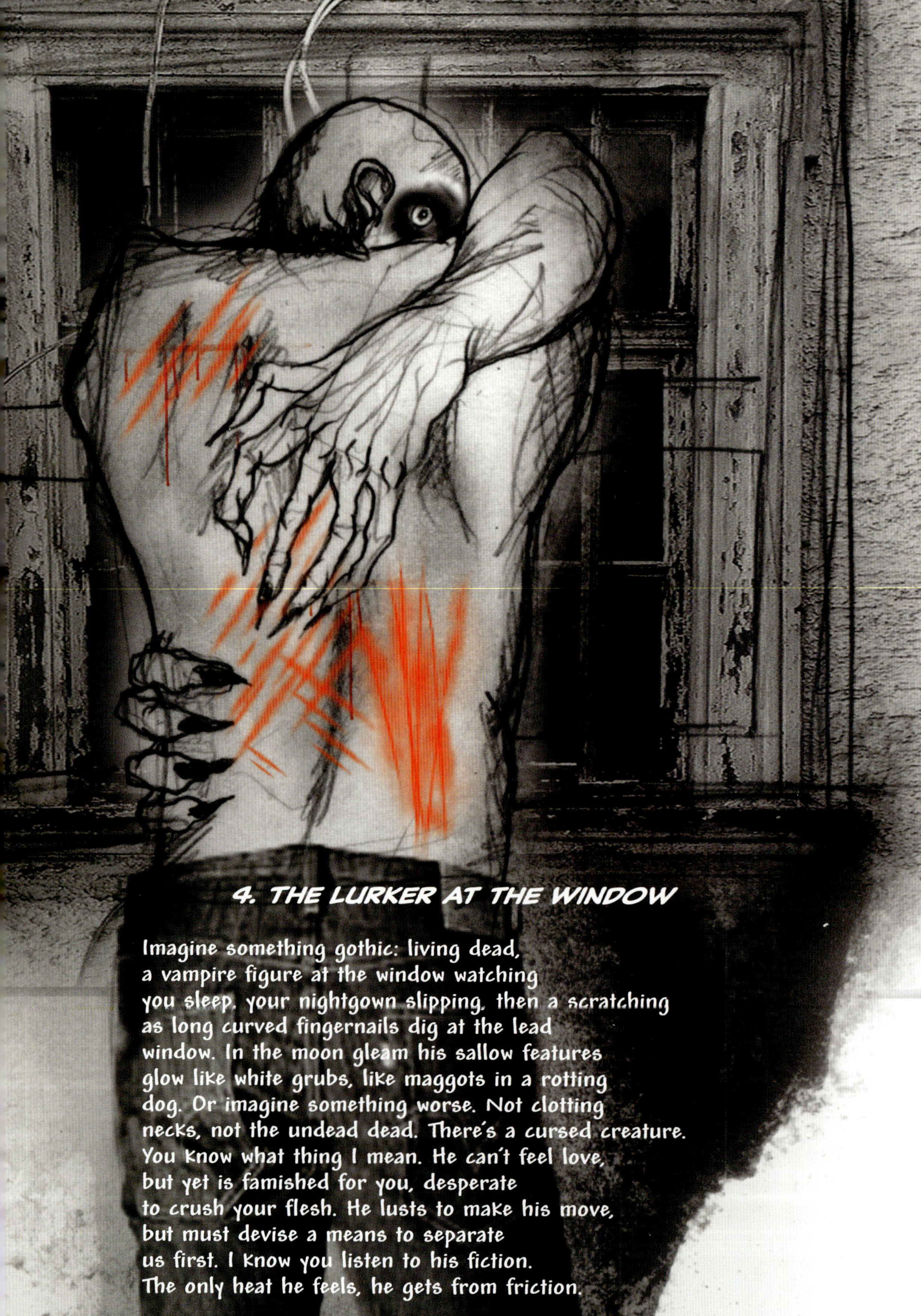

4. THE LURKER AT THE WINDOW

Imagine something gothic: living dead,
a vampire figure at the window watching
you sleep, your nightgown slipping, then a scratching
as long curved fingernails dig at the lead
window. In the moon gleam his sallow features
glow like white grubs, like maggots in a rotting
dog. Or imagine something worse. Not clotting
necks, not the undead dead. There's a cursed creature.
You know what thing I mean. He can't feel love,
but yet is famished for you, desperate
to crush your flesh. He lusts to make his move,
but must devise a means to separate
us first. I know you listen to his fiction.
The only heat he feels, he gets from friction.

5. THE SECOND DEATH OF DRACULA

Jonathan tossed the box from the cart it rode
and we prized the lid back with a screeching sound.
Lying in the coffin on the ground,
I saw the Count, covered with soil the rude
fall from the gypsy wagon to the road
had scattered over him. He was death, bound
in a wax image, and his red eyes glared
with the vindictive awful gaze
I knew so well. I saw their baleful hate
turn to triumph as the last sun flared.
But then the great knife flashed and swept on high.
I shrieked as the blade sheared through the white neck
and the Bowie knife plunged through the heart. And yet
a wonder happened then before our eyes:
just as that body turned to dust and ceased,
those twisted features settled into peace.

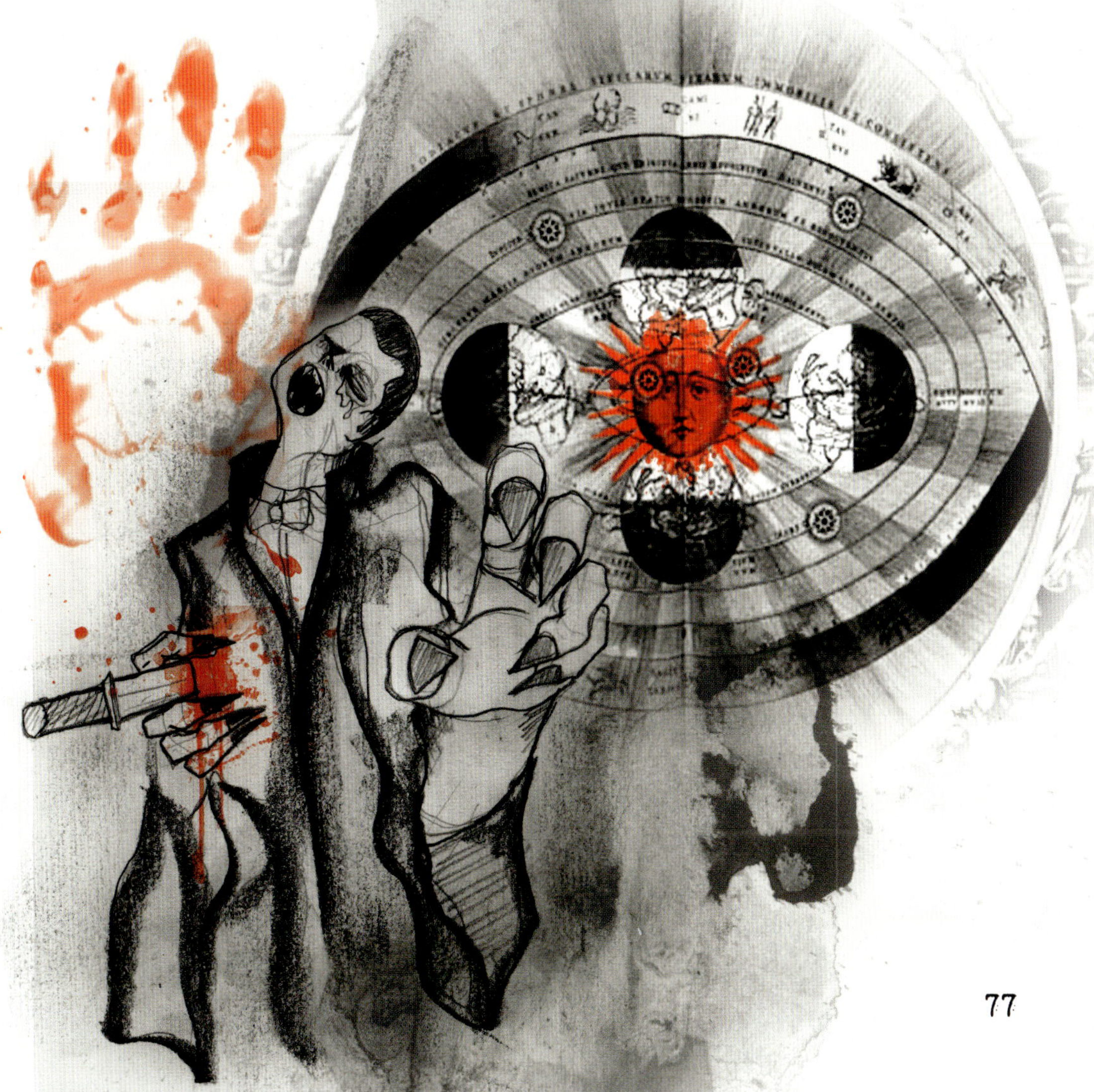

SNAKE PEOPLE

1. THE WORMS OF THE EARTH

The sun, it burns, it burns, and turns our skin
from lovely glossy green to bubbling red,
the moon's white flame will blast our eyes to dead
white bulbs, and every star's a javelin,
and so we burrow deeper in the soil
and live and breed and swarm in slippery night.
Only when mists baffle the sharp starlight,
when the moon drowns its visage in black oil,
do we dare surface from the caves and tombs.
We, who once walked the earth, almost like men,
now swarm like nightmare thoughts out of our den
and watch you hesitate in lighted rooms,
and watch you douse the lamp and stare in vain
at our dark faces at your windowpane.

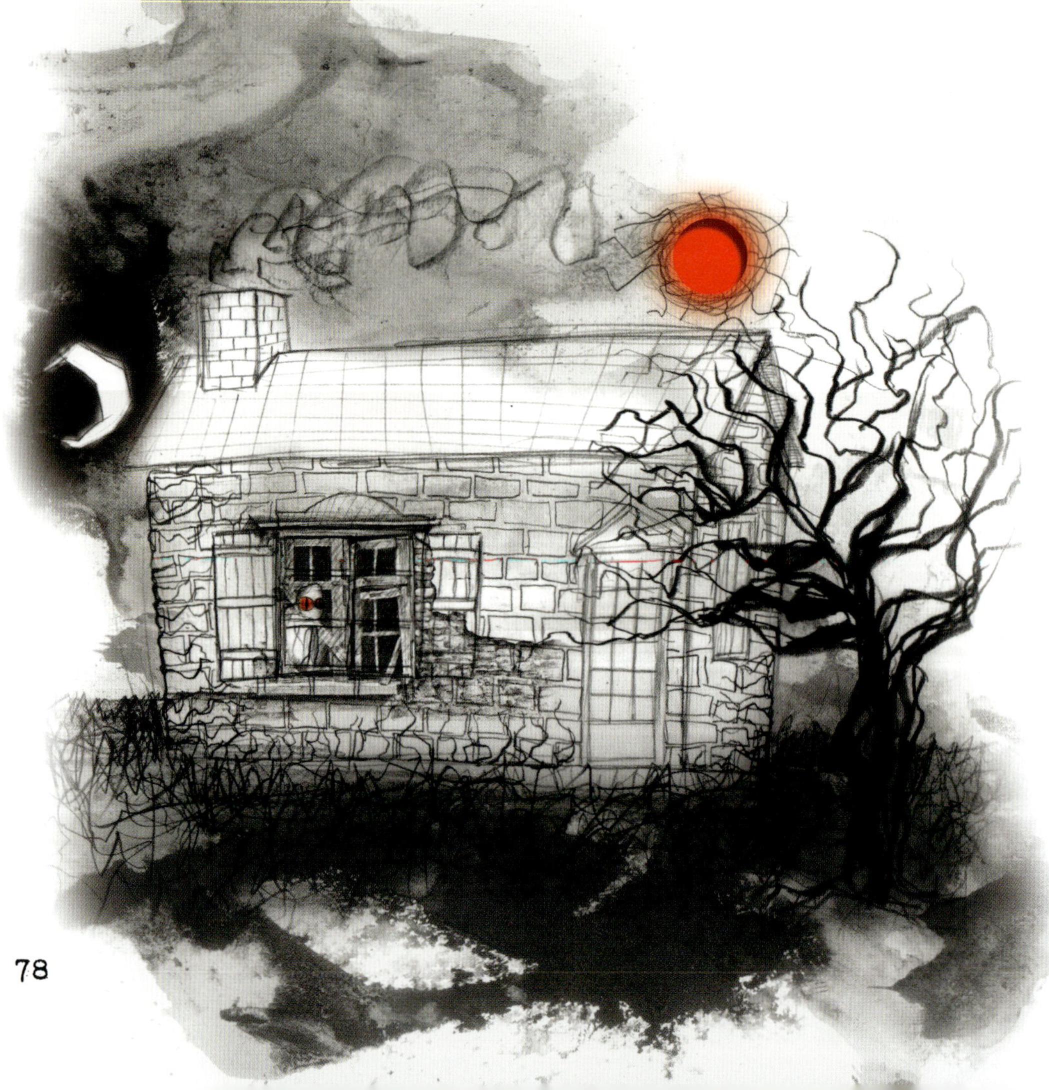

2. CLAWS IN THE DARKNESS

Huh! What a shock. I thought I saw dark faces
for just an instant at my windowpane
before the light went dark. One of those cases
of too much Chinese food for lunch, and pain
in the intestines twisting round like fears
in the unconscious, winding eels and snakes
of dread. No, I'm no wimp, but all it takes
is mu-shu pork and drink a couple beers
and then for dinner eat all-you-can-eat
baby back ribs and stuffed potatoes, and
you'll see the faces, too, you'll understand
the way I shiver underneath the sheet
imagining I hear, once the light's fled,
the scratch of claws on wood beside my bed.

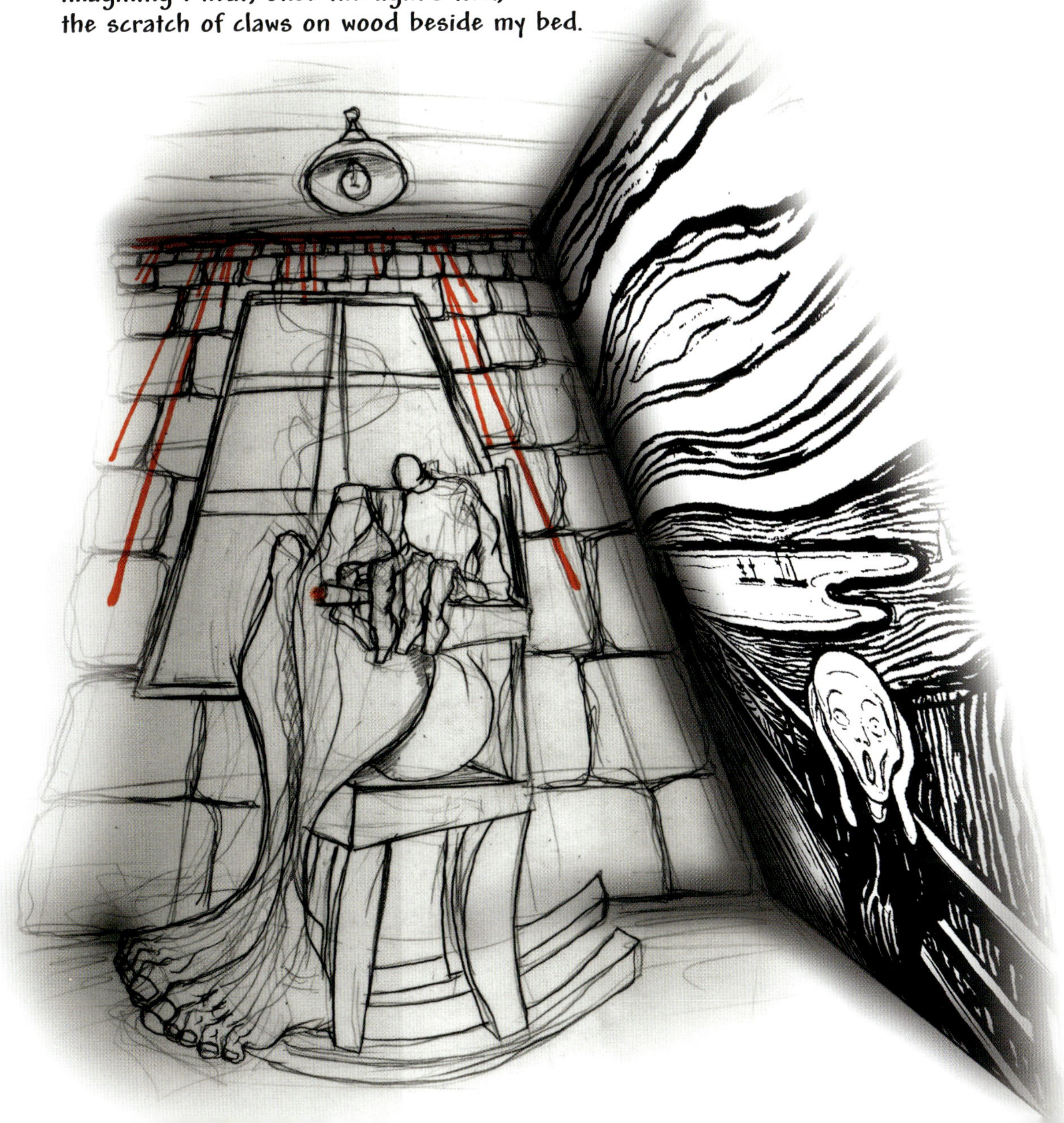

THE WEREWOLF OF GREEN KNOLLS

1. POOCH

The frat boys playing pool yell, "Hose her! Hose her!"
when Dan and I walk in the bar, and Daniel
just grins and takes a bow while I, brown-noser
that I am, toady, doormat, flunky, spaniel,
duck my head low. "What yours, sweetheart?" the bar-
man asks, but Danny cuts me off, "Get her
a Miller Lite." The bar-man smiles a far-
off, sad, I've-seen-this-one-before smile. Cur,
tail-wagger, mongrel, pooch, I tremble out
a "Thanks," and take the beer. Here in Green Knolls
you take what man you find, or masturbate
at home. Tonight he comes then leaves without
a kiss. I hate what I've become: his hole,
a pussy, jellyfish, invertebrate.

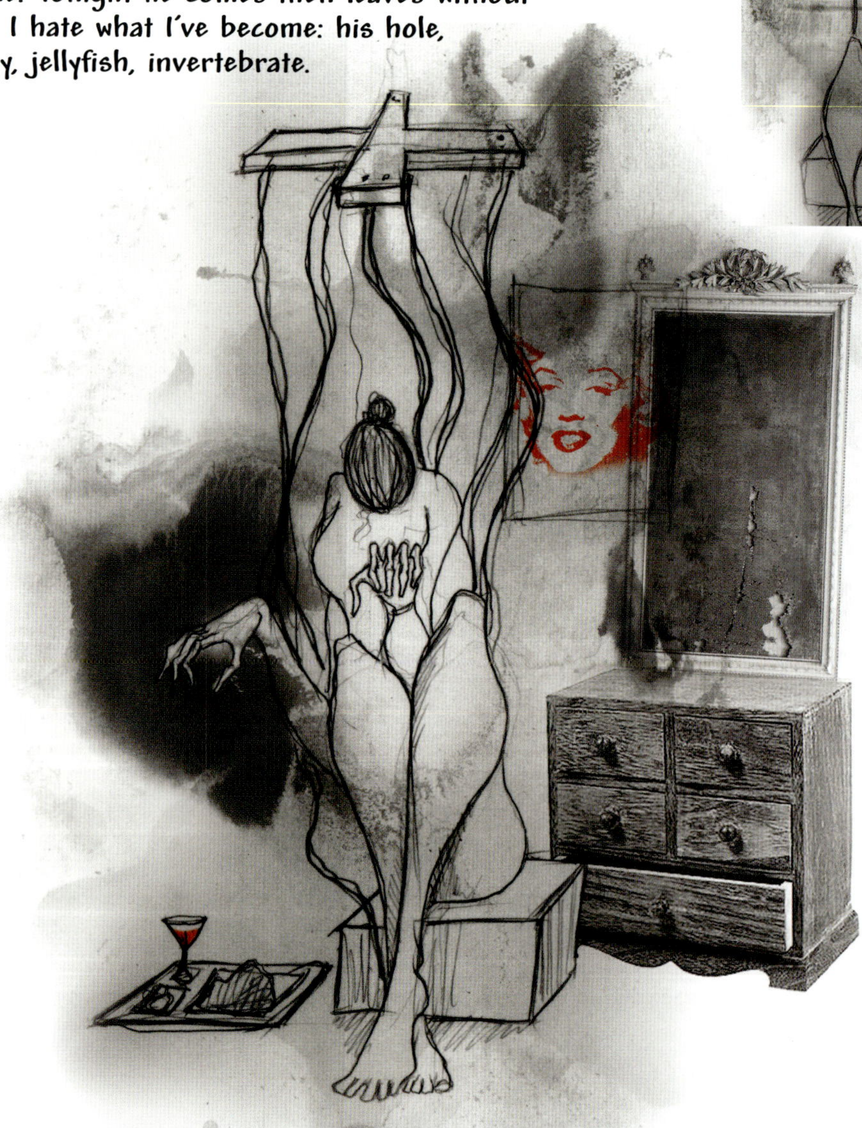

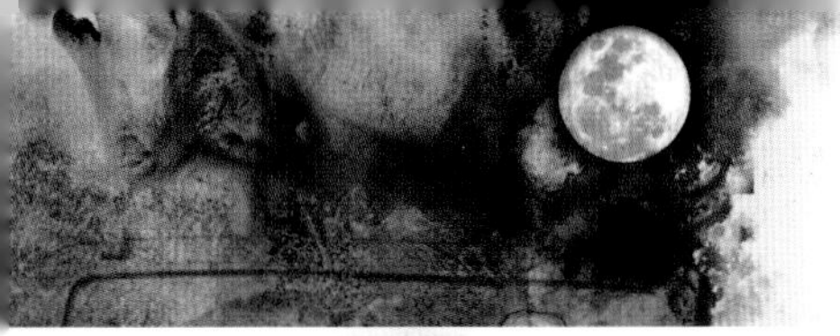

2. SNARL

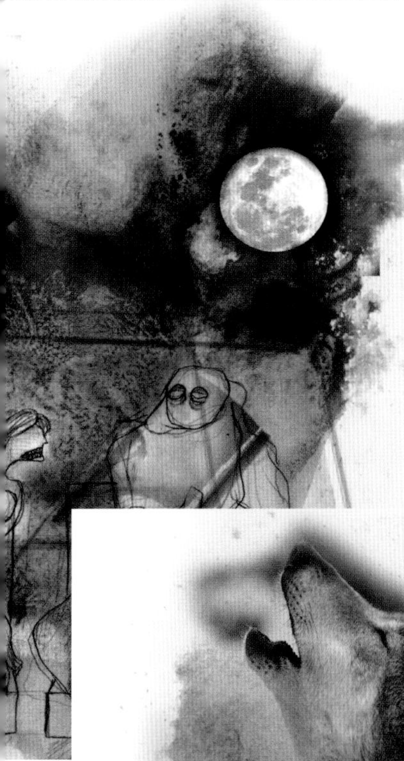

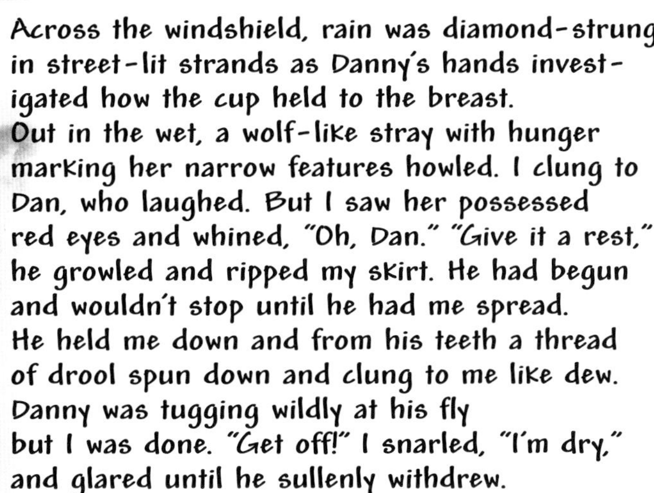

Across the windshield, rain was diamond-strung
in street-lit strands as Danny's hands invest-
igated how the cup held to the breast.
Out in the wet, a wolf-like stray with hunger
marking her narrow features howled. I clung to
Dan, who laughed. But I saw her possessed
red eyes and whined, "Oh, Dan." "Give it a rest,"
he growled and ripped my skirt. He had begun
and wouldn't stop until he had me spread.
He held me down and from his teeth a thread
of drool spun down and clung to me like dew.
Danny was tugging wildly at his fly
but I was done. "Get off!" I snarled, "I'm dry,"
and glared until he sullenly withdrew.

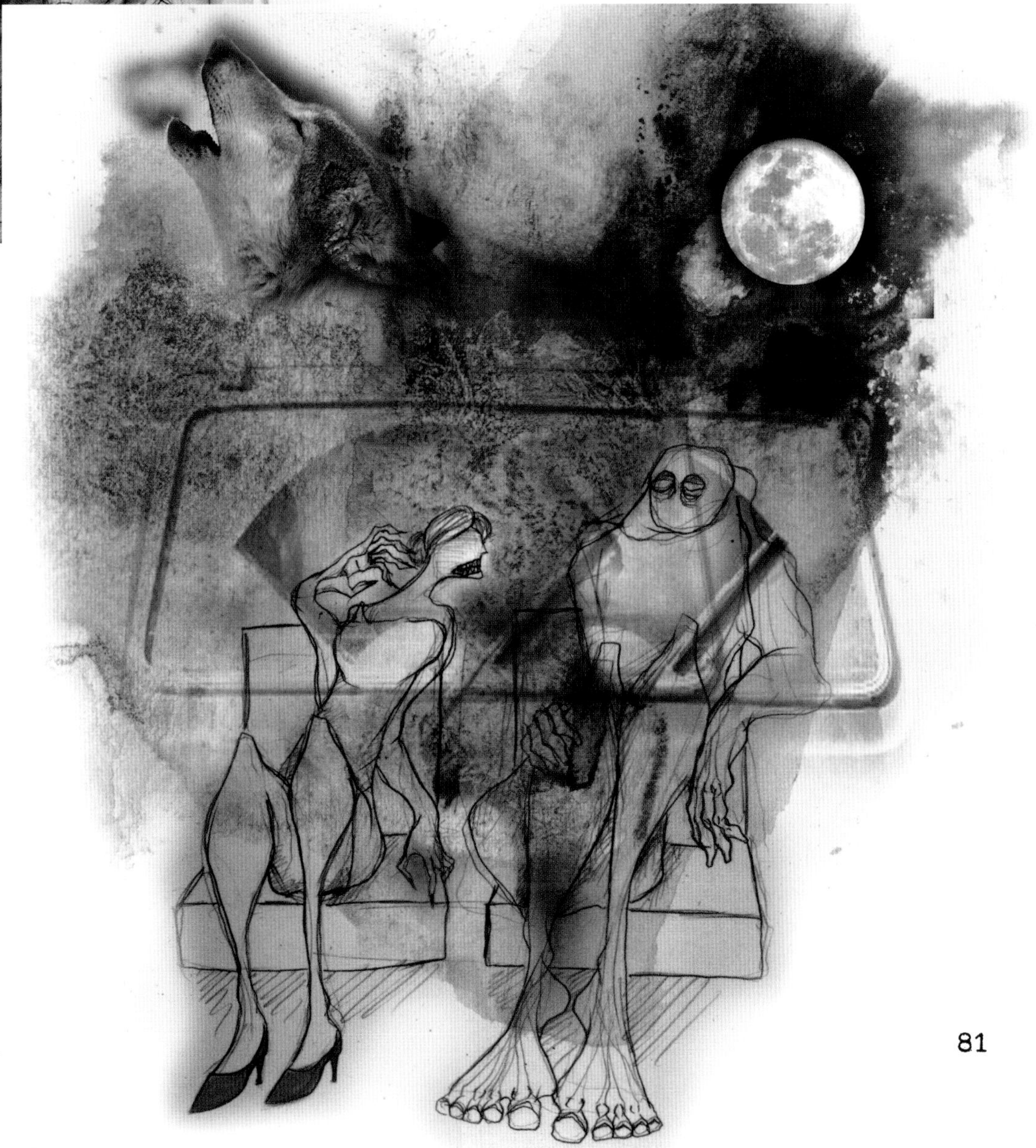

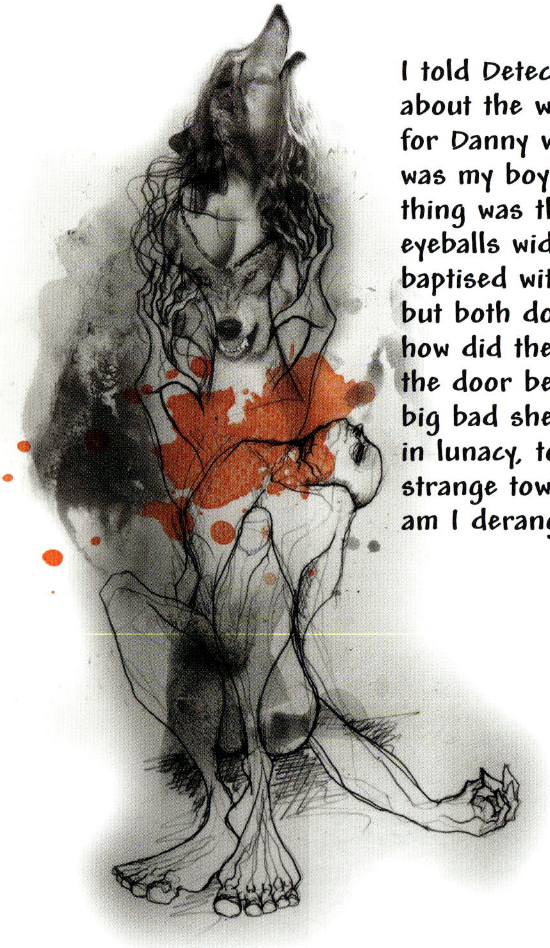

3. LITTLE PIGGY

I told Detective Abernathy-Todd
about the wolf, then couldn't help but weep
for Danny with his ripped-out throat. The creep
was my boyfriend, after all. The odd
thing was the way they found us: Danny, his
eyeballs wide and throat a gash, and me,
baptised with blood, out cold, my clothes slashed free,
but both doors locked. So try to answer this:
how did the wolf get in? And how'd she close
the door behind? The wolf got in, somehow,
big bad she-wolf. It makes me want to howl
in lunacy, to change my life like clothes,
strange towns, new man. By my chinny chin-chin,
am I deranged to welcome the wolf in?

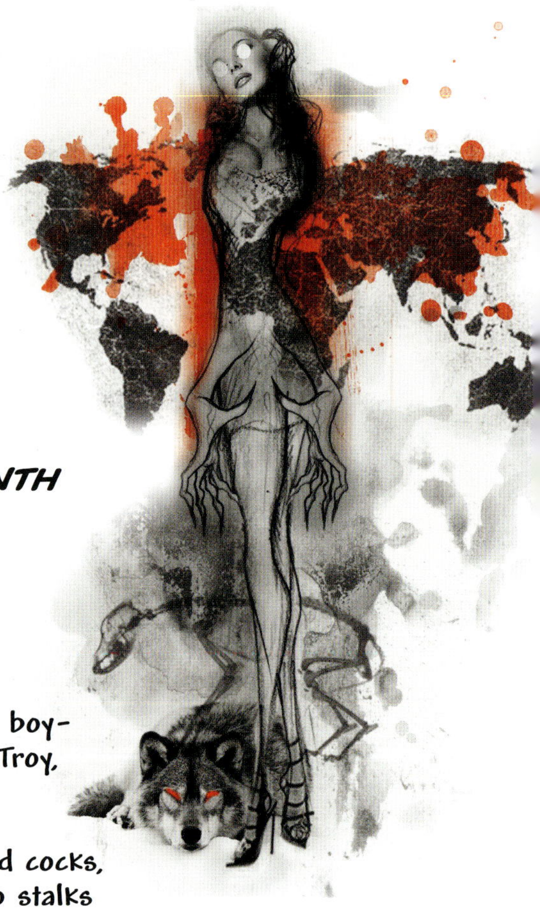

4. THAT TIME OF MONTH

The problem is I find it hard to switch
back to a woman after the full moon
chips off a piece, blood hunger a typhoon
of whirling teeth inside my narrow bitch
skull as I skulk the trashcan alleyways
and spread my dangerous loins for yipping boy-
dogs. While they snap and nip, I burn like Troy,
like Alexandria, my red eyes blaze
like Tokyo, Nagasaki, burn like silver
moonlight, white fire, burn like their hot red cocks,
their hot wet blood on my wild tongue. Who stalks
me now? Another dog. His haunches shiver.
He smells the blood, the sex. His nostrils flare.
He walks toward death in her sleek coat of hair.

5. WOLF'S BEST FRIEND

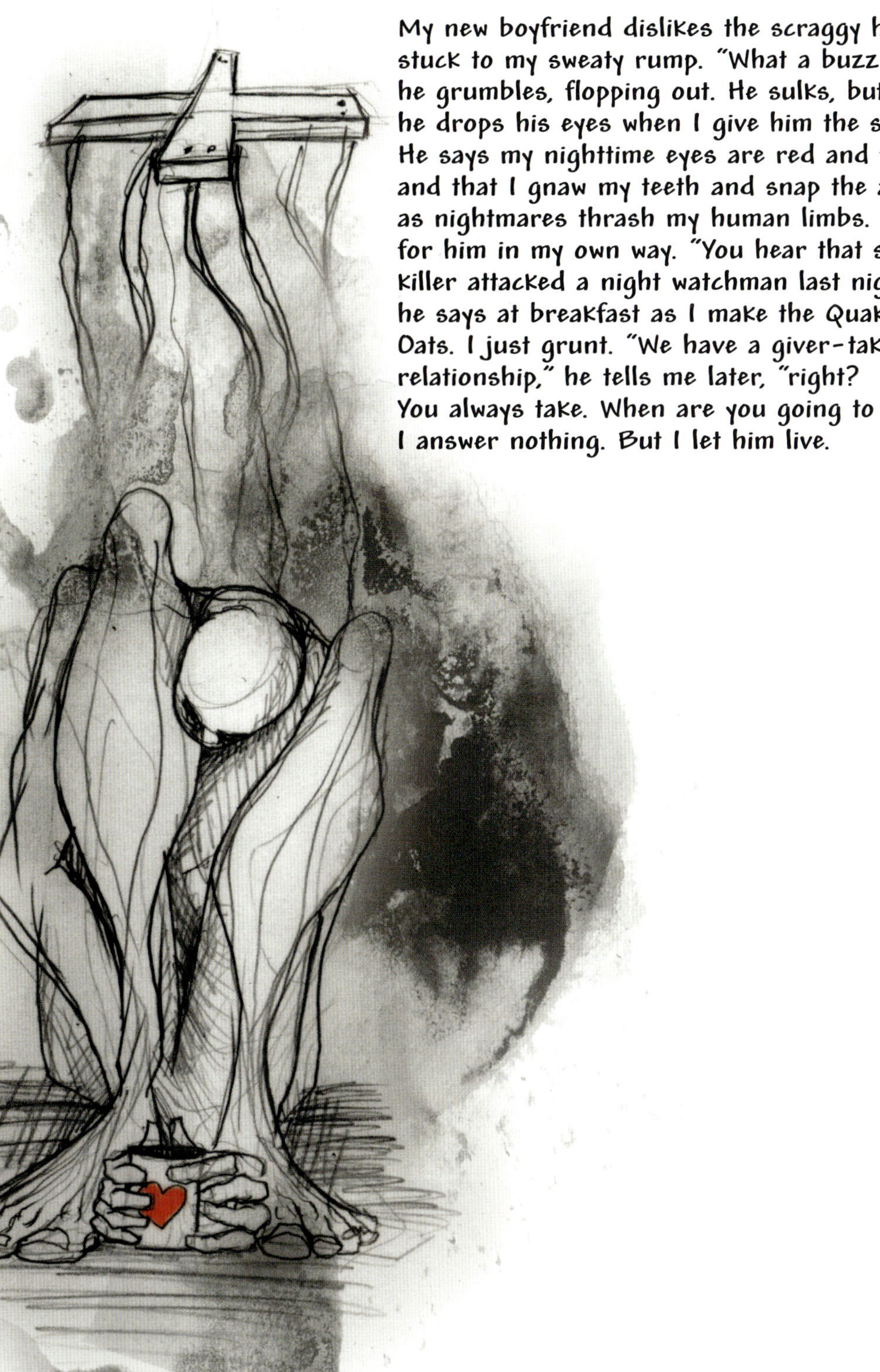

My new boyfriend dislikes the scraggy hair stuck to my sweaty rump. "What a buzz-kill," he grumbles, flopping out. He sulks, but still he drops his eyes when I give him the stare. He says my nighttime eyes are red and feral and that I gnaw my teeth and snap the air as nightmares thrash my human limbs. I care for him in my own way. "You hear that serial killer attacked a night watchman last night?" he says at breakfast as I make the Quaker Oats. I just grunt. "We have a giver-taker relationship," he tells me later, "right? You always take. When are you going to give?" I answer nothing. But I let him live.

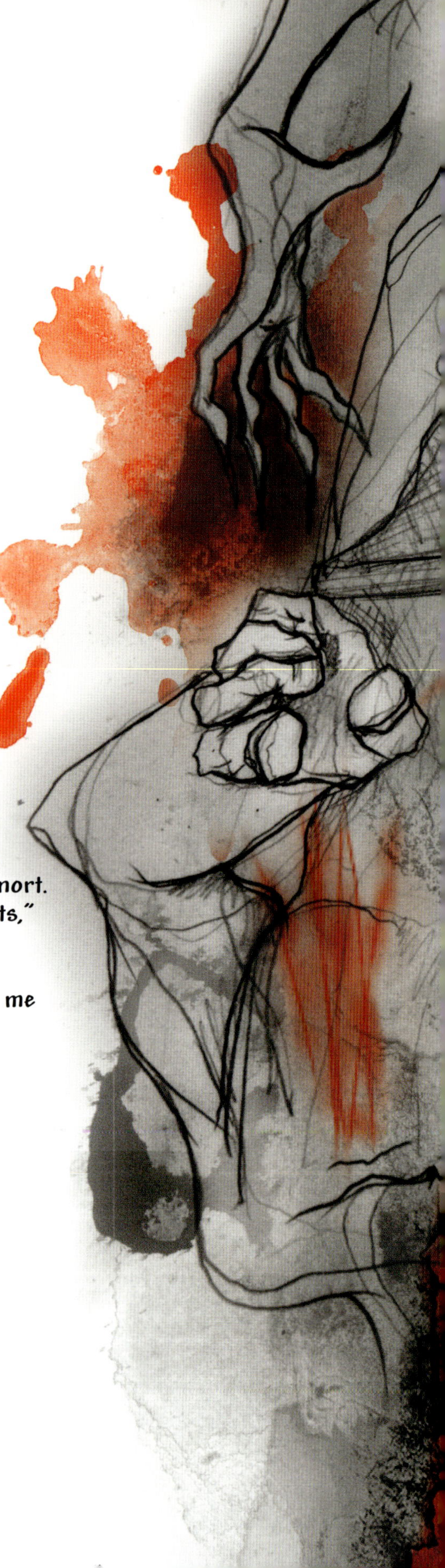

6. WHINE

"I'm wearing antiperspirant," he says
peevishly when I snuffle, chuff and sniff
at his armpit. I don't answer, but gaze
at his pale limbs, blood-animated. "If
you want, I'll take a shower," Nathan blurts
when I push my nose into his crotch and snort.
I give his rump a nip. "Hey! Don't, that hurts,"
he whines, but it was just a taste. I sport
with him a while, lick him until I find
he's hard enough. He moans and moons at me
until I let him take me from behind.
After I come, I growl and then push free.
I bite his lip when Nathan tries to kiss.
He sighs, "Oh, well." I go to take a piss.

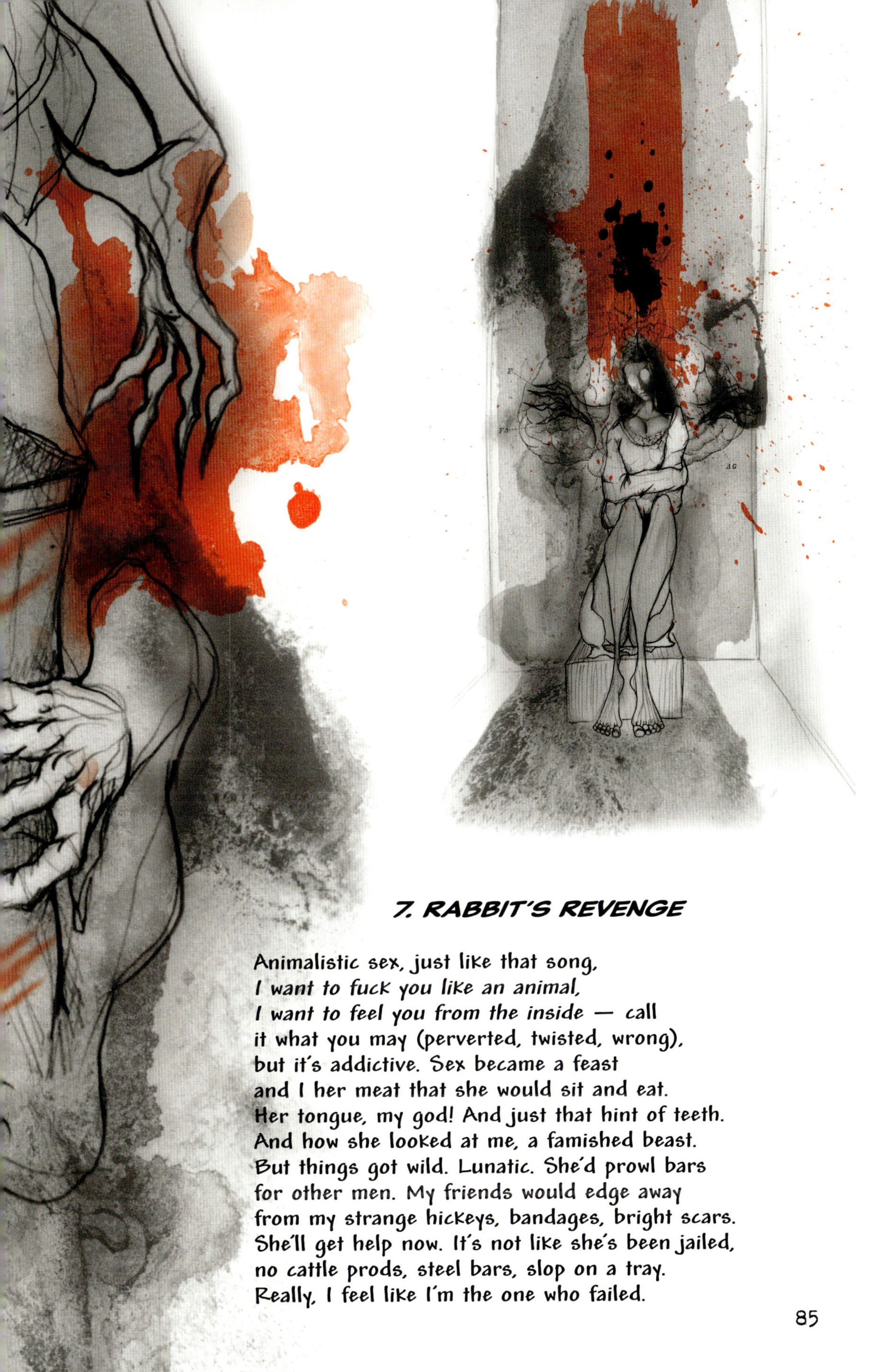

7. RABBIT'S REVENGE

Animalistic sex, just like that song,
I want to fuck you like an animal,
I want to feel you from the inside — call
it what you may (perverted, twisted, wrong),
but it's addictive. Sex became a feast
and I her meat that she would sit and eat.
Her tongue, my god! And just that hint of teeth.
And how she looked at me, a famished beast.
But things got wild. Lunatic. She'd prowl bars
for other men. My friends would edge away
from my strange hickeys, bandages, bright scars.
She'll get help now. It's not like she's been jailed,
no cattle prods, steel bars, slop on a tray.
Really, I feel like I'm the one who failed.

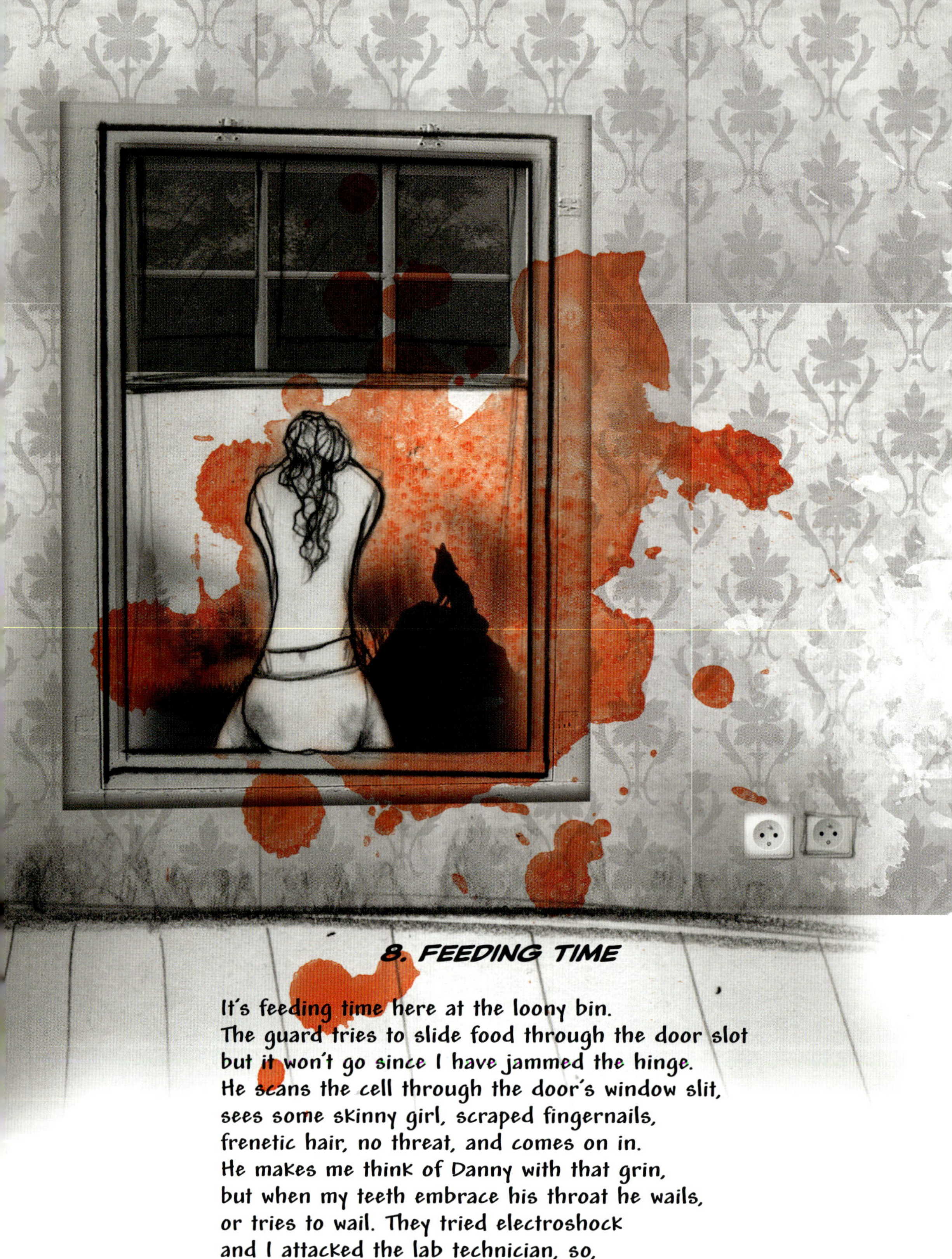

8. FEEDING TIME

It's feeding time here at the loony bin.
The guard tries to slide food through the door slot
but it won't go since I have jammed the hinge.
He scans the cell through the door's window slit,
sees some skinny girl, scraped fingernails,
frenetic hair, no threat, and comes on in.
He makes me think of Danny with that grin,
but when my teeth embrace his throat he wails,
or tries to wail. They tried electroshock
and I attacked the lab technician, so,
this comfy padded cell. How could they know
there are some things you can't keep in with locks?
I prowl the parks and people run from me:
haunted harlot, demon, woman, free.

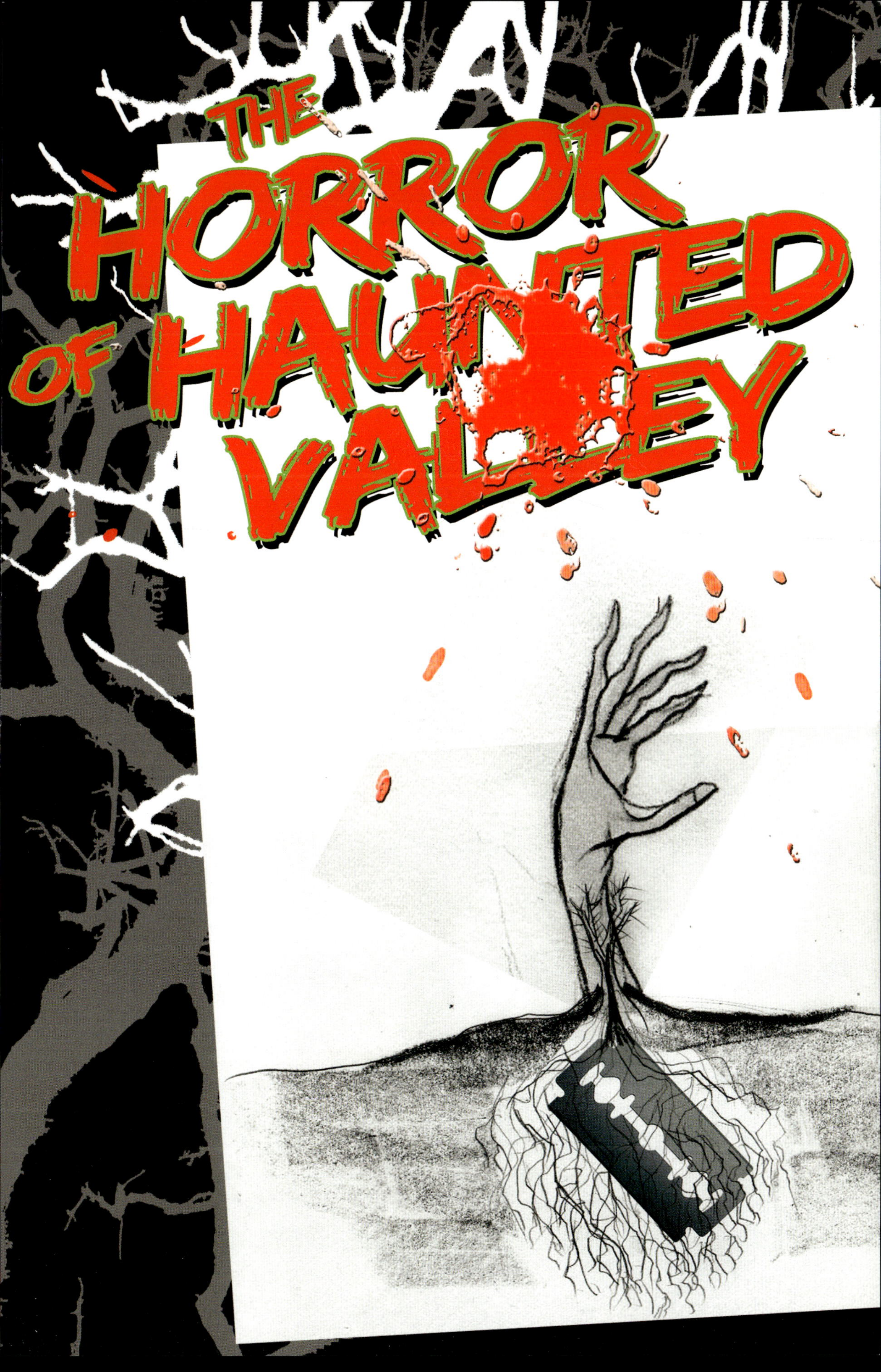
THE HORROR OF HAUNTED VALLEY

1. Red Glow in the Woods (Case 001: Dan Weiss, 13, Andrea Troyer, 14)

'Drea and me come up to where the red
glow raygunned through the branches like Red Vines,
skinny, you know, and long, and straight. And red.
There was a crater there between two pines.
"Looks like your face!" says 'Drea, so I pinched
her in the nipple, yelling, "Titty-twist!"
She pulled my hair till I let go. We inched
through the night woods. I felt like when I kissed
'Drea between her legs down in the cellar
that day, all hot and loose inside my jeans,
when we caught sight of the ship. "It's interstellar,
sci-fi stuff," I breathed. "It's like in dreams."
"Let's go back," 'Drea whispered urgently.
I stood up then. "No way. I gotta see."

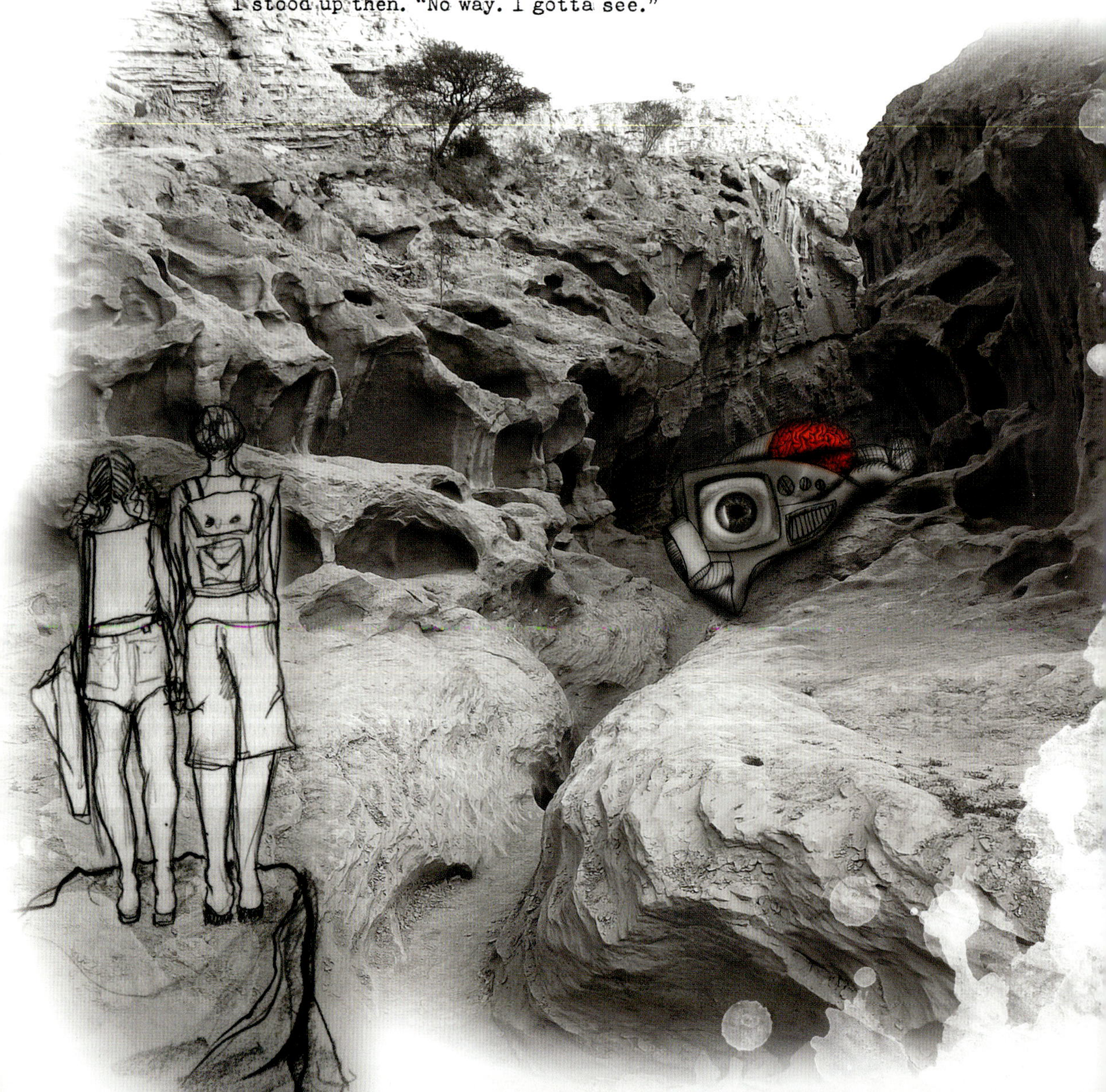

2. Bagged Cats (Case 002: Anthony Miller, 18, John Fitzgerald, 19)

Anthony had caught a one-eyed cat
and had it in a burlap sack to play
with later, and we got some Boone's Farm — that
sweet crap will make you sick, but it's too gay
to do the kitty sacrifice without
some booze and that's all Anthony could rip
off from the Circle K. A few miles out
of town I swear I saw the mothership
go screaming down into the black treetops.
"Let's check it out!" says Anthony, and so
I grab the bulging, yowling bag, we power-
chug wine, and go to find the UFO.
"We're fucking lost!" says Tony in an hour.
"No, wait." I say, "Red lights. Must be the cops."

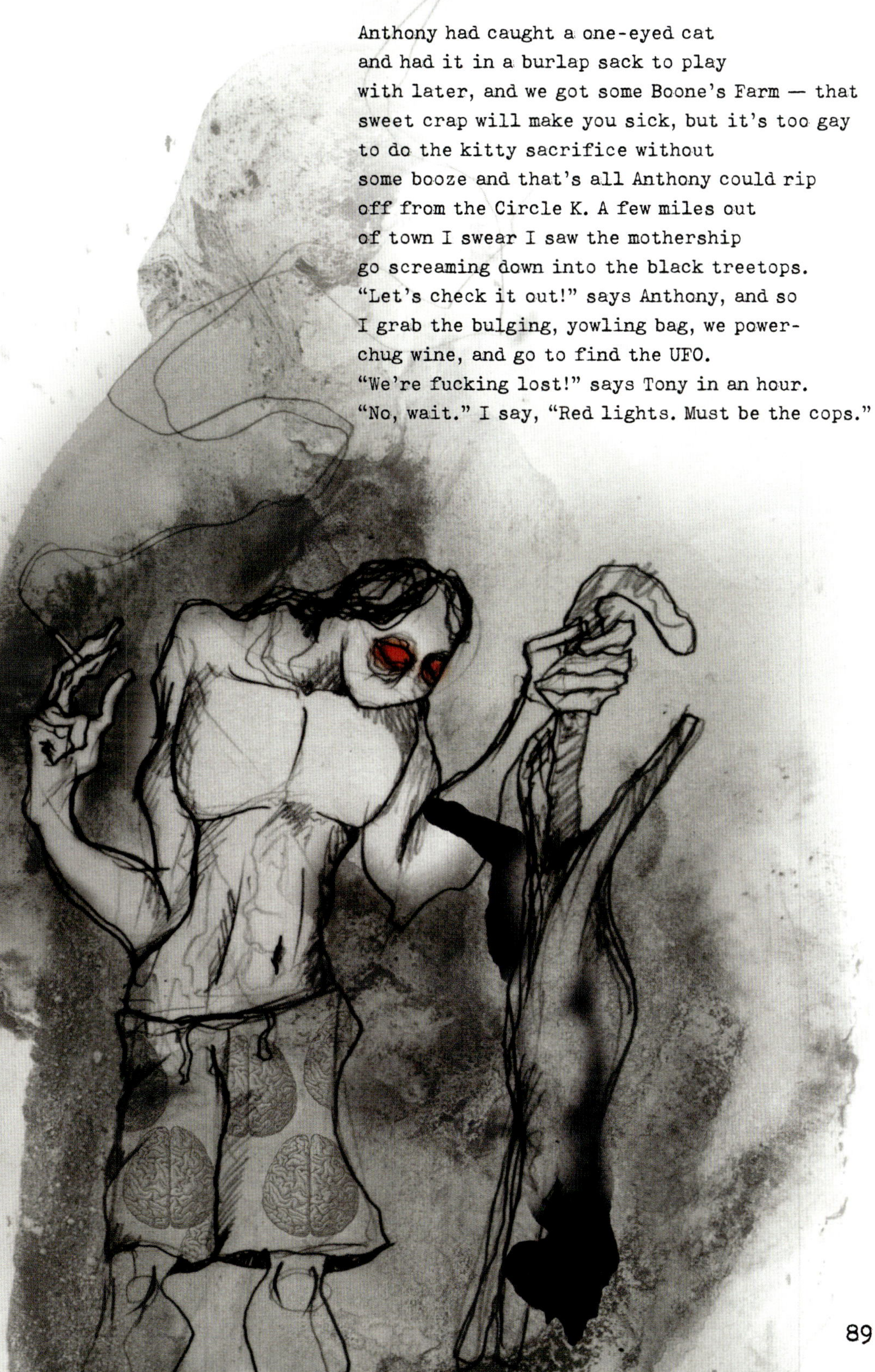

3. The Fire Sacrifice (Case 003: Sheriff Kim Oja, 37)

I heard tell from that Heldman girl she'd found
a circle in the woods with totems, evil
runes, charred animal bones stacked in a mound,
Budweiser cans and porno mags. Some devil
cult, hair band fantasy, that's spread among
the meth-heads is my guess (based on graffiti,
rumors, the missing pets). What's with the young
these days? I know we're living in a shitty
backwoods nowhere town, but Jesus fuck!
Just get an X-Box. Now two kids are missing,
plus two school thugs. So when I find the truck,
skull painted on the hood, I think, "That's promising."
I stumble through the woods. At dark, I tire,
but now I see a reddish glow. A fire?

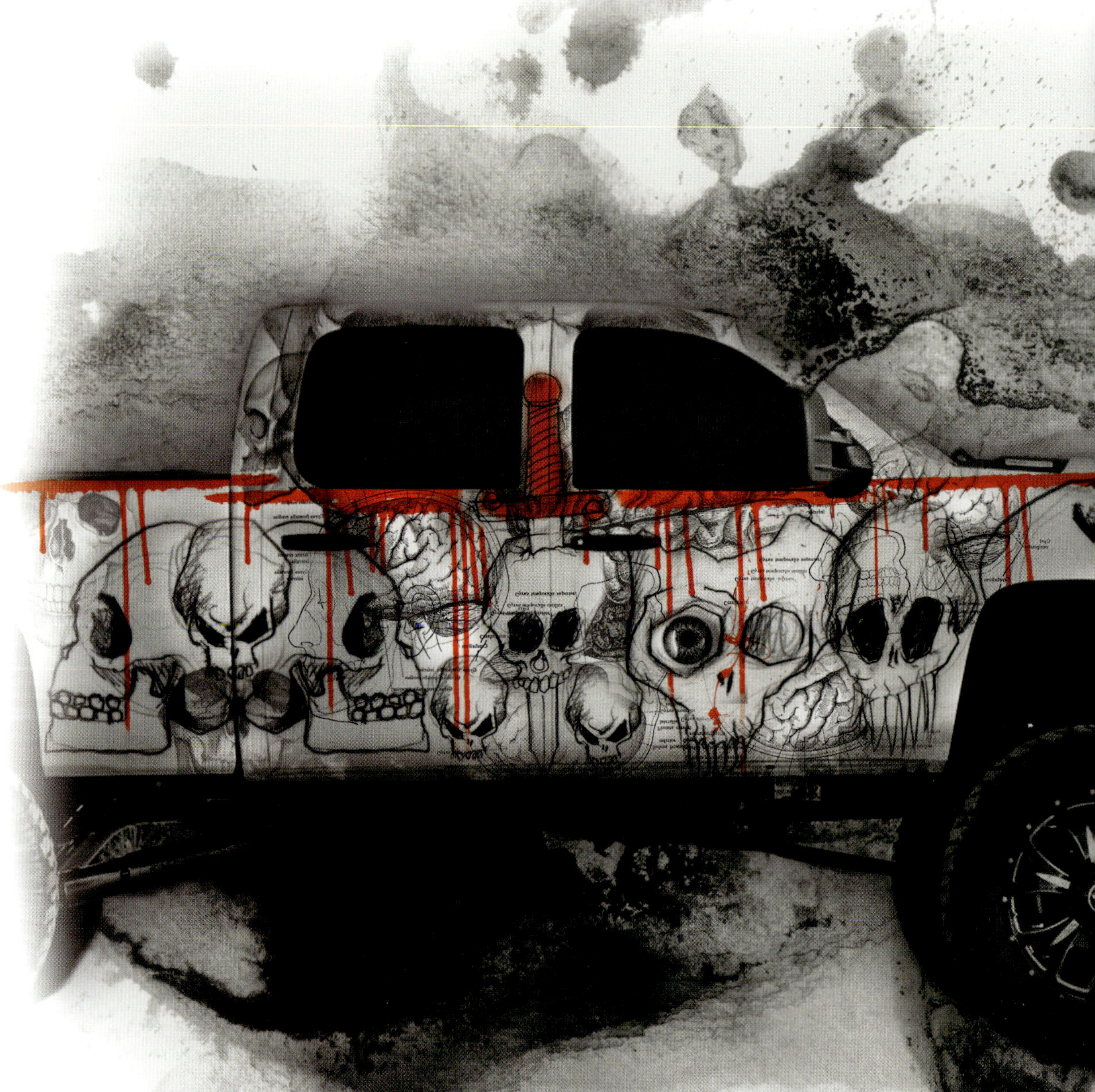

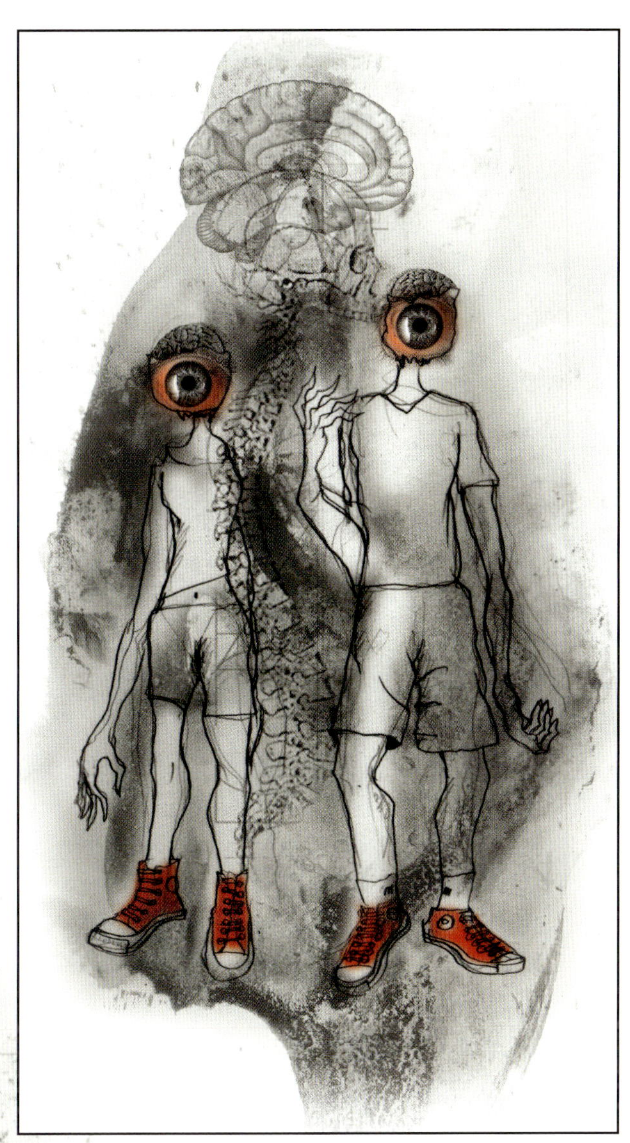

4. Picnic in the Woods (Case 003, Addendum: Sheriff Kim Oja, 37, Dan Weiss, 13, Andrea Troyer, 14, Anthony Miller, 18, and John Fitzgerald, 19)

They're after me. Before me, just more trees.
Long-distance running through the brush is rough:
the brambles tangle up my feet, but please,
don't let me falter. What I've seen would crush
my soul if I had time to think: the weird
red glow inside their eyes like flashlight beams
through skin. I'm not a coward but I feared
those children gnawing at two tweaker teens
the way you'd munch on KFC, and while
I watched I saw the dead eyes of one teen
switch on like taillights, then that mangled pile
of eaten limbs stood up, alive. I've been
running since. Of course I lost my head.
How do you kill a thing already dead?

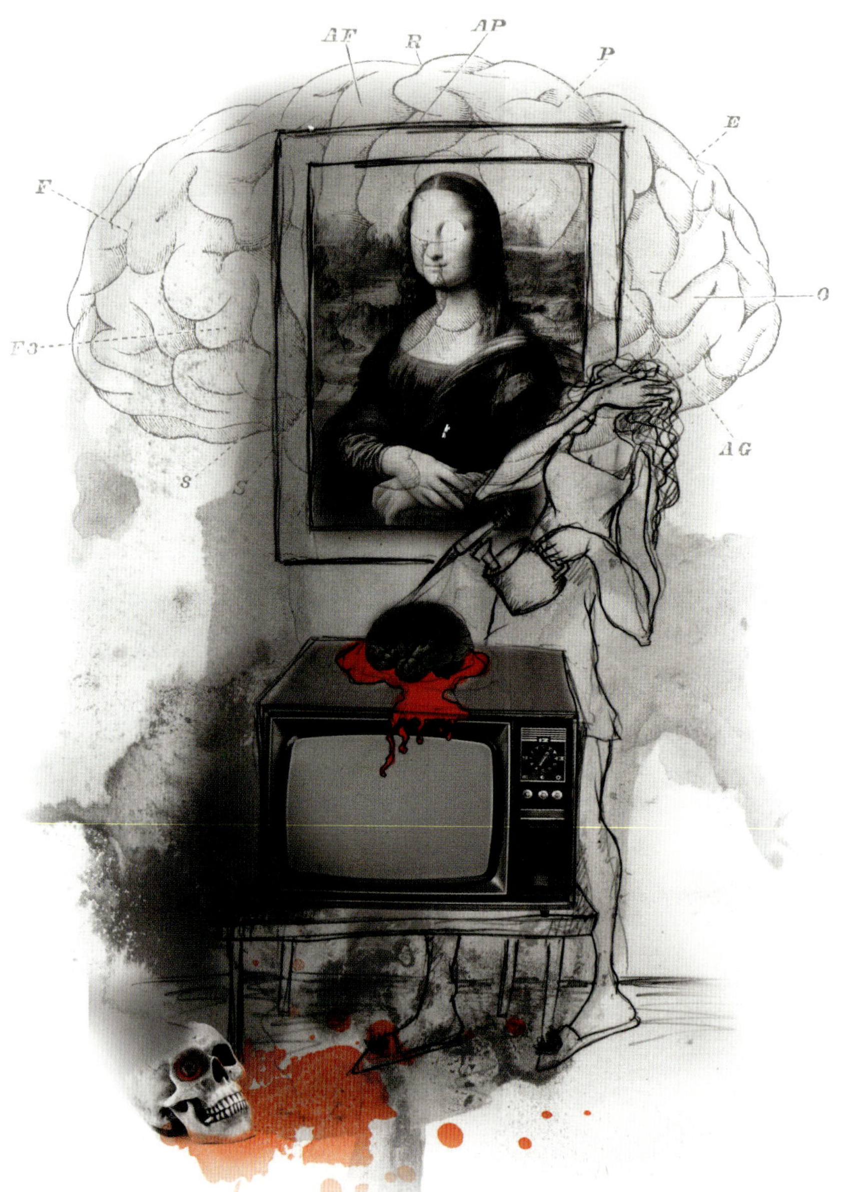

5. No Refunds, No Returns (Case 004: John Fitzgerald, 19, Kathy Strong, 20)

When we broke up, I told him, “You walk through
that door, we’re done, no refunds, no returns,”
but then tonight I looked up from the blue
glow of the screen where 70’s sideburns
were trapped in time likeon on some sci-fi show
and I heard stumbling footsteps on the porch,
a scrabbling at the knob, saw two DayGlo
eyes peering in the pane. Dad’s old blowtorch
was in his sculpture studio. I ran
for it and hit the flint just as the door
crashed in. The thing that used to be my man
pawed at me with his zombie hands. Hardcore.
In retrospect, I did what was humane:
“You stoner Fuck!” I screamed, and cooked his brain.

6. Priest of the Strange (Case 005, Bilal Shaw, 33, Proprietor, Golden Dawn: An Esoteric, Theosophical and Masonic Bookstore)

Something strange has landed in our town,
extraterrestrial like on TV.
It started with a red flash you could see
across the county, something wailing down
into the forest like a flaming angel.
I'd been expecting this for quite some time,
and so I took my staff and cape to climb
the wooded hills to where I thought the angle
of the descent would land the alien craft.
I've spent my whole life seeking arcane secrets
of the lost past. I failed. Still, no regrets
— no girlfriend, money, house, and they all laughed
at me — but now! I've found the craft. No fear.
I step into the light, "My friends, I'm here!"

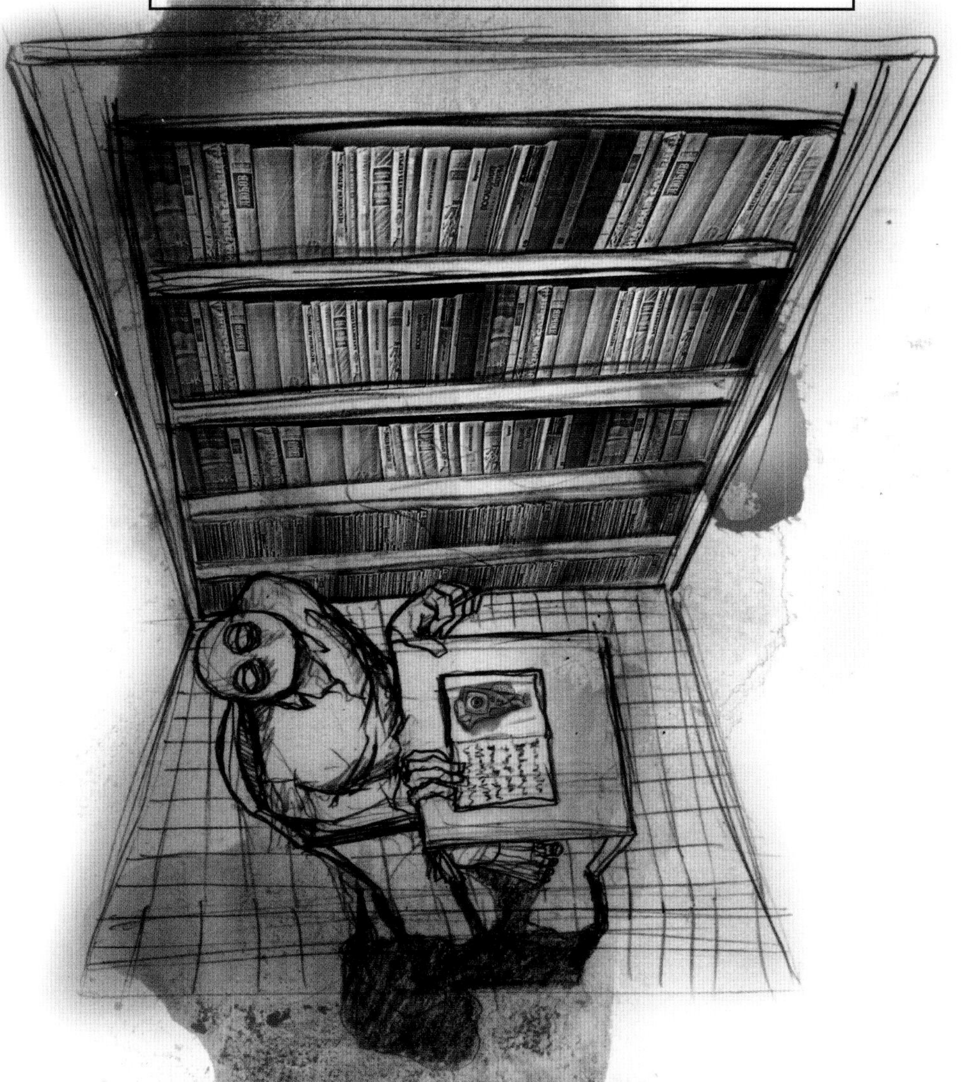

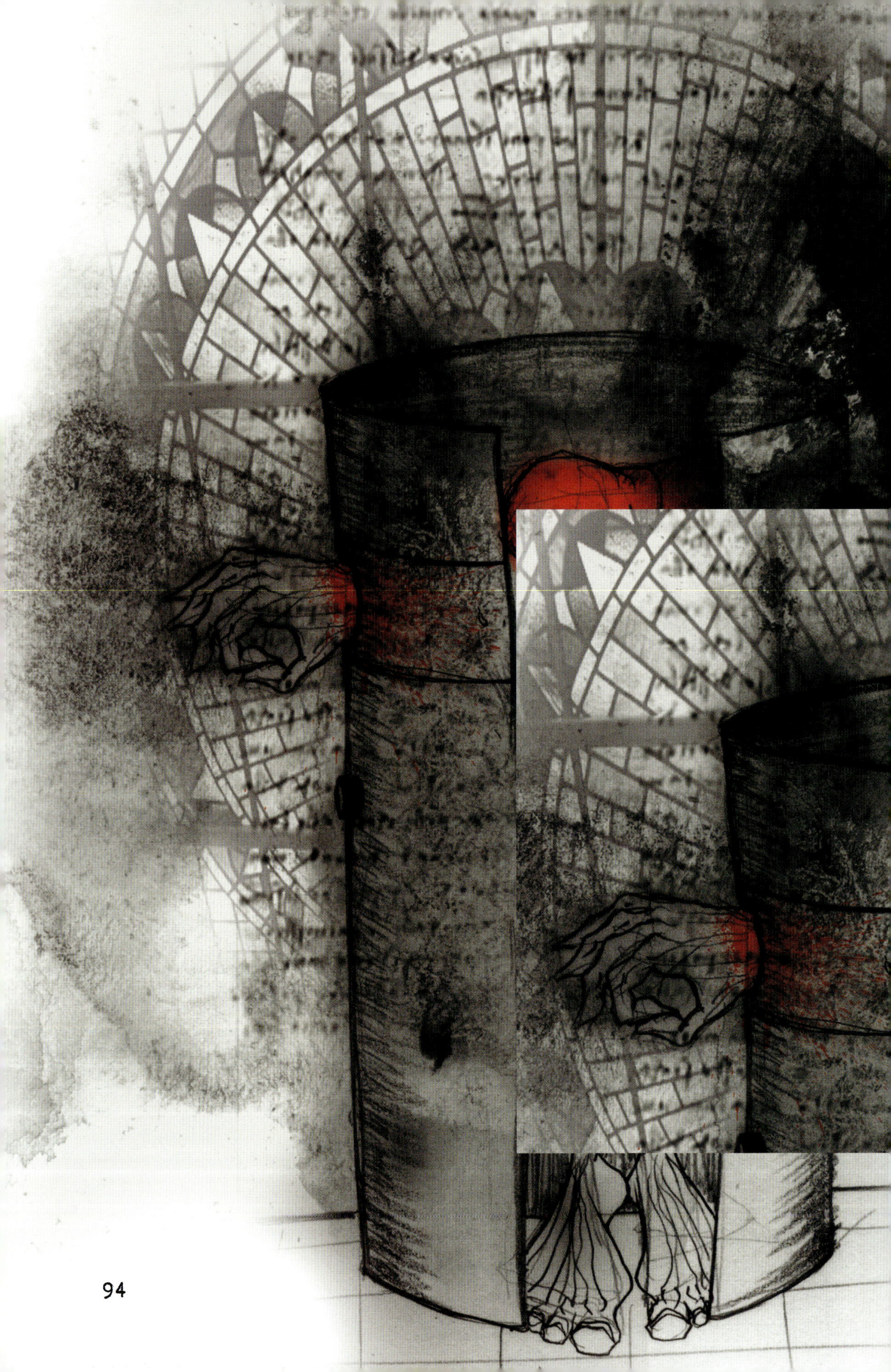

7. Unholy Ghost (Case 005: Addendum, Bilal Shaw, 33)

I'm in a tube with silver walls that lightning-
crackle when I reach two fingers out,
and then my fingers glow. I guess it's frightening.
I hear my far-off mouth begin to shout.
Last thing I knew, I stepped into the light
and now I feel a thing inside my brain.
My mind, my mind's not right, my mind's not right,
there's something worming in me. Oh! The pain.
What do you want, I'm here to help, you want . . .
but no, that's terrible, you were supposed
to come to us like Jesus, and you can't
ask me — but they won't follow me. They're closed
like turtles, and they — no! The pain! Stop, Lord.
No more! I'll be your priest. They'll hear your word.

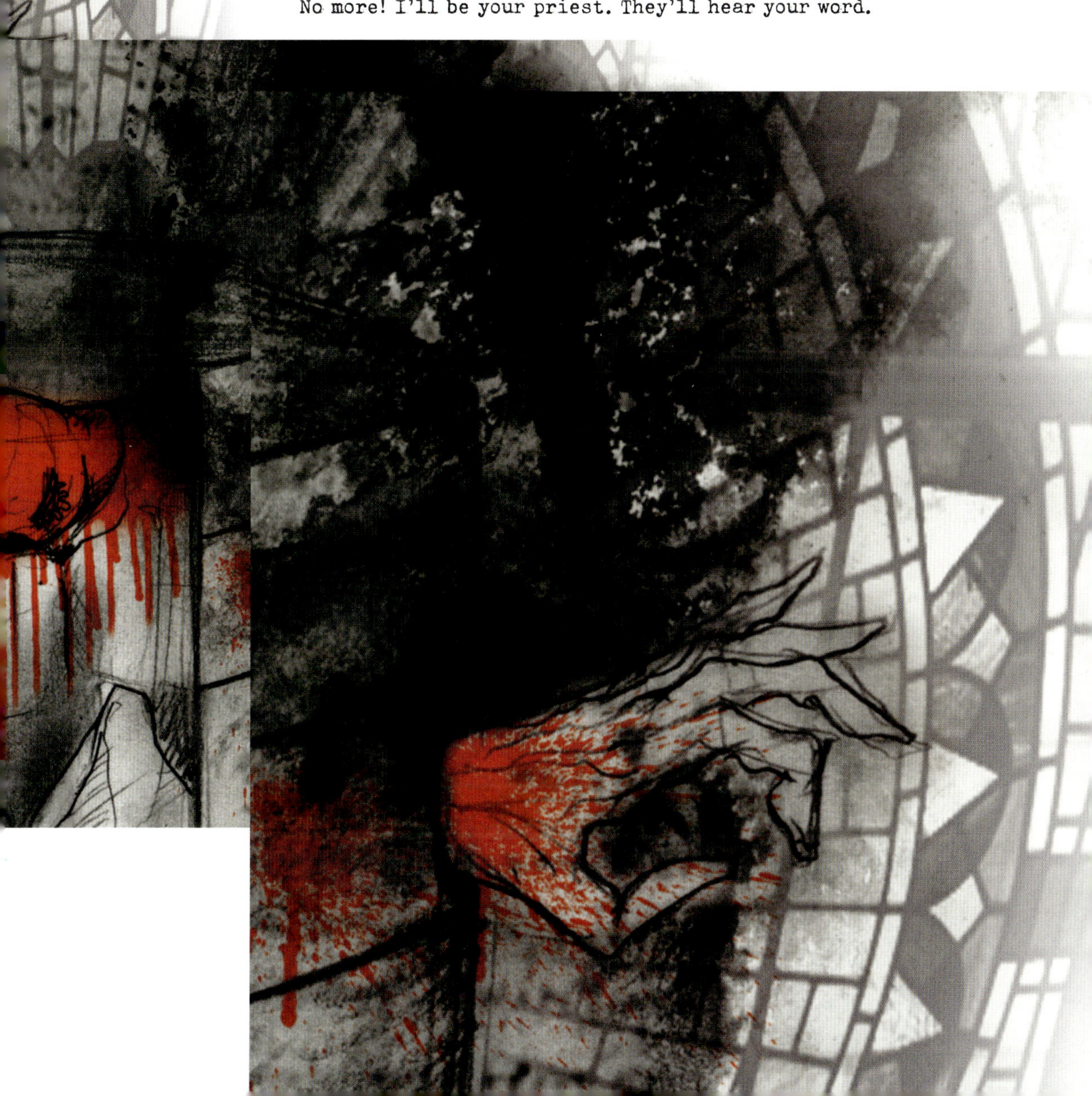

8. Illegal Alien (Case 006: Ronaldo Alcalay, age unknown)

I've spent my days outside the Home Depot
praying for day work with the other men,
I've dug your ditches, picked your grapes. You know
you need my wife to scrub your tub for ten
dollars an hour if she's lucky, so
maybe I am an illegal alien
but this town doesn't run without my crew,
my family, my pickup truck with shovel,
rake, machete, chainsaw, though it's true
I saw you all start running, start to grovel
once the red-eyed demons broke into
the town hall, ate the mayor's brain. My hovel
is poor, my skin is brown, but I will not run.
This is my town, my chainsaw, and my shotgun.

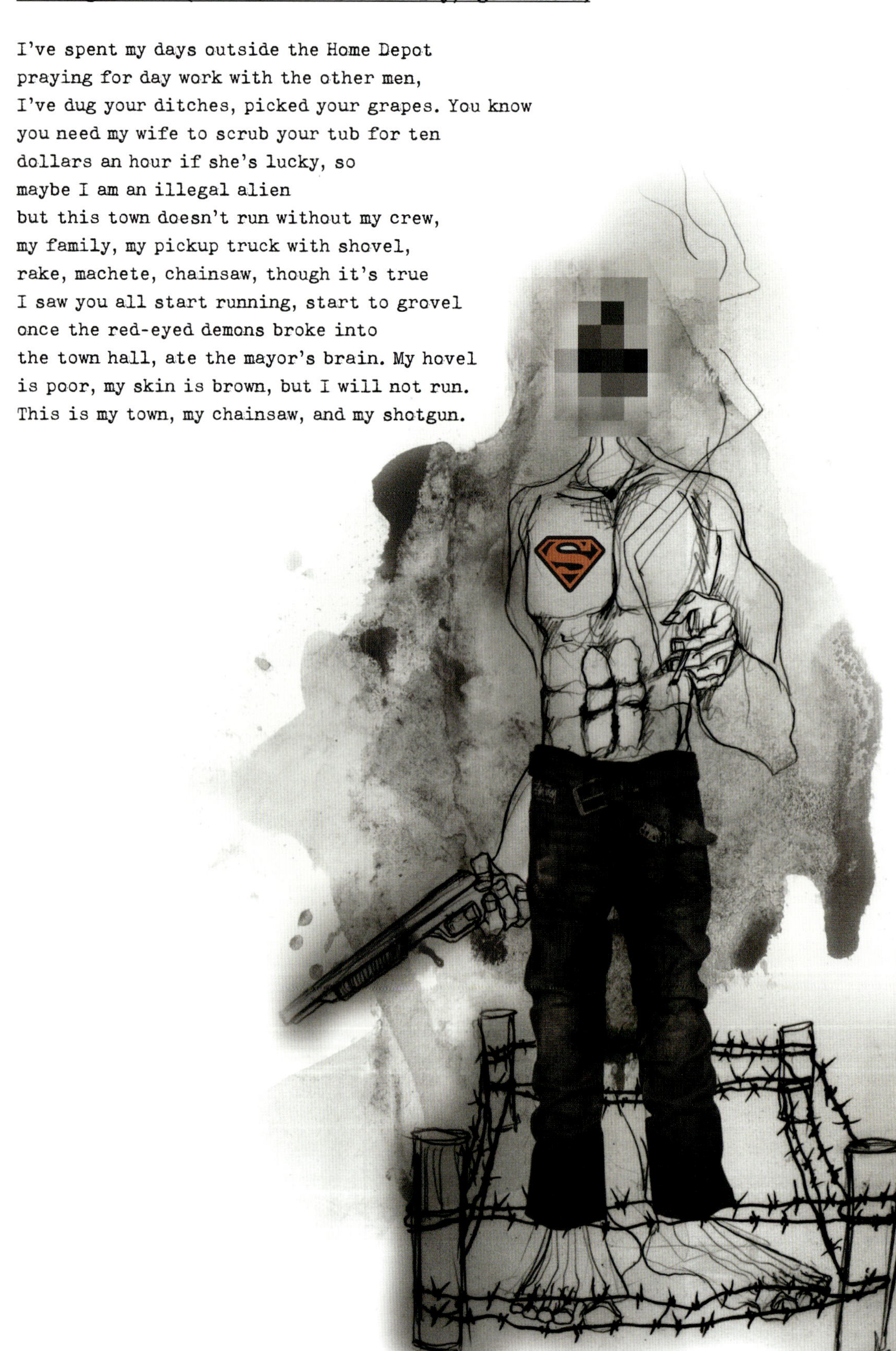

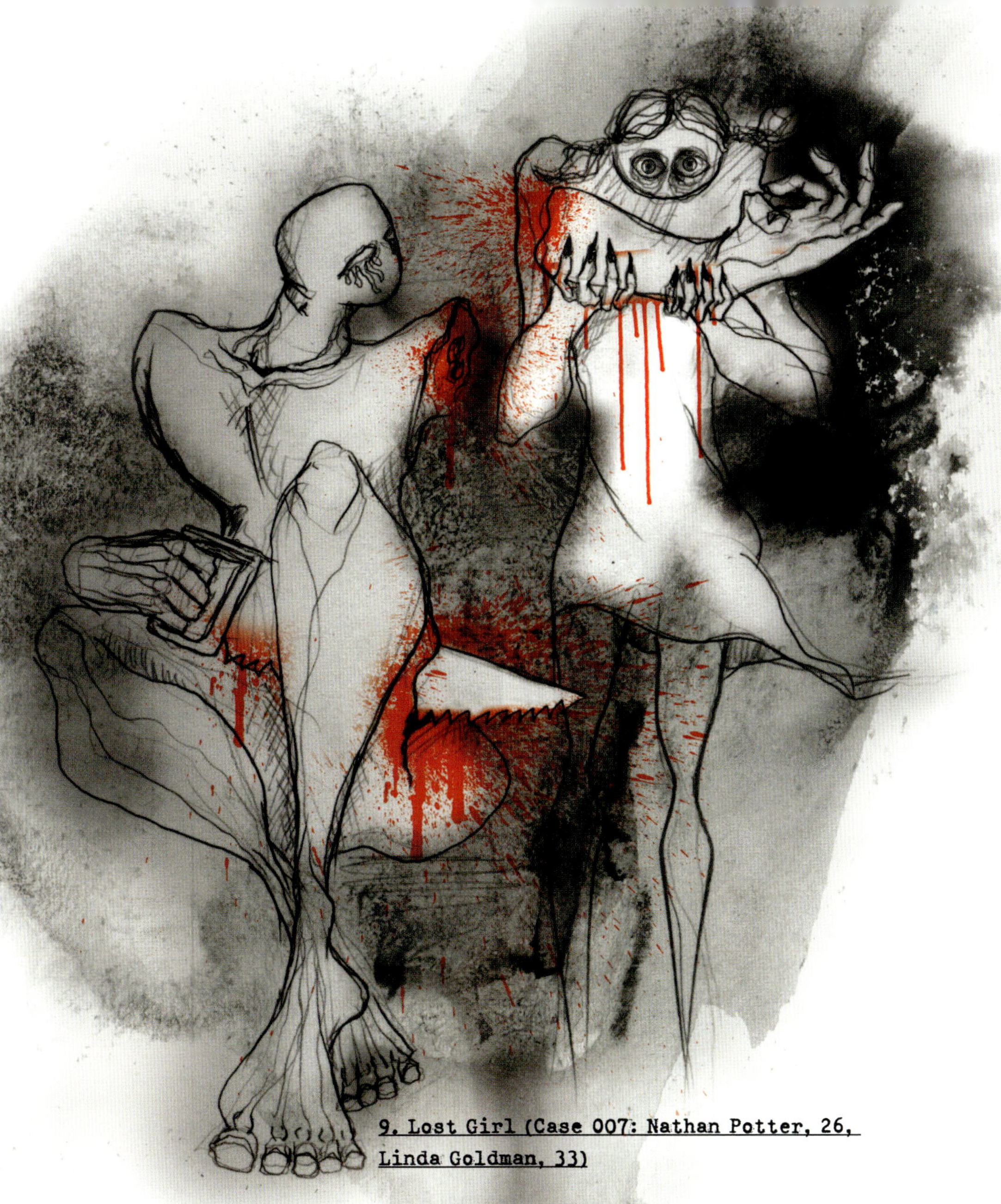

9. Lost Girl (Case 007: Nathan Potter, 26, Linda Goldman, 33)

She comes out of the woods with a strange walk.
My heart, like a fish flopping on the deck,
spasms inside my chest, and the dark shock
of seeing Linda alive again wets
my eyes and drops me to my knees — an error
as it turns out, despite my feelings for her
— she moans and claws at me, a gorgeous horror.
And as she bites my thigh, despite my terror
somehow I can't resist. I understand
the reason why this dead girl walks again:
the creatures have replaced her lovely brain
with alien larvae, but life's empty, and
there are worse ways to die. She's beautiful
and so I let her eat until she's full.

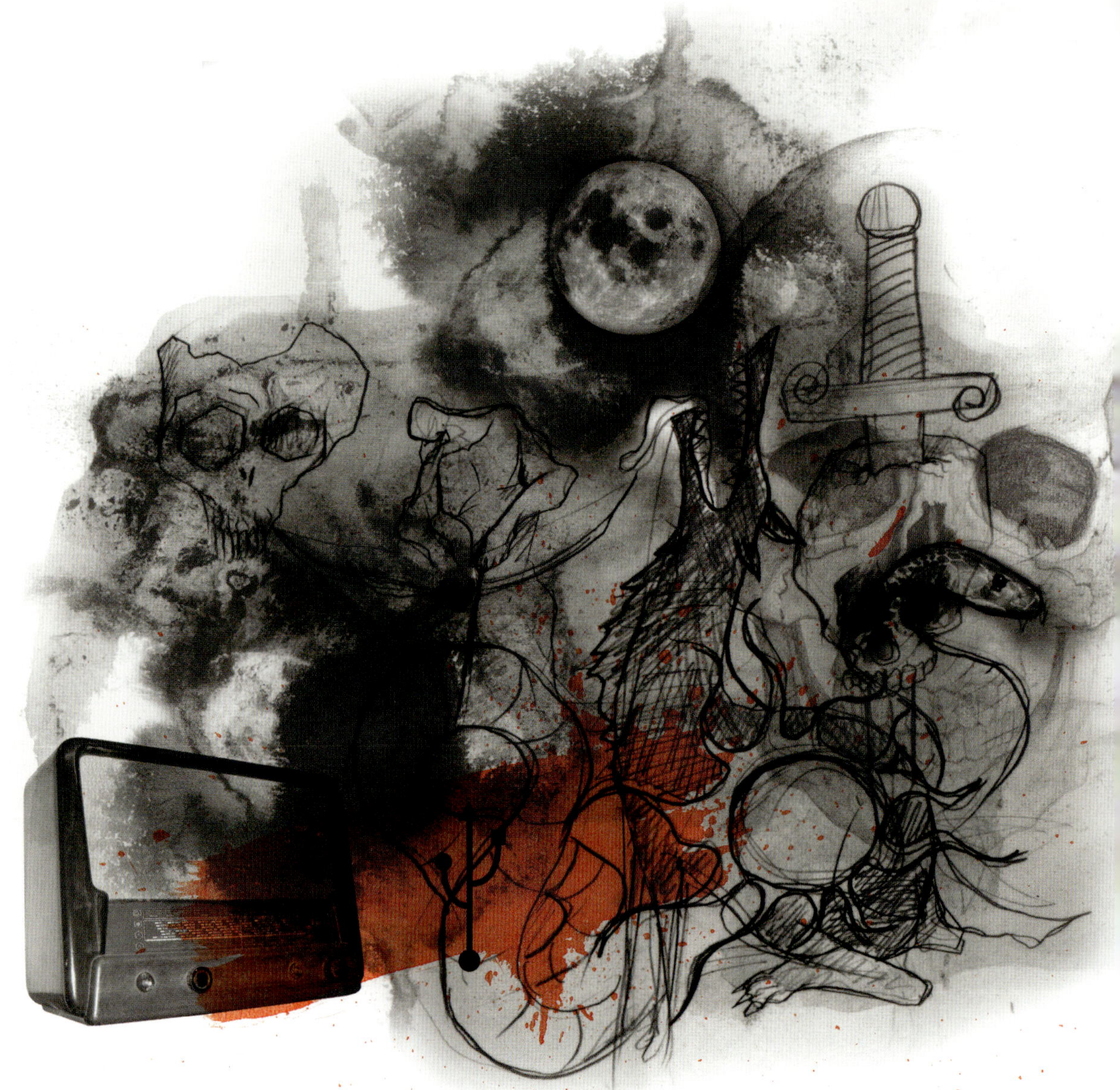

10. Revelation Now (Transcript: NSA Radio Intercept, Speaker Thought to Be Bilal Shaw, 33)

The wolf has swallowed up the sun; the snake
has risen from the seas; the archer leaves
the rabbit on the moon for galaxies
beyond; the drowned are walking from the lake.
Today's the day that ends all days. The night
of nights will come tonight. Something like that,
anyway. Truth is, my mind's a bat
shuddering through elliptical strange flight.
But I do know our masters need a harvest
and so, my followers, I send you forth
to gather fuel for the hungry larvae.
Something wicked this way comes, a birth
whose name has never passed through human lips.
It's like that movie: *Dark Apocalypse.*

11. New Under the Sun (Case 008: Brian Turner, Infantry Team Leader, 40)

We thought we'd seen it all, our buddies blown
into the sky by IEDs inside
the Triangle, lasers killing from a drone,
but now they've got us telling folks to hide,
to barricade themselves inside their homes,
telling them the government has lied
for all these years about the UFOs,
"For your own safety." Yeah, right. My ass.
We thought we'd seen it all, but eyes that glow,
the ship still there after our bombing pass,
a zombie army led by some dick-blow
in Birkenstocks who should be selling hash
or doing yoga? *That* is new. We're beat.
That's also new — our army in retreat.

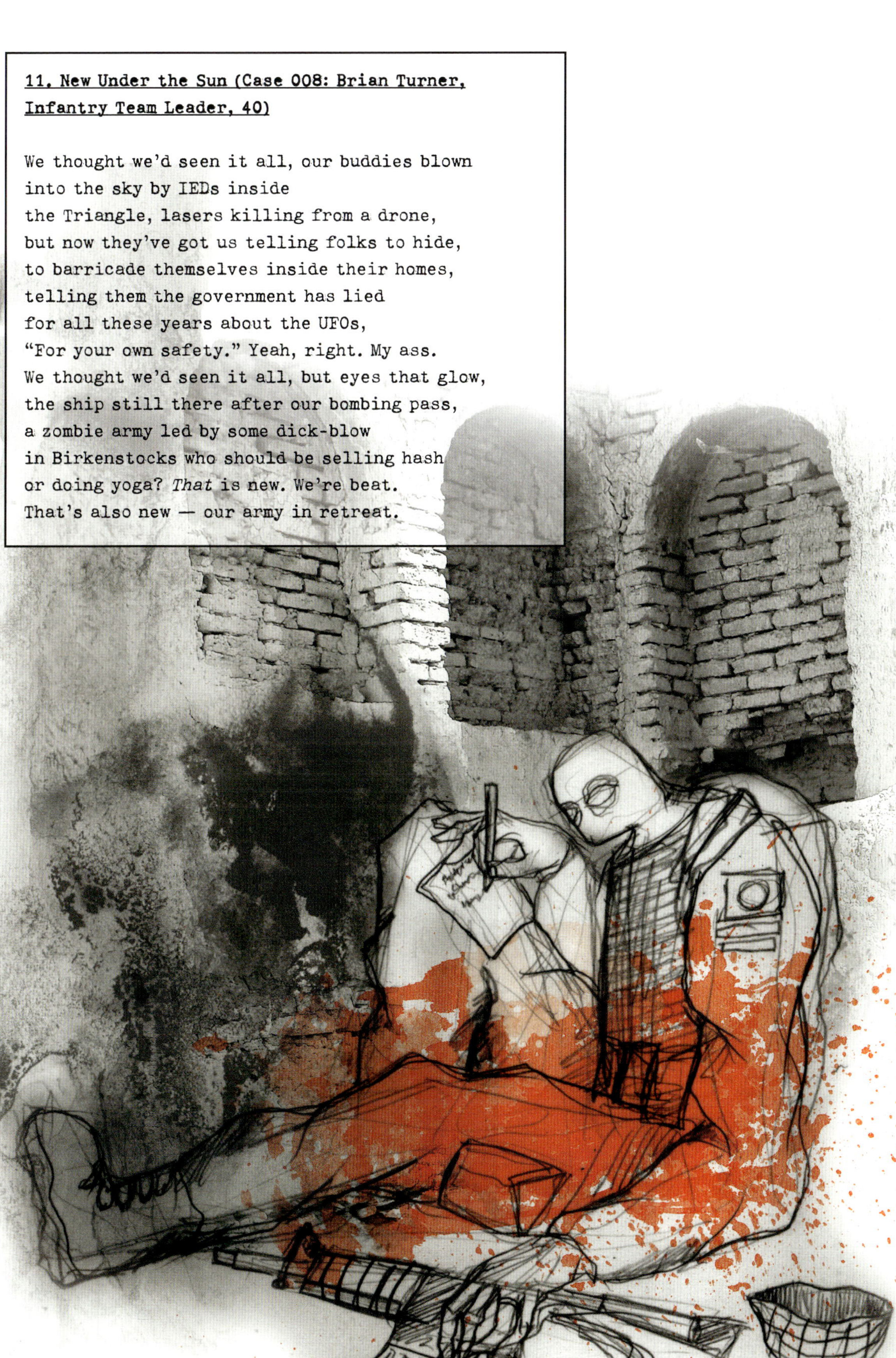

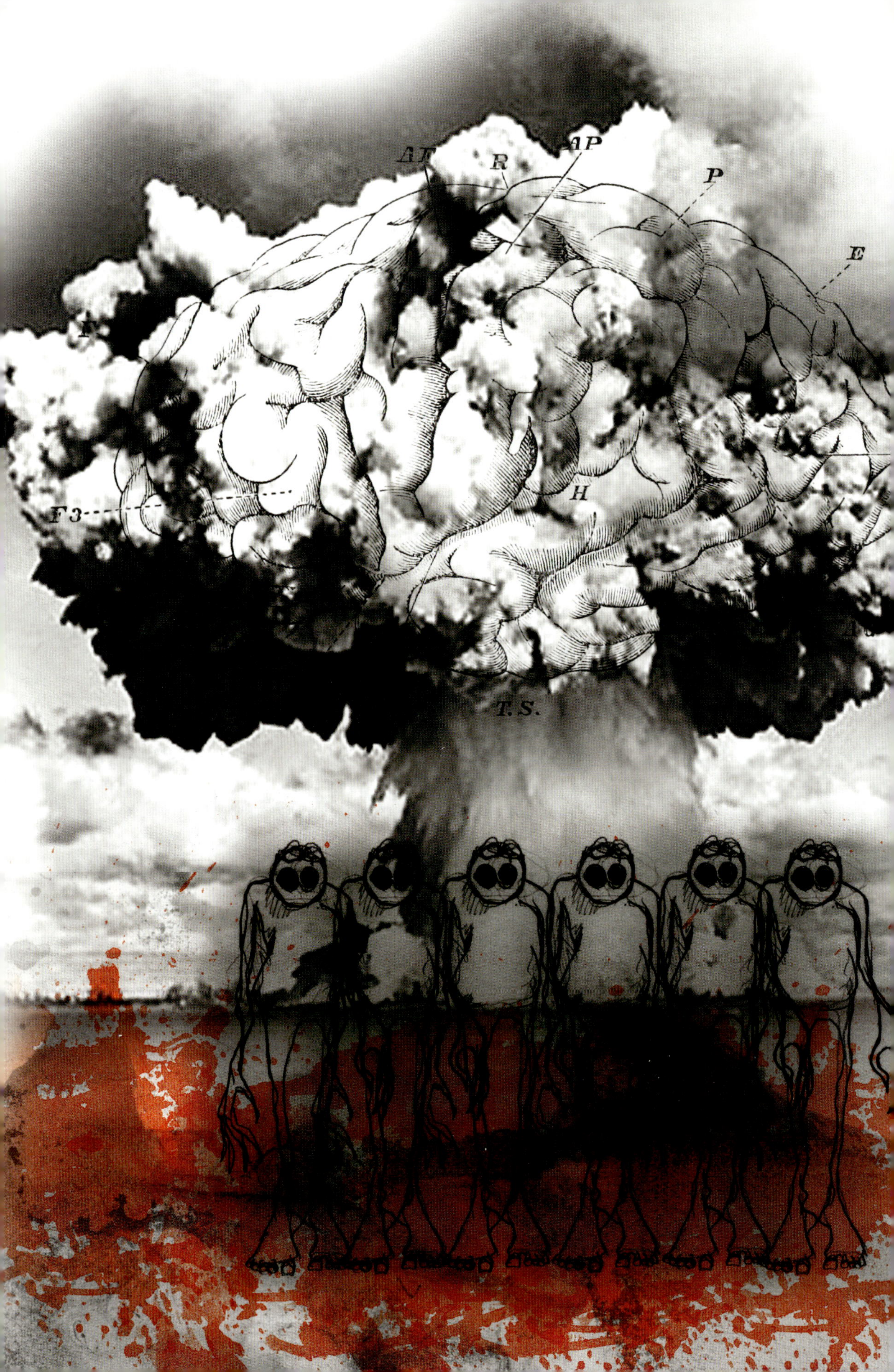

R
AP
P
E
F3
H
T.S.

12. Diary Entry: Brian Turner, in the Bunker

We set them off, a razzmatazz of rockets
that beat like fists against a locked steel door.
No luck. Tactical nukes did nothing more.
First New York went and then D.C. Just pockets
of army men and cops held out, like Kim
and me here in the bunker taking cover
with Strong and Swan. America is over.
Now Swan's gone missing. When Strong goes after him
I tell her, "Kathy, give it up. You *know.*"
I see now why they called her Captain Strong
down at the school. She looks at me real long
and says, "Brian, I know. Still, I must go."
At least she'll die for something when she dies.
I let Kim hold me, and begin to cry.

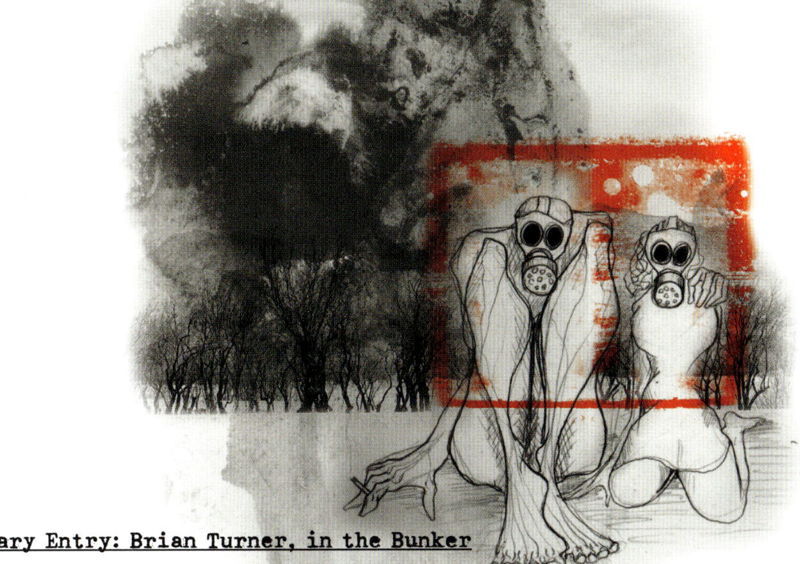

13. Diary Entry: Brian Turner, in the Bunker

Okay, I know, the goddamn world is dead.
Now there's just Kim and me. I can't believe
we're all that's left — Adam and fuckin' Eve.
I tell you when I lost my addled head
Kim kept hers and shut my mouth while creeps
went creeping by the vine-draped bunker entrance.
What a great gal. Sure thing I am entranced.
So fine, let all the world go to those freaks,
no movie ending like *War of the Worlds*
where all the aliens die off. At least
there's Kim who says, "Stop writing" while she twirls
her bra. At least I'm in this hole with her.
Two comforts: that I'm no effing officer,
and that before I die I get the girl.

14. Final Diary Entry: Kim Oja, in the Bunker

They got my Brian yesterday when he
went out to scrounge for food. I heard him scrabbling
at the steel door and swung it wide to see
his red eyes glowing, torn skin, slack mouth gabbling
that stuff they use for language, sounds like snails
beneath your heels. I gave him one between
the eyes then sat and wept. So here's the tale
of history, of empire, love and dream:
it's all come down to me. If they get me
there's nothing left, but on the other hand,
I'll starve and die alone if I stay free.
There's nothing left both ways. I understand
what I must do. No reason I should hide.
I put my shotgun down and walk outside.

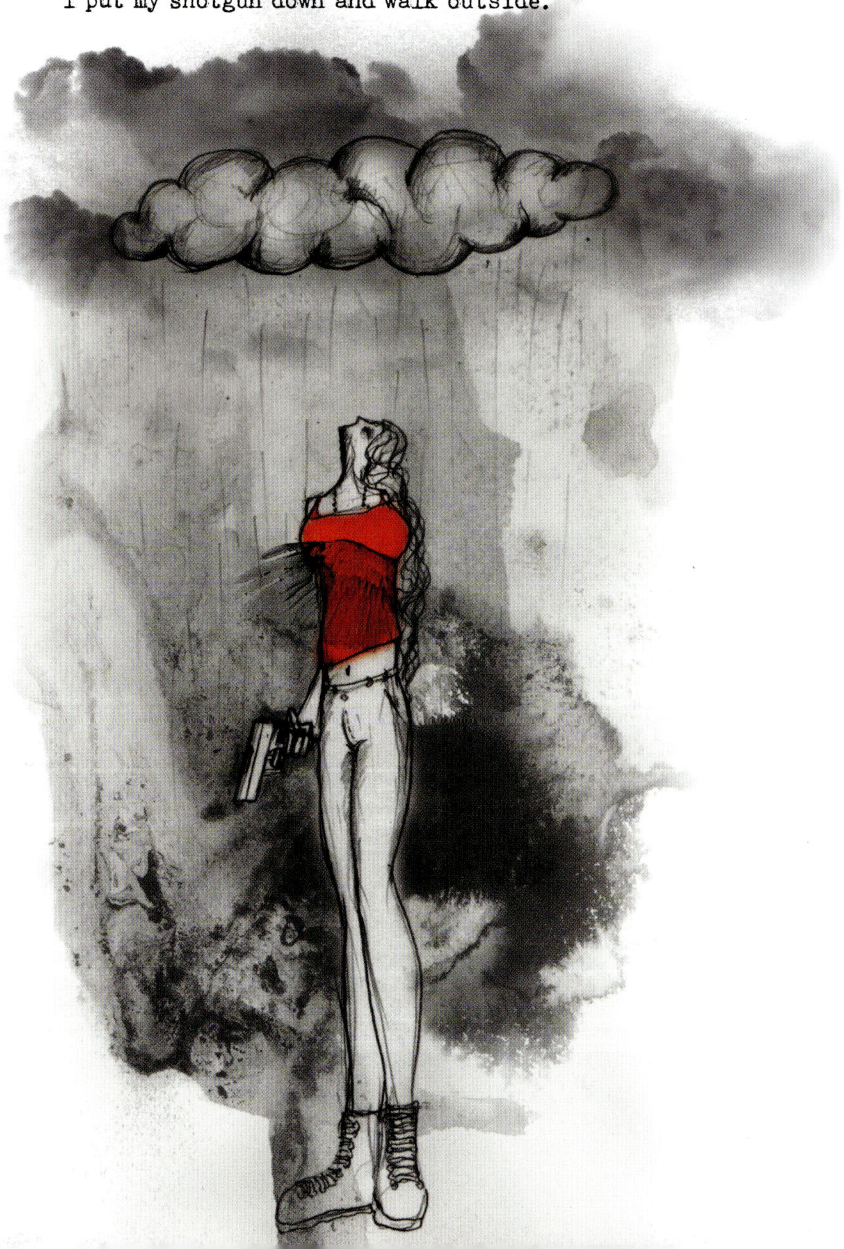

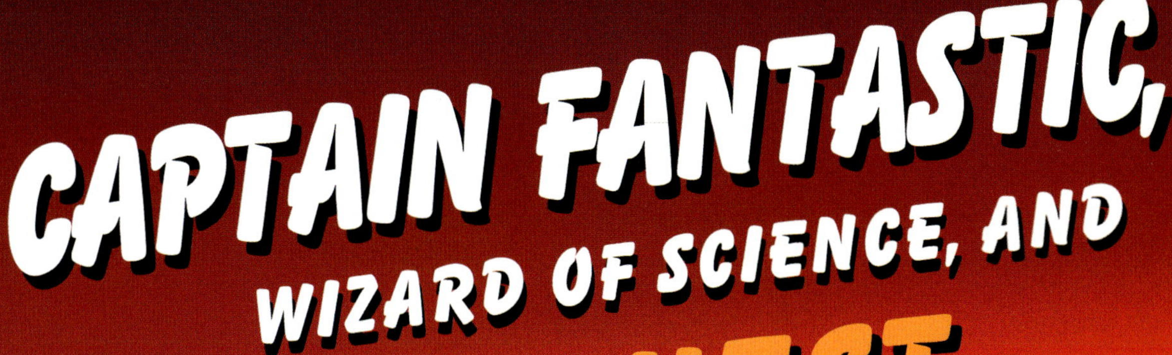

THE QUEST for the NEW UNIVERSE

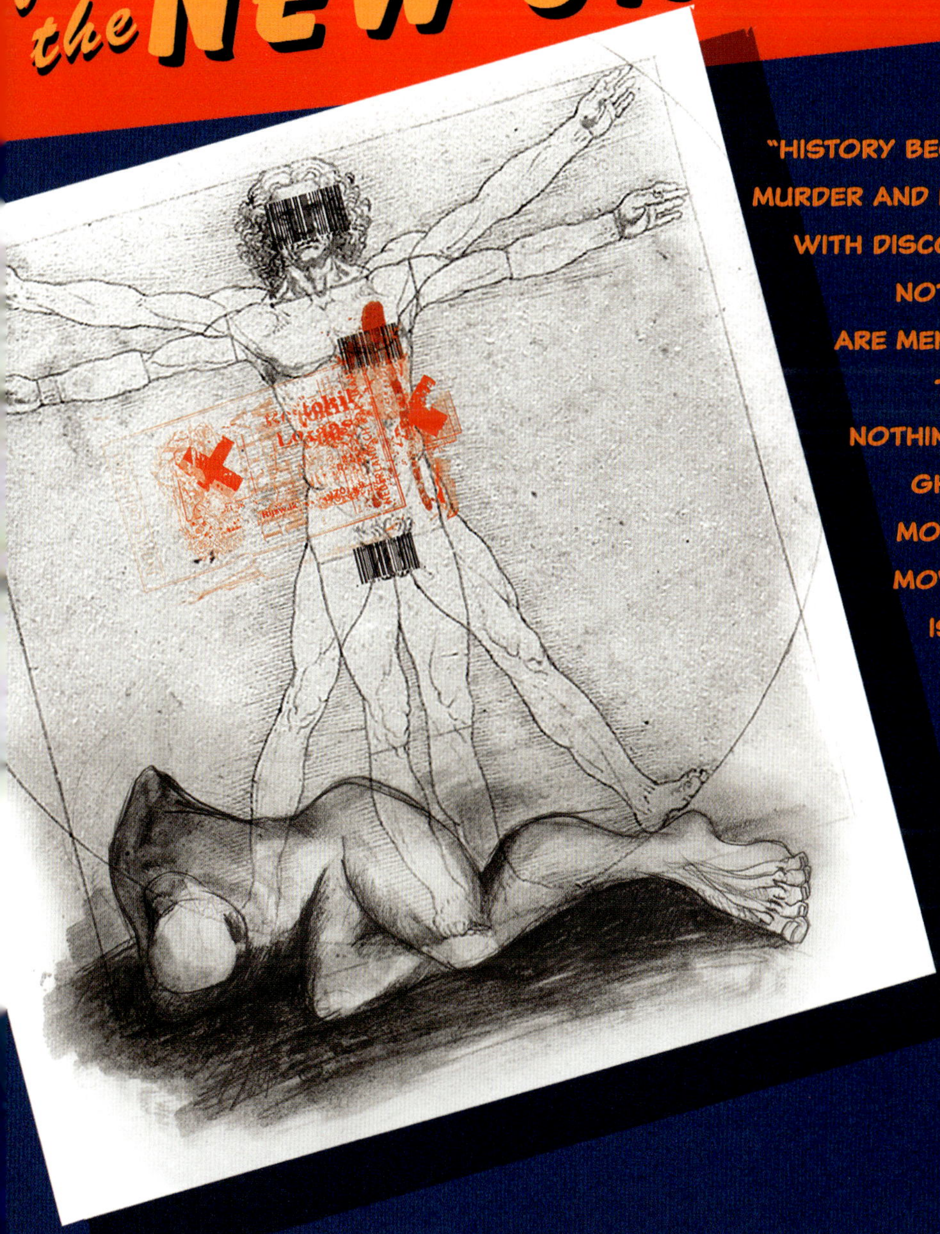

"HISTORY BEGINS FOR US WITH MURDER AND ENSLAVEMENT, NOT WITH DISCOVERY. NO, WE ARE NOT INDIANS, BUT WE ARE MEN OF THEIR WORLD. THE BLOOD MEANS NOTHING; THE SPIRIT, THE GHOST OF THE LAND MOVES IN THE BLOOD, MOVES THE BLOOD. IT IS WE WHO RAN TO THE SHORE NAKED, WE WHO CRIED, 'HEAVENLY MAN!'"

—FROM *IN THE AMERICAN GRAIN,* BY WILLIAM CARLOS WILLIAMS

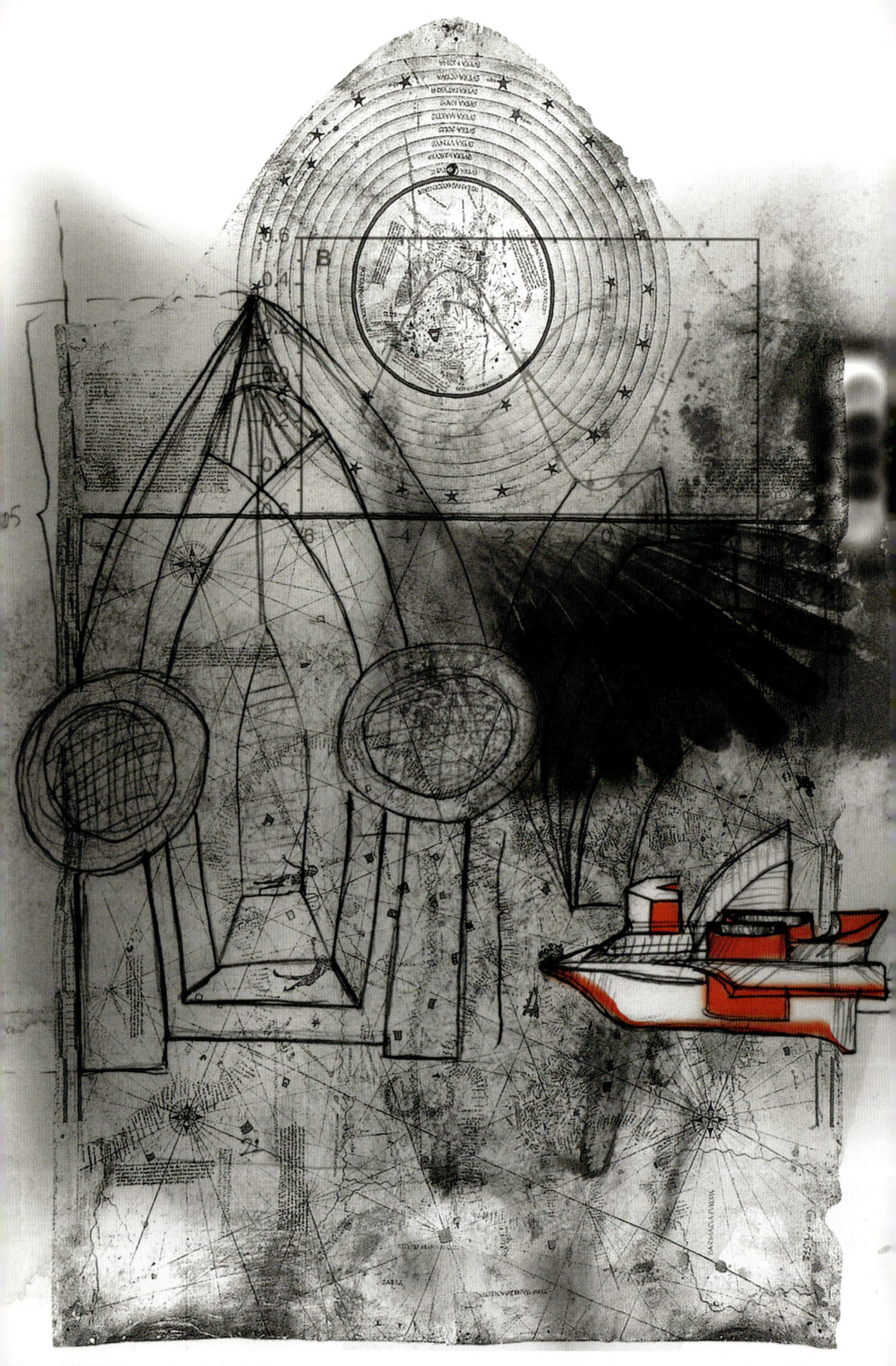

1. CAPTAIN FANTASTIC IN "AMONG THE FLAT EARTHERS!"

The Devil science drives me crazy, some
say, since I want to blast off from the Earth.
They say that in uncharted space is death,
that strange and undiscovered country from
whose airless grave no traveler returns,
that all of space-time is a tabletop
and I'll sail off the edge and drop and drop
through black holes, dead skies. But this planet turns,
I say, and the blue Earth is a bright ball
spinning through spheres, not flat. They're like ship mice,
frightened, seeking their nests, not Paradise.
Not me. Space dust pocks the hull as I fall
(or rise) through space — my atom shields unfurled —
and shoot myself into the unseen world.

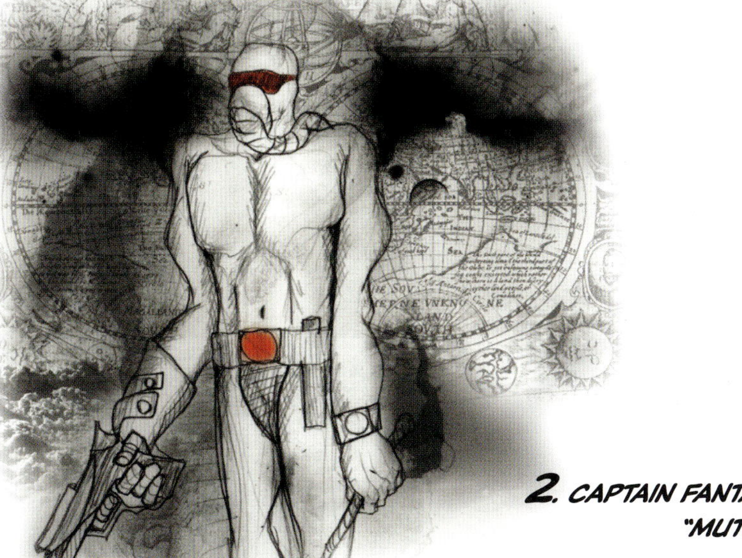

2. CAPTAIN FANTASTIC IN "MUTINY IN SPACE!"

I'm having serious trouble with the crew
despite the stellar charts I've made. They eye
me, fingering their guns. I know they view
me as a lunatic who made a lie
of fertile planets, gold, plutonium,
of asteroid belts to mine, and alien earths
where we'll be seen as gods. So I play dumb
until one night when they're in sleeping berths
I have my officers collect their guns.
I have the leaders whipped until they screech,
disintegrate Frank Adler when he runs,
put five men in the lock and give a speech:
"We are explorers, each one of us a hero"
— then run the airlock pressure down to zero.

3. CAPTAIN FANTASTIC IN "LOST IN SPACE!"

While floating through a spaceship cemetery
I lose the metal tether. Just static
from the ship — faint, now gone. I've wrestled scary
monsters and lived, but though it's less dramatic
this emptiness is worse — just space to catch
at with my silver-suited hands — and fear
comes rushing howling from the cargo hatch
inside my brain. The tiny atmosphere
inside my pressure suit makes a small ship
where I can live until I die, distending,
compressing with each breath. The homing chip
leads to my rescue (that's the happy ending)
but still at night in solipsistic dreams
I try to fill the emptiness with screams.

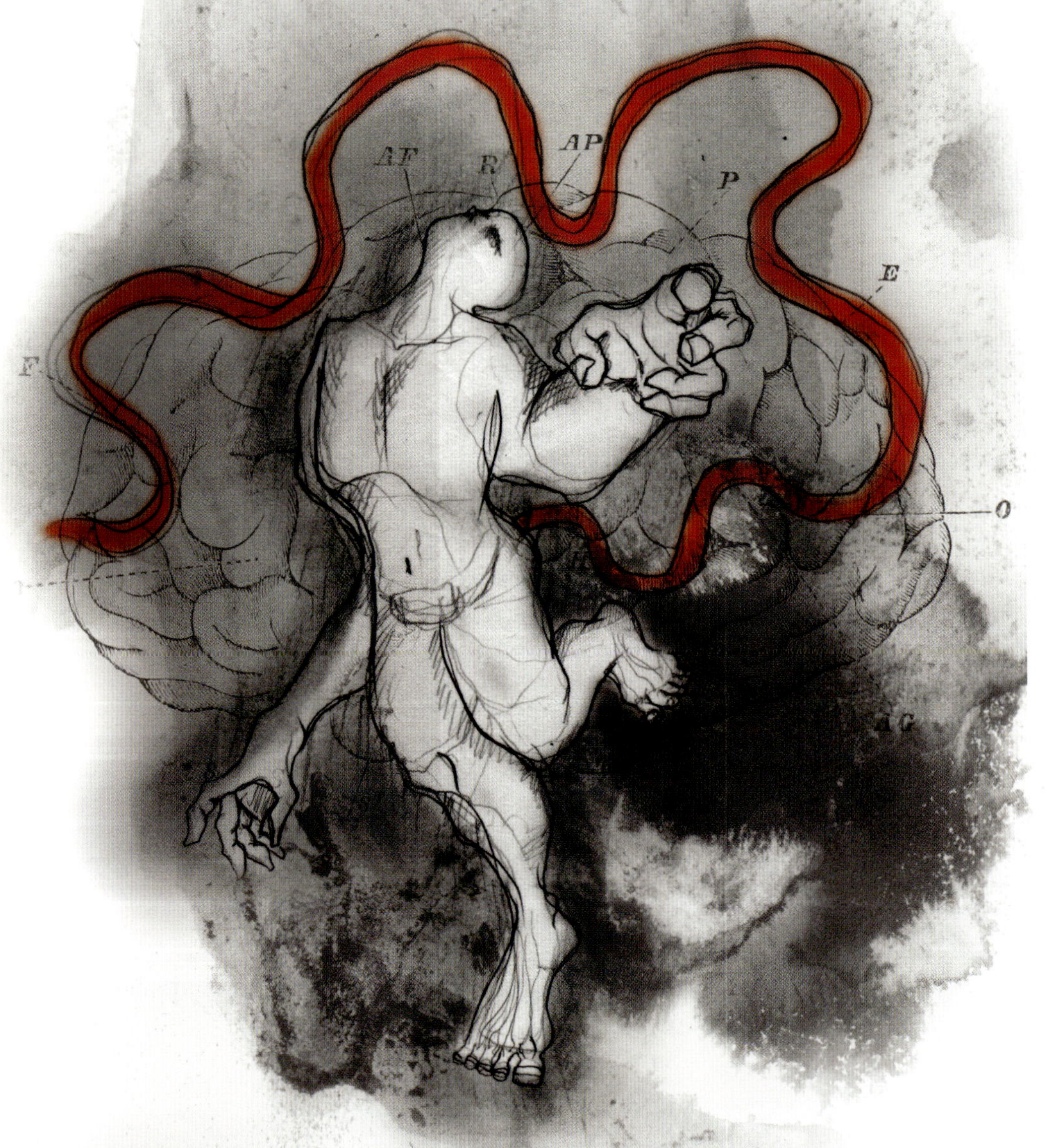

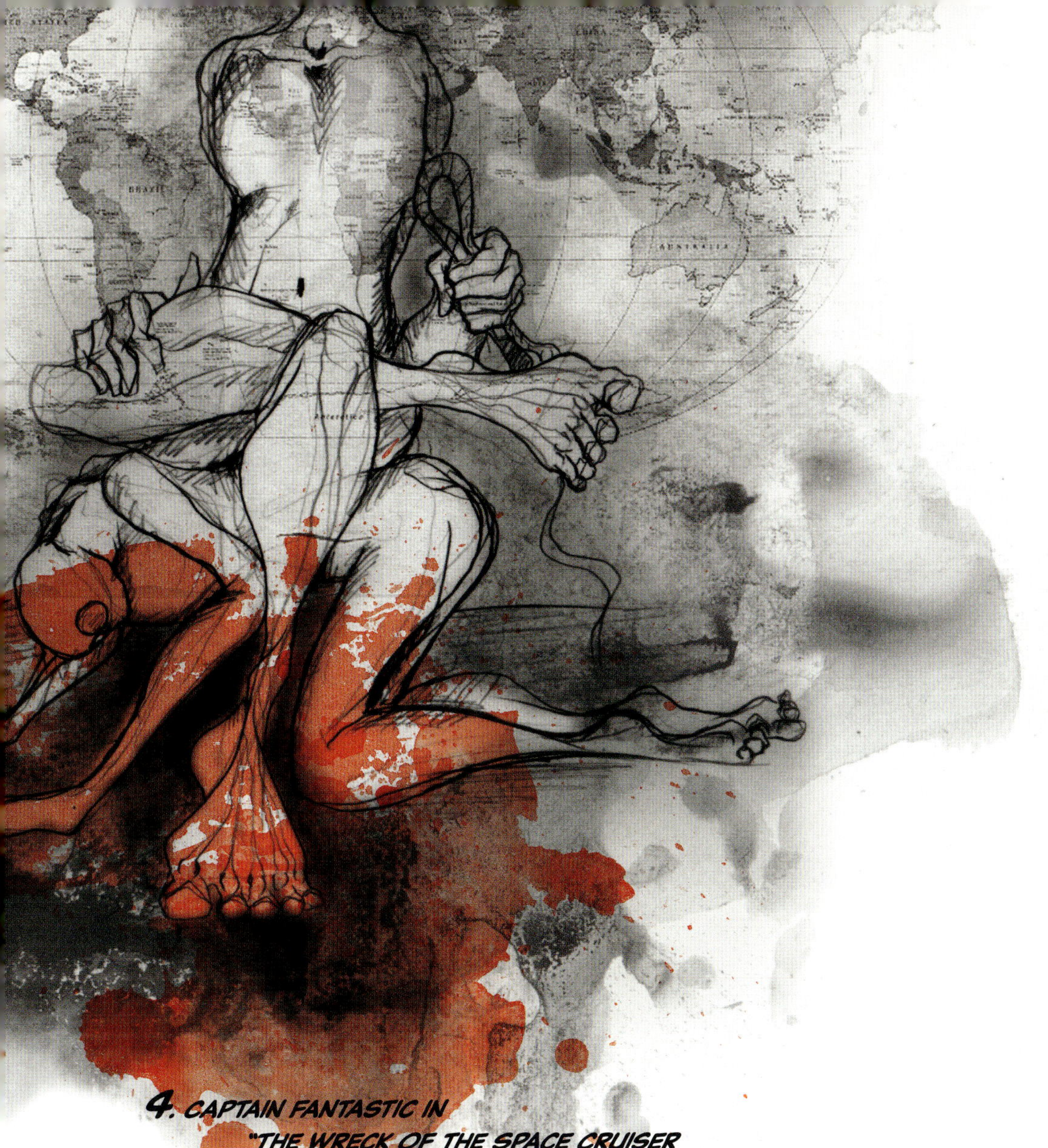

4. CAPTAIN FANTASTIC IN "THE WRECK OF THE SPACE CRUISER SANTA MARÍA!"

I felt secure, no asteroid, black hole
or aliens on the screen, so went to sleep.
The navigator working the helm stole
a few winks since the universe seemed deep,
peaceful, and smooth as water in a bowl.
The whole crew was asleep and left a boy
alone to steer. The distant stars like coals
went dead. We drifted darkly like a toy
boat swept by tides through coral reefs of dream,
and hit the asteroid belt so quietly
that only I woke up. And then a scream
of bulkheads shattering, then fire, then we
abandoned ship. Later — it gave me no joy —
I had the crewman shot, and hung the boy.

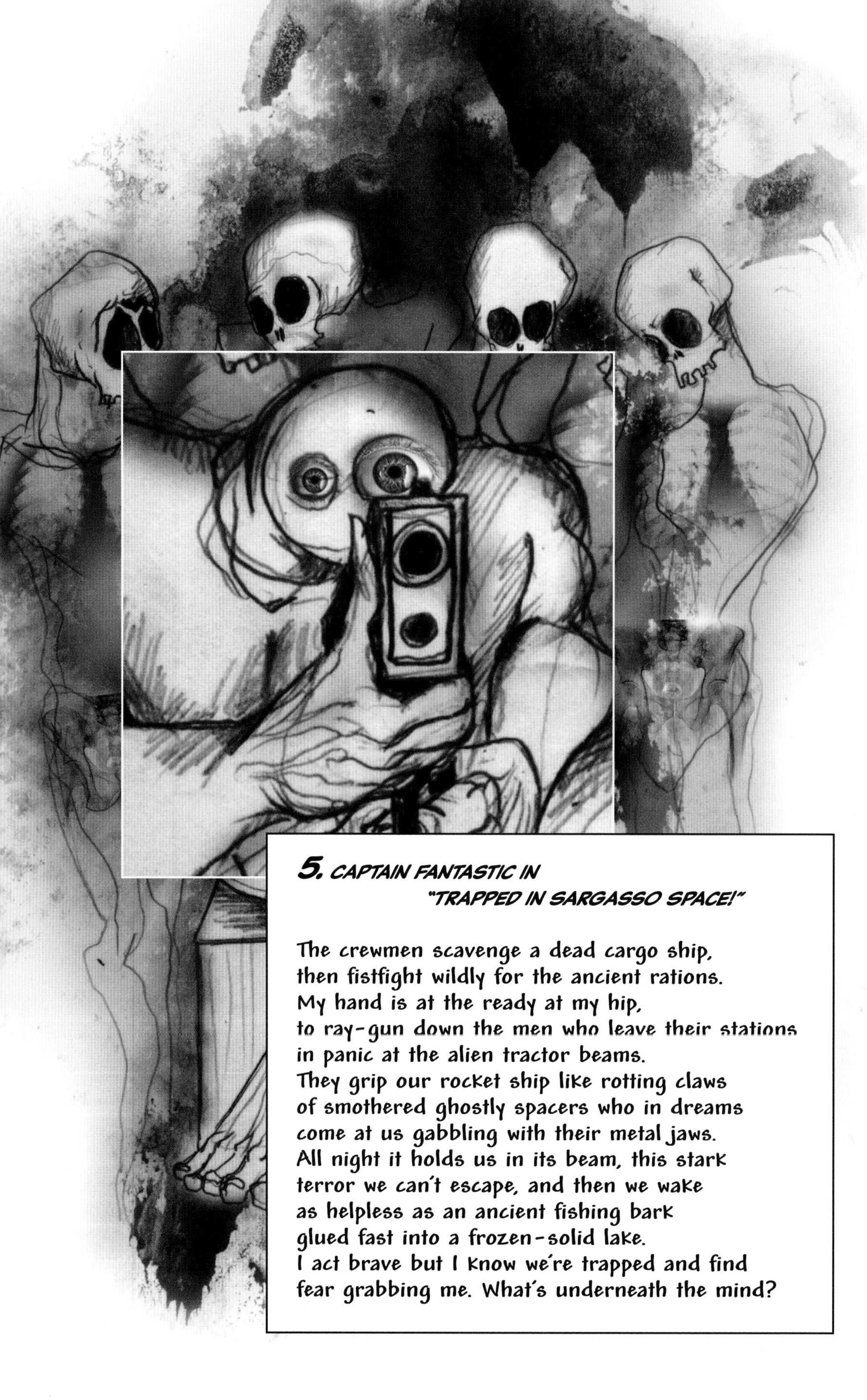
5. CAPTAIN FANTASTIC IN
"TRAPPED IN SARGASSO SPACE!"
The crewmen scavenge a dead cargo ship,
then fistfight wildly for the ancient rations.
My hand is at the ready at my hip,
to ray-gun down the men who leave their stations
in panic at the alien tractor beams.
They grip our rocket ship like rotting claws
of smothered ghostly spacers who in dreams
come at us gabbling with their metal jaws.
All night it holds us in its beam, this stark
terror we can't escape, and then we wake
as helpless as an ancient fishing bark
glued fast into a frozen-solid lake.
I act brave but I know we're trapped and find
fear grabbing me. What's underneath the mind?

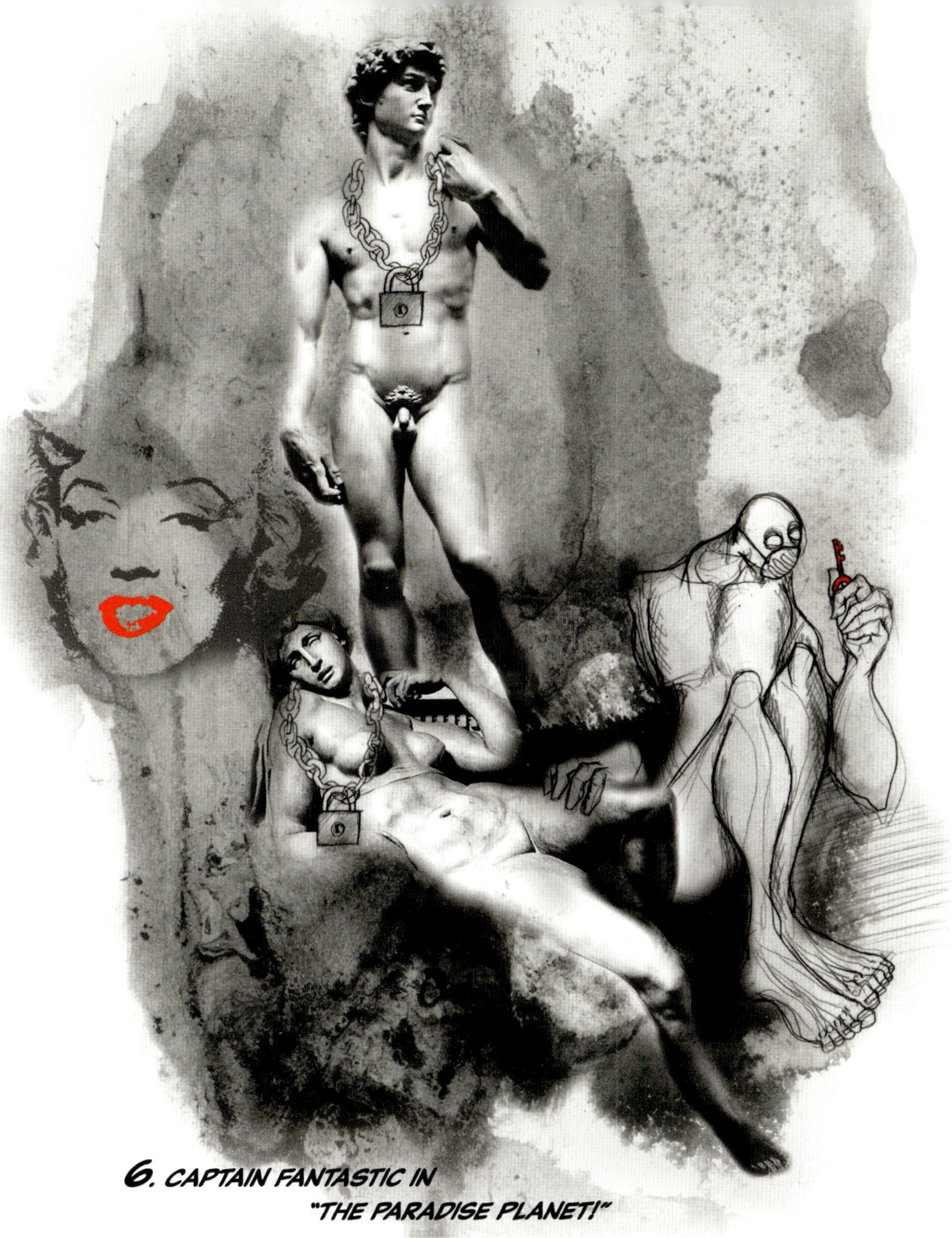

6. CAPTAIN FANTASTIC IN "THE PARADISE PLANET!"

When the ship lands we see nude creatures and
ray-guns in hand we disembark, unfurl
the red imperial banner, pierce the land
with flags and claim this green planet. A girl
watches, as naked as her mother bore
her, with an open face without a trace
of shame. Others approach, perhaps two score,
bearing rich cloths as gifts, each large-eyed face
smiling an alien smile, as pure as we
were once upon a time—before the fall.
Harsh life: the old ones must be in their graves
for all of these are young and beautiful,
their slim bodies painted, manner friendly.
In my report I say: "They'll make good slaves."

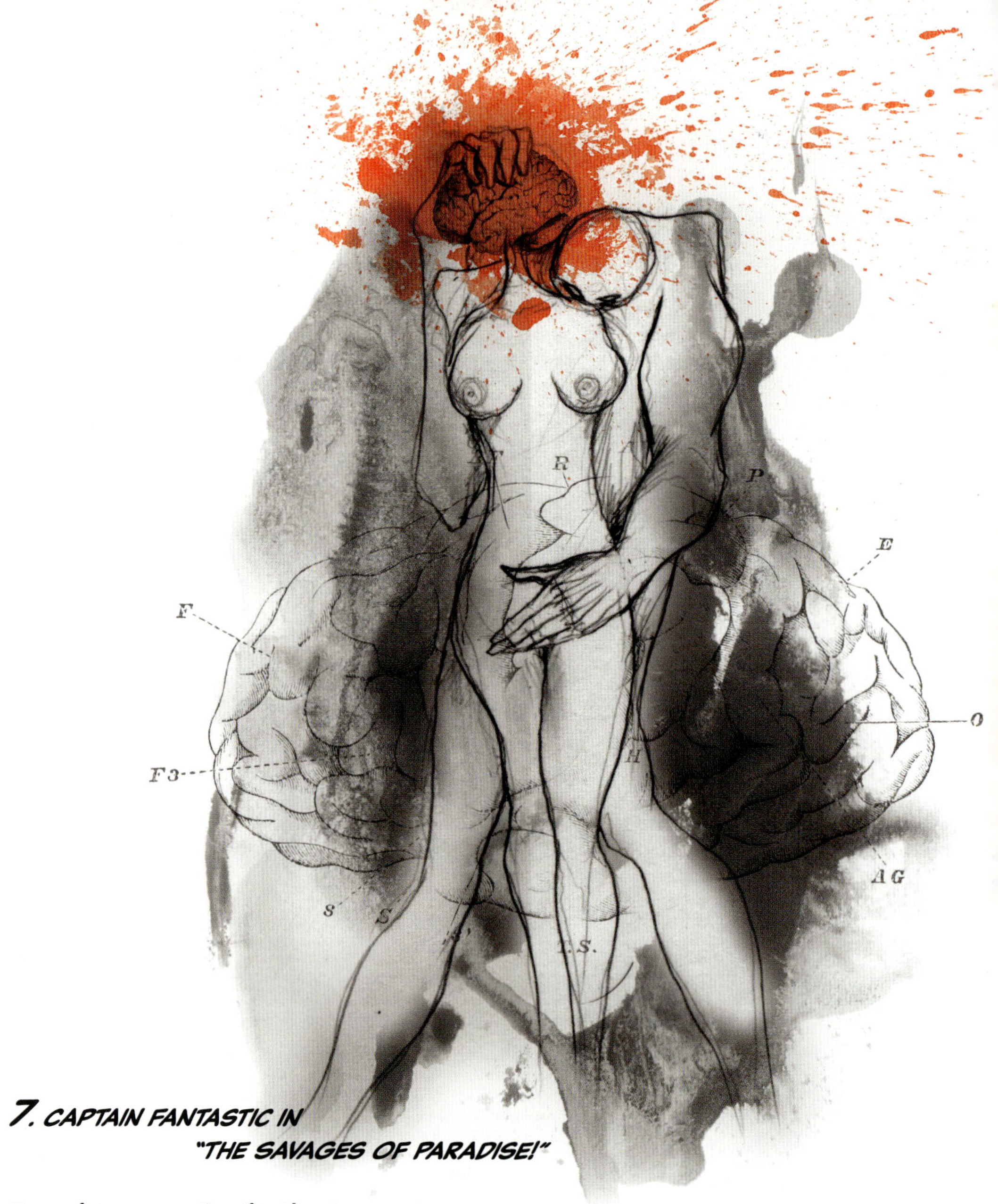

7. CAPTAIN FANTASTIC IN "THE SAVAGES OF PARADISE!"

Back home on Earth, the Inquisition scans
the brains of citizens each week. One trace
of faithlessness and you are sent by trans-
port to the mines of Mars. Out here in space,
the high priest rules, and even I must dread
the brain-scans and nerve tortures. On Paradise
the savages are ignorant, don't read
or know how to make war or sacrifice
their babies to the psycho-tanks. The crew
disdains them, but their calm dark faces show
intelligence, and one has spent the blue
nights in my arms. She smiles and doesn't know
to love me is a sin. I stick my spur
inside and moan, but cannot fathom her.

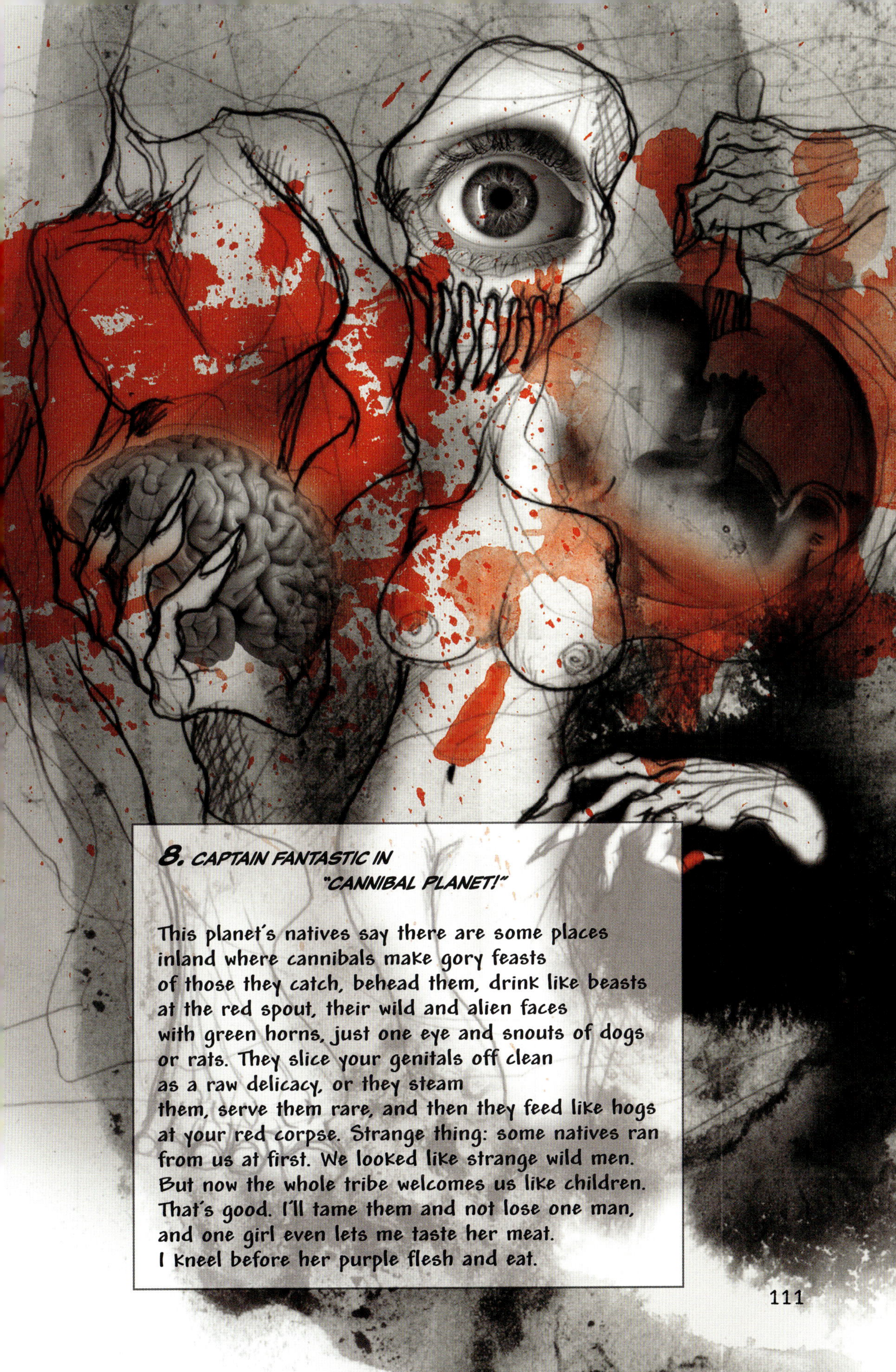

8. CAPTAIN FANTASTIC IN "CANNIBAL PLANET!"

This planet's natives say there are some places
inland where cannibals make gory feasts
of those they catch, behead them, drink like beasts
at the red spout, their wild and alien faces
with green horns, just one eye and snouts of dogs
or rats. They slice your genitals off clean
as a raw delicacy, or they steam
them, serve them rare, and then they feed like hogs
at your red corpse. Strange thing: some natives ran
from us at first. We looked like strange wild men.
But now the whole tribe welcomes us like children.
That's good. I'll tame them and not lose one man,
and one girl even lets me taste her meat.
I kneel before her purple flesh and eat.

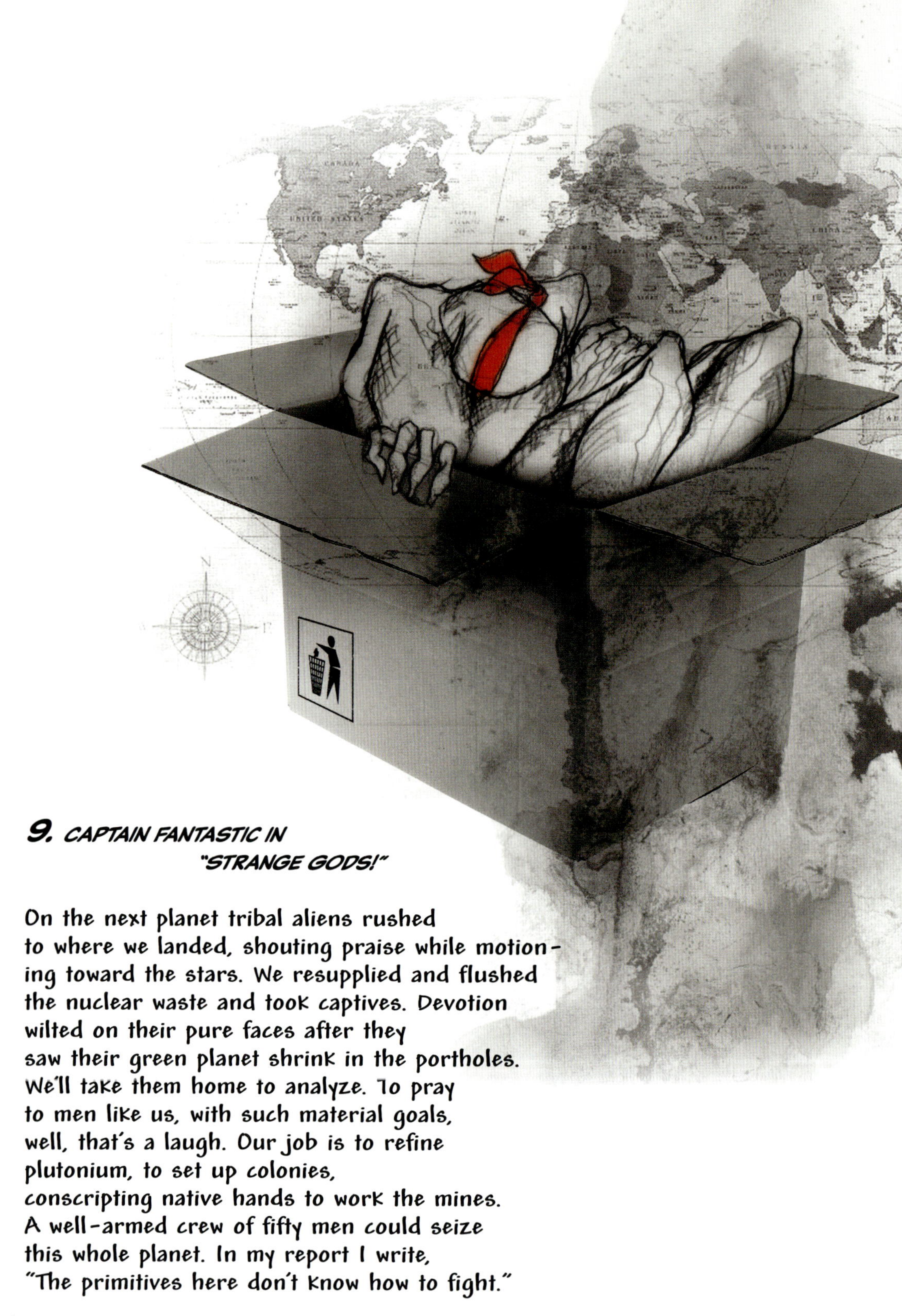

9. CAPTAIN FANTASTIC IN "STRANGE GODS!"

On the next planet tribal aliens rushed
to where we landed, shouting praise while motion-
ing toward the stars. We resupplied and flushed
the nuclear waste and took captives. Devotion
wilted on their pure faces after they
saw their green planet shrink in the portholes.
We'll take them home to analyze. To pray
to men like us, with such material goals,
well, that's a laugh. Our job is to refine
plutonium, to set up colonies,
conscripting native hands to work the mines.
A well-armed crew of fifty men could seize
this whole planet. In my report I write,
"The primitives here don't know how to fight."

10. CAPTAIN FANTASTIC IN "RETURN TO THE PARADISE PLANET!"

We land on Paradise but this time not
one soul comes out to greet us. All have fled.
We wander the abandoned village, caught
in painted time. We sheath our guns and shed
our fears, meandering enchanted through
green groves of trees, with gorgeous alien fruit
we cannot name. Later, I climb up to
a cool sweetwater lake and leave my suit,
helmet and airpack like some brilliant rocks
piled on the shore, with my ionic gun
tossed down like a tree branch while I float, vulture
in Paradise. Above me, alien flocks
migrate across the sky, blotting the sun
as I dry off, then dress myself in culture.

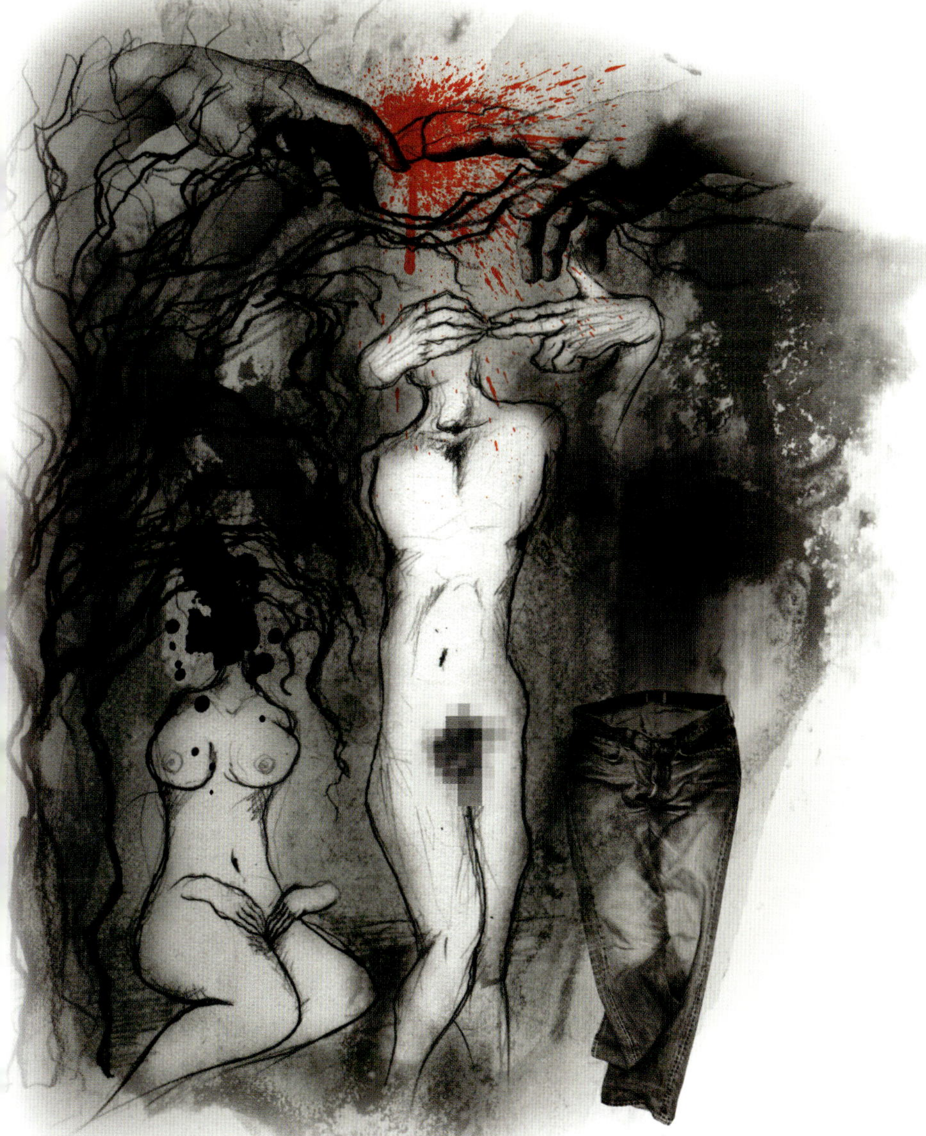

11. CAPTAIN FANTASTIC IN "THE PLANET OF WOMEN!"

On the red planet of the lizard men
I saved a scientist from certain death
— he was to be cooked in green sauce and then
served to the Queen — and when he caught his breath
after we fled from dinosaurs, ray-guns
flashing, the scientist told me of an earth
inhabited by women, gorgeous ones,
and not one man. Now, sleeping in my berth,
I dream of landing on the virgin breast
of a new world, pushing through jungle trails
to find a secret spot where blue undressed
girls dance. I'd stroke their tentacles and tails.
With just one alien kiss I'd be destroyed.
That's why I point my rocket at the void.

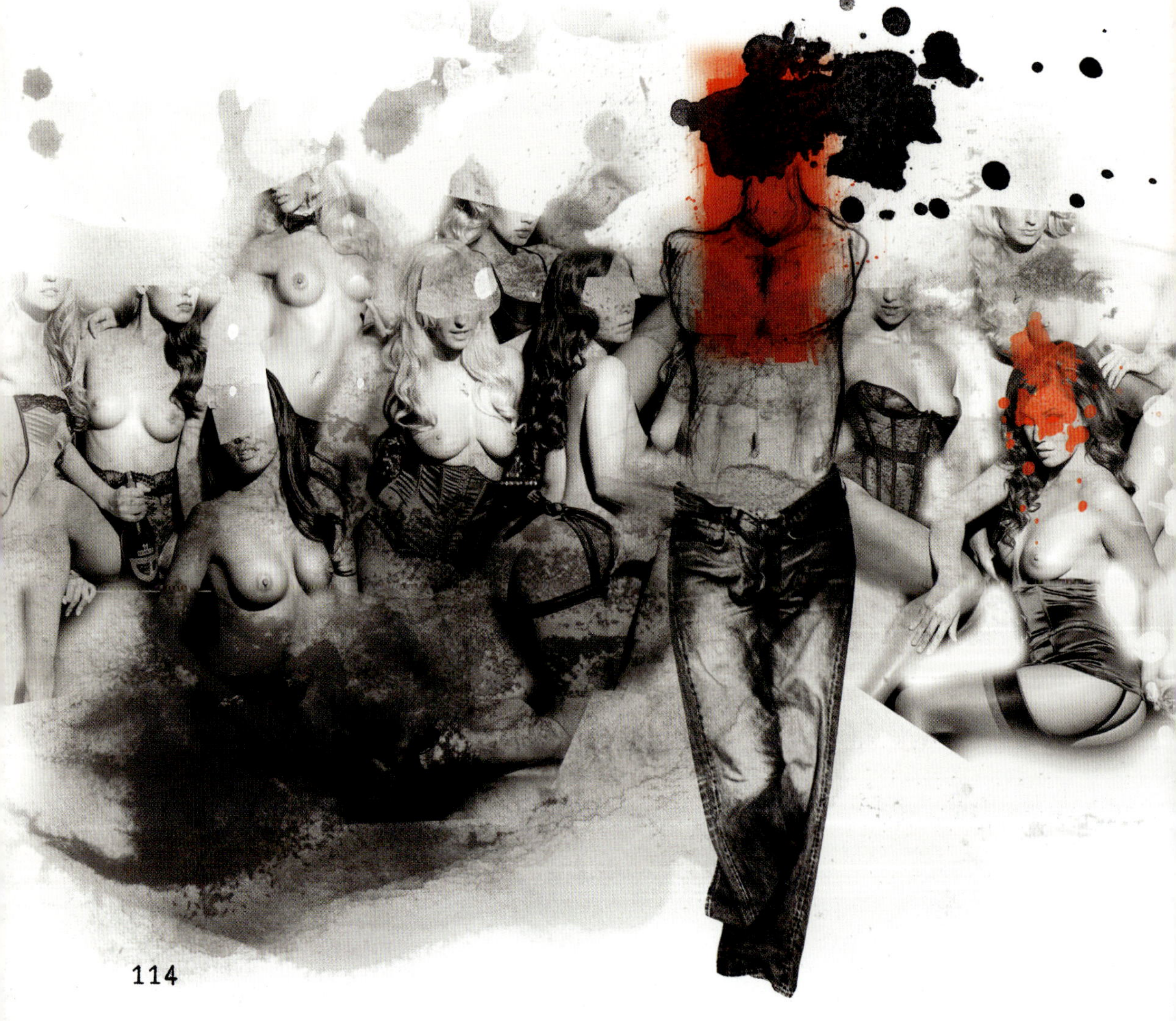

the TOMB in the WOODS

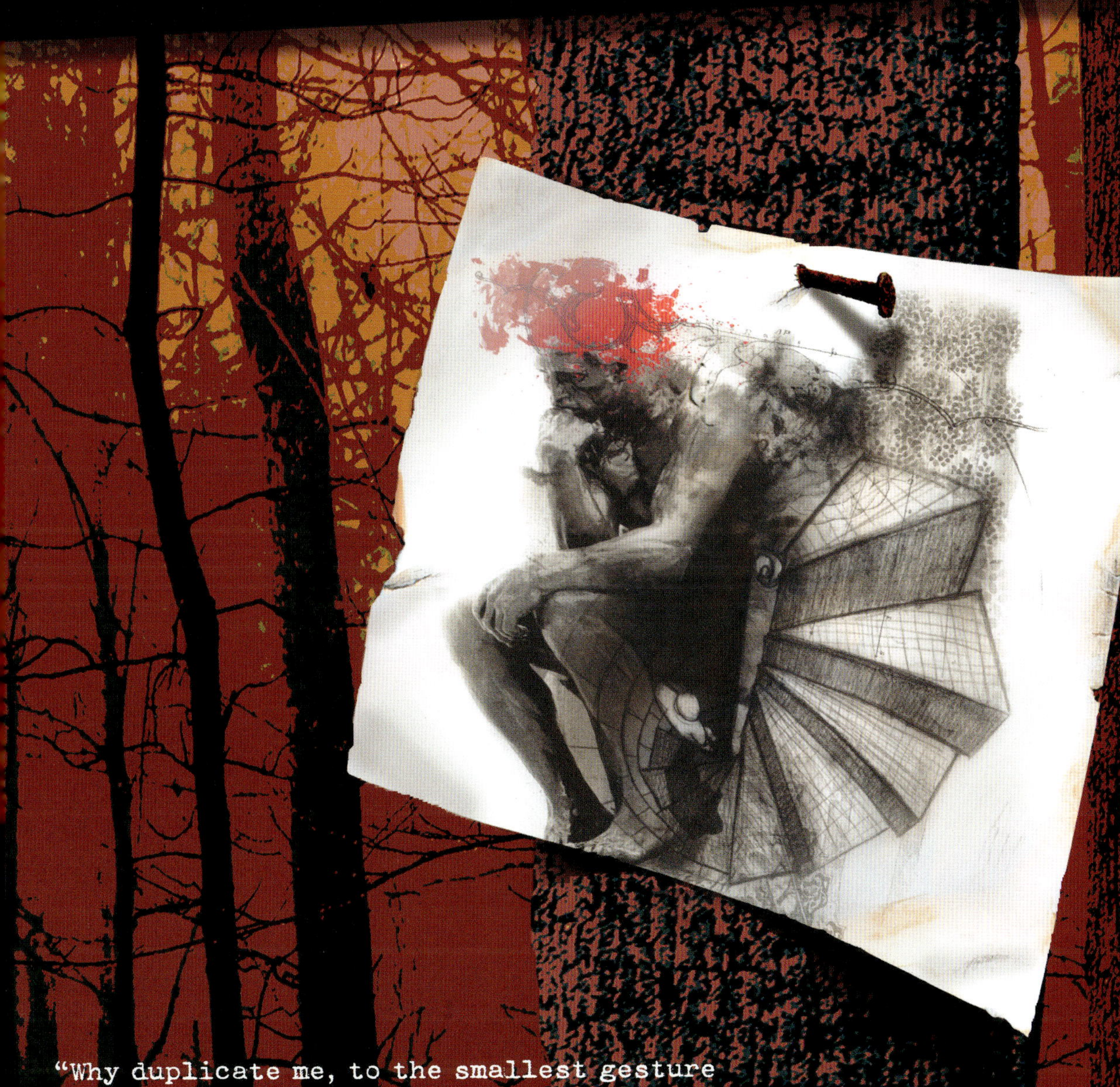

"Why duplicate me, to the smallest gesture of my hand? Why suddenly reflect there in the shadows? You, uncanny brother, you are the other me...."

—Jorge Luis Borges, from "To the Mirror"

1. PROLOGUE

This little Buddha coiled into a ball,
this Jesus laid out in his cave (his death),
they wait till the seed bursts in the wet earth
and a green snake coils up intestinal,
emerges from a hole, its bladelike head
swaying upon a slim green stem, its jaw
hinging apart as if its spreading maw
might eat the sun and bring life to the dead.
All this is just a tale to tell a man
who knows he'll end within a hundred years:
death is a start, so give up your grave fears.
Enter the labyrinth, fallopian,
sheath-wet, the way you enter sleep's dark lie.
Who can tell how many times we've died?

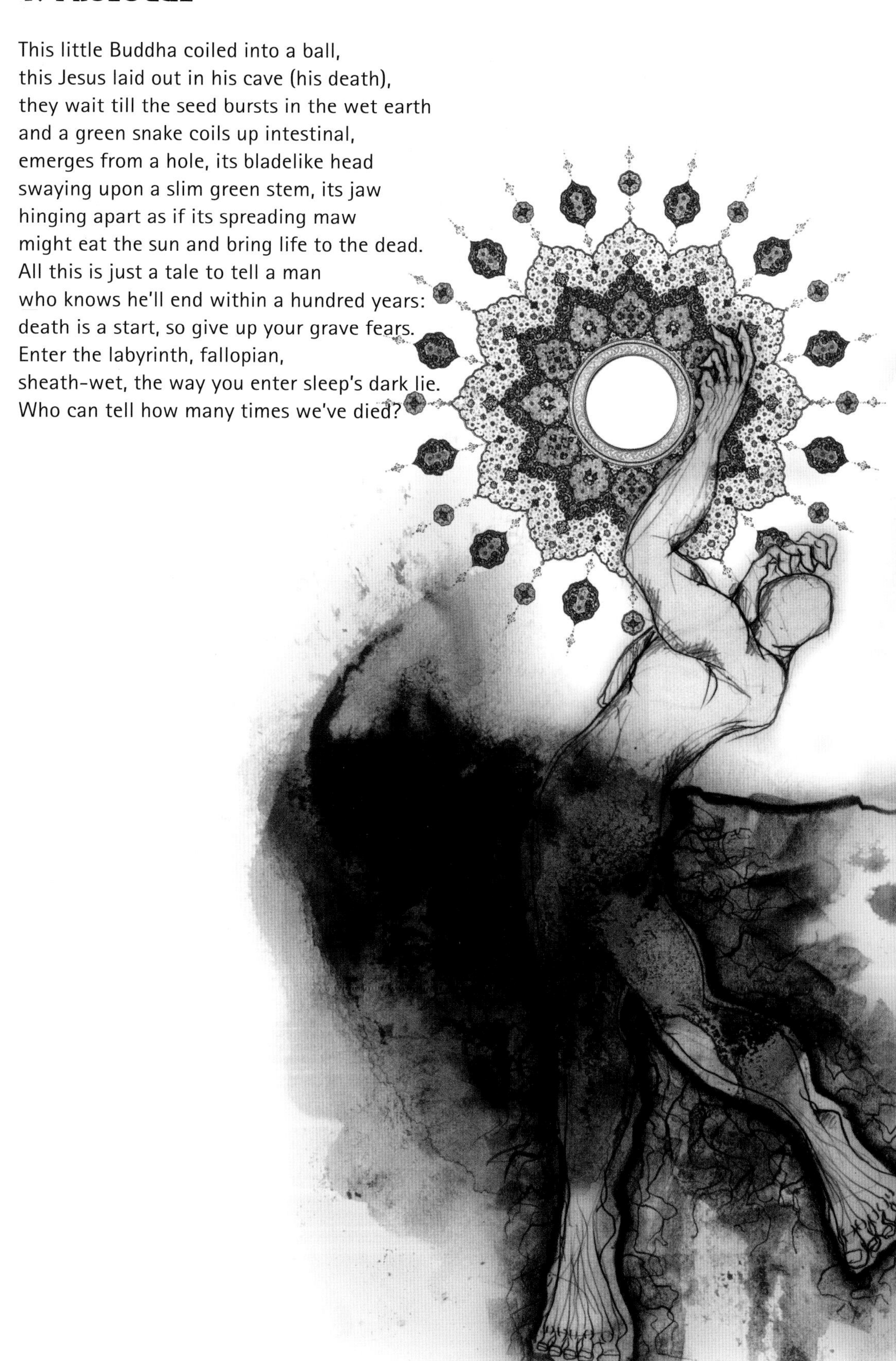

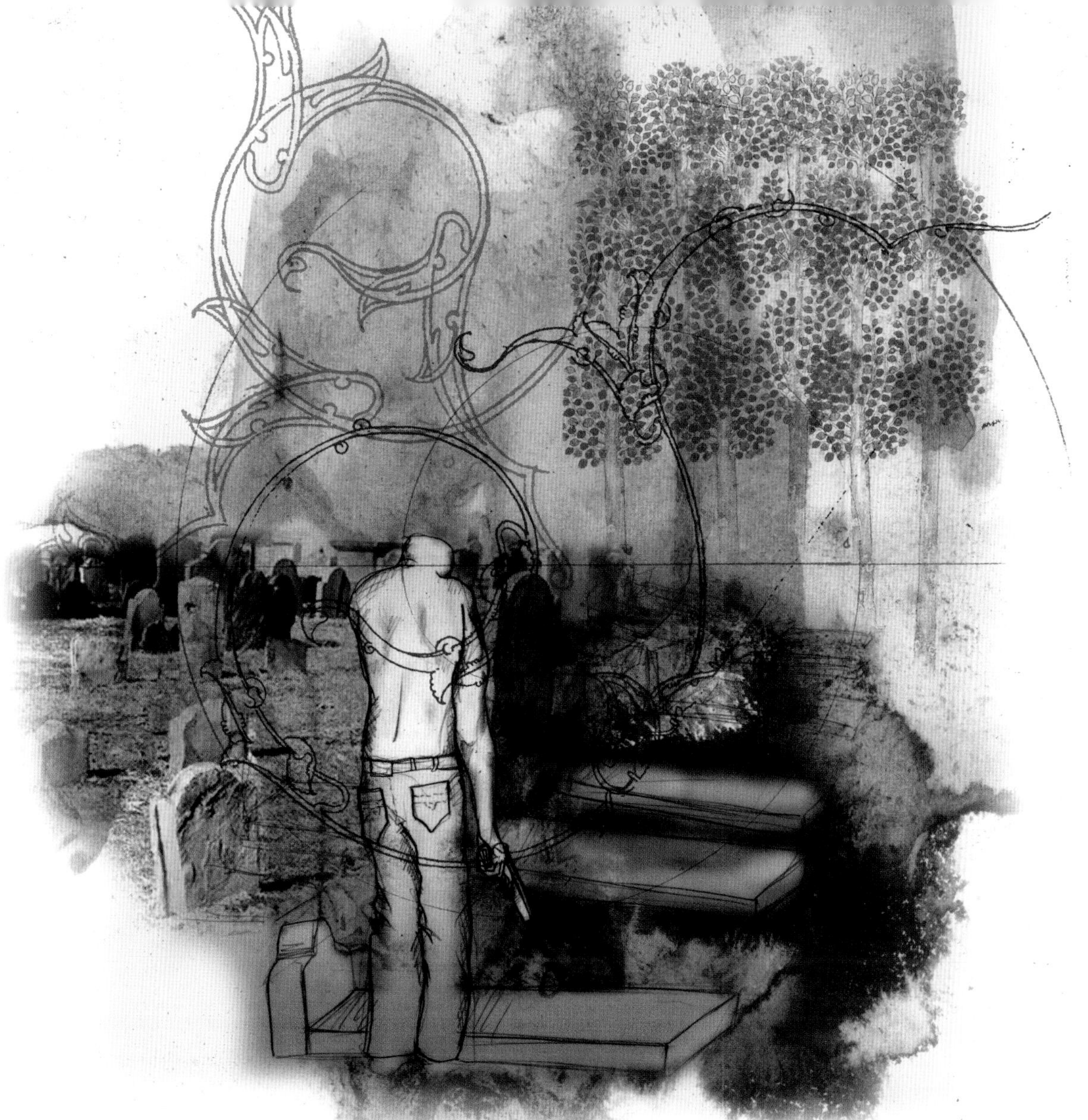

2. IN A FOREST SAVAGE, ROUGH AND STERN

Tonight I find myself in a dark wood,
losing my way. Though the straight way is lost,
the new moon rises, scimitar of blood,
and casts a panther light upon the mossed
tree boles, a swift and feral spotted light
showing a twisted path that, hang the cost,
I'll follow, though I spend my life tonight.
With rapier and pistol near to hand,
I feel my way inside with sightless sight.
A clearing. Gross, primeval statues stand
before a blackened tomb. With my steel blade
I pry it open, walk below the land
in labyrinthine halls the ancients made.
My mind is dark. I lie, "I'm not afraid."

3. EACH OPEN ARCHWAY BREATHES OUT CLUTCHING DREAD

I walk among the houses of the dead.
I see them laid out on stone shelves, with rings
of muted fire, dark armor, and gold thread
wound in their tresses, laid among the things
of their lived lives, their pale limbs smooth and cold,
yet whole and undecayed. The vision stings
my eyes with sudden tears, and I feel old,
my sinews shivering as if with flu.
I am a character in a tale told
by unknown gods and when the tale is through
I'll lie among these warriors and queens
and stare forever from dead orbs into
the dark, the dark unknowing, dark that means
we are bobbing puppets playing scenes.

4. JUST PUPPETS ON A STAGE OF DARKNESS

Well, there'll be time enough for me to rage
against the gods, there will be time, a time
to murder and create, to be a page
or king, then die, so though breath might rhyme
with death, I'll suck it in my chest and fate
along with it. I take a lungful, mime
confidence and stride through a metal gate
and down a spiral stair into the deeps.
Listen. Is that something my fears create?
A tiny skittering as something creeps
behind me down the stairs like my dark other,
a living shadow come to kill what keeps
it trapped, reflection in a glass. Don't bother.
We all will die. Will we be free then, brother?

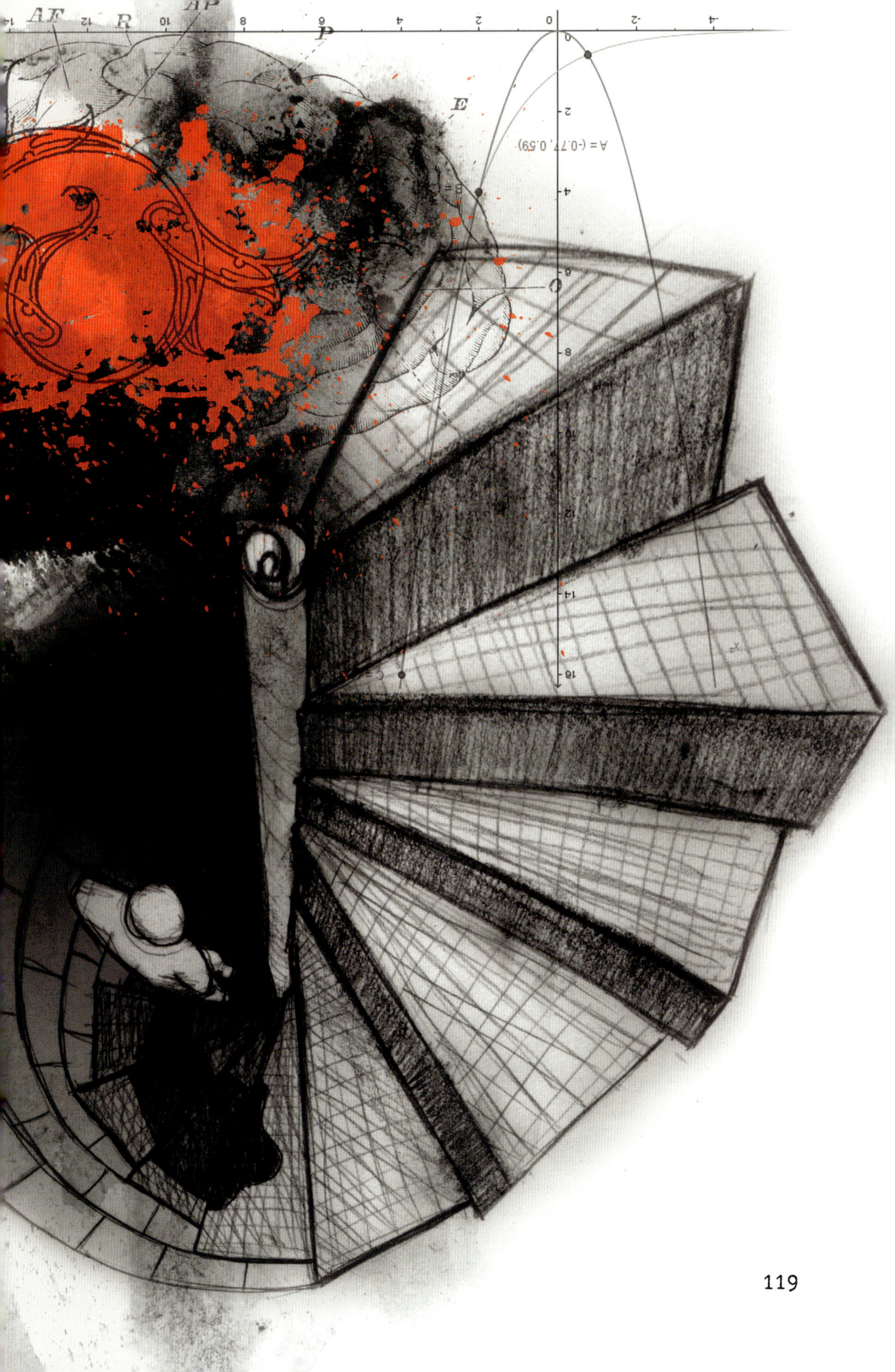

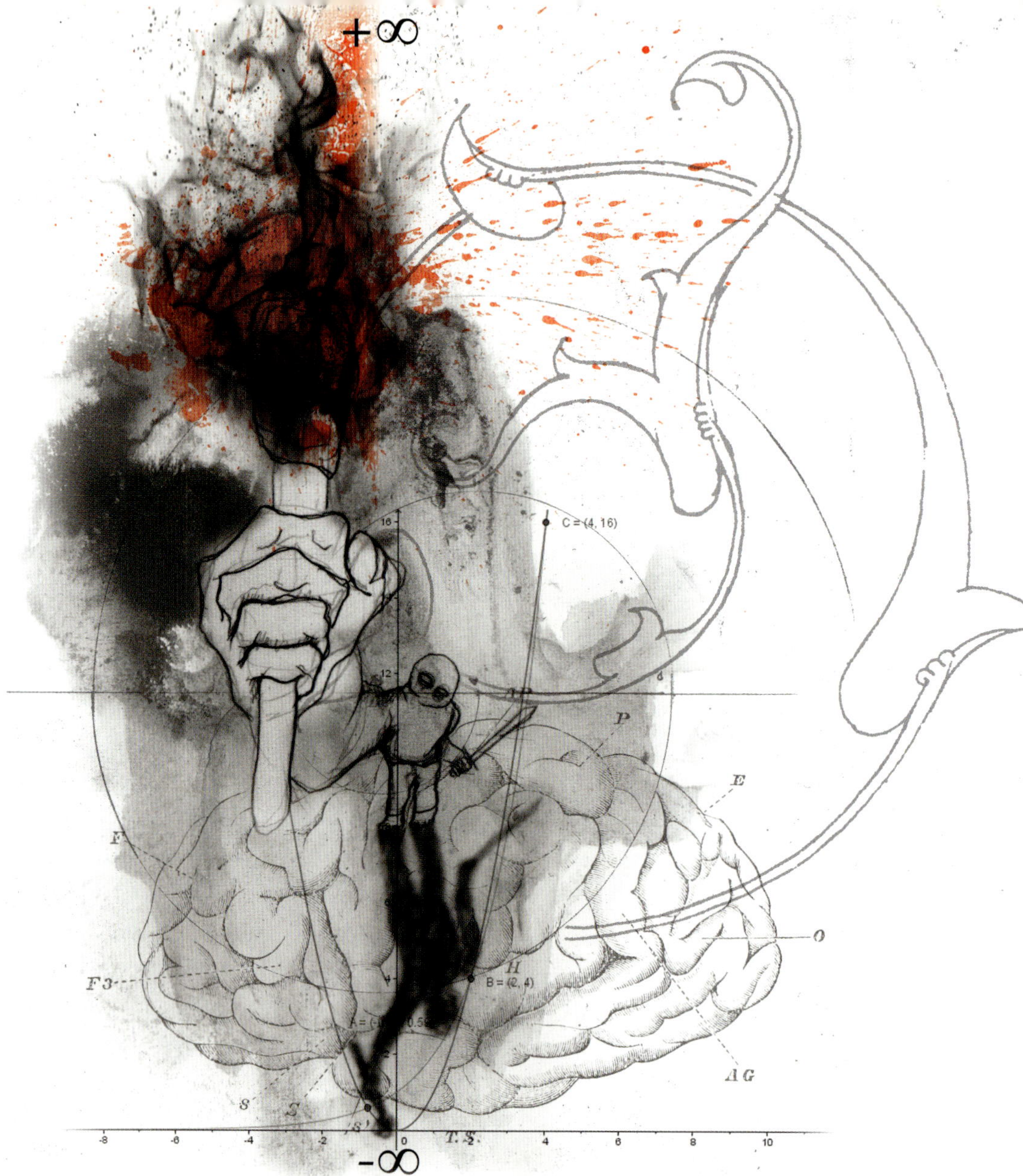

5. I HEAR THE DARKNESS WHISPERING

I hear the darkness whispering, and blade
in hand I whirl, and see just torchlight leaping,
and shadows lapping at the shore, to fade
each time I thrust the light. And then the creeping
back. I descend until the darkness seems
to crowd against my hemisphere of weeping
torchlight, until I walk through deeper dreams
than any dreamer's dreamt, below the well
of nightmares, underneath the maniac screams
that strike like lightning through this darkened hell,
descend until it seems like an ascent.
How long I journey down I cannot tell.
Perhaps I'll find out what the darkness meant.

6. GIANT COILS OF DARKNESS WINDING

When my torch gutters out, at first I'm blind,
then darkness slowly opens its red eyes.
I think at first they must be in my mind,
those crimson gems, blood bright. But then they rise
on giant coils of darkness, and see me.
The secret chamber where the treasure lies
is guarded. I strike my flint and see
round crystals, jeweled orbs and gold in kegs,
and skeletons. The treasure isn't free;
the price is life. Some dark thing grabs my legs
and trips me, coiling, choking out my breath.
I scrabble for my sword among the eggs.
I'm dead, I think, but slice away at death
until it dies, then slump down to the earth.

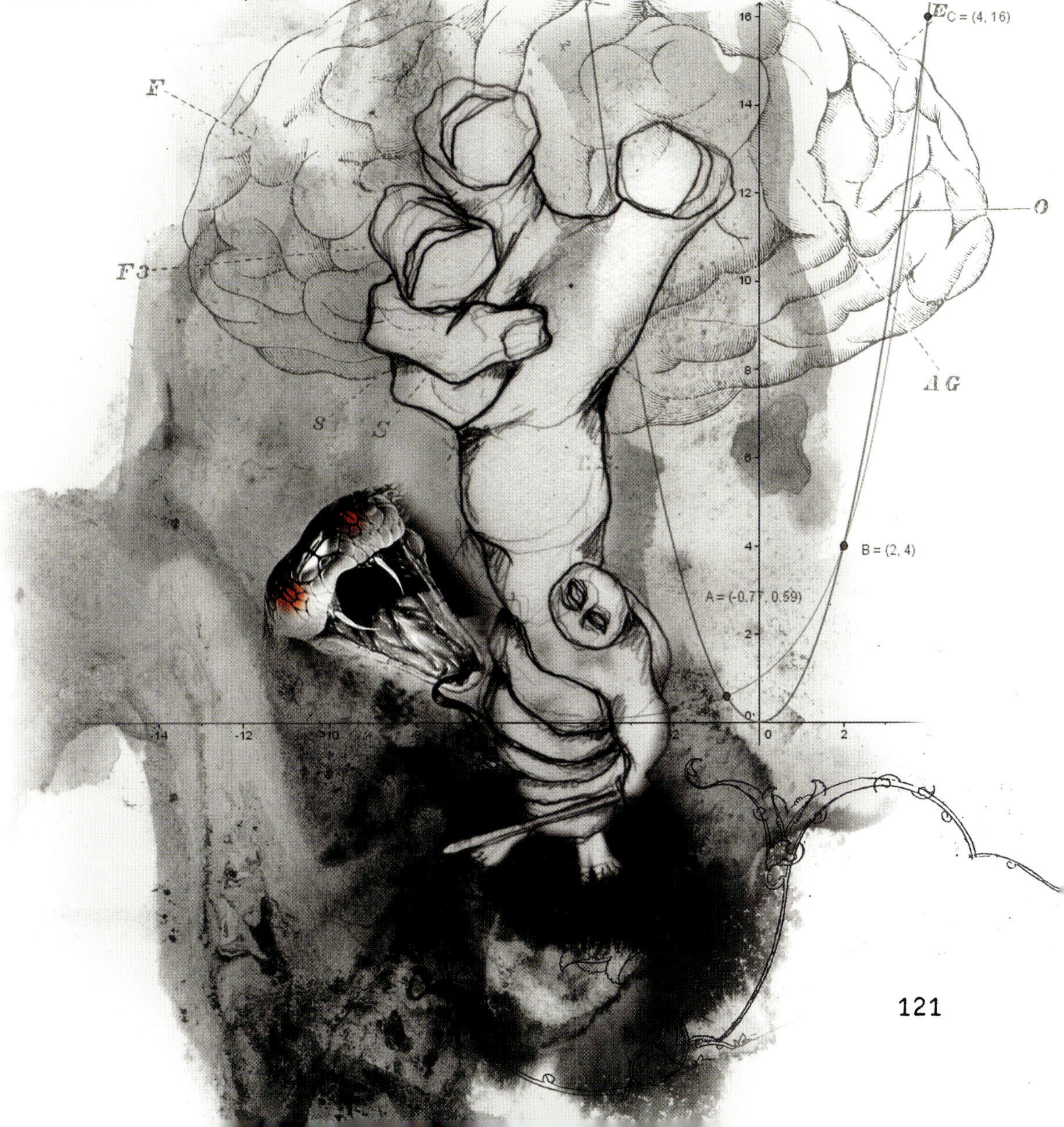

7. THE CLIMB OUT OF THE UNDERWORLD

I strike a flint and torchlight gleams on mail
and helmets sloughed off of the men embraced
to death by the great guardian snake, from tail
to fangs some sixty feet. Dead now. I taste
the rank slime of its heavy shaft, blunt head,
and drooling poison mouth, and spit. I waste
no time, but gather jeweled eggs and shed
my heavy armor for the climb to day,
then shed my clothes, and then my fears. The dead
wait on their shelves, a small light shows the way,
my shadow licks my heels, my darkened twin,
as we climb from this grave, born from decay
into a new world, naked. From within
I wriggle like a snake with a new skin.

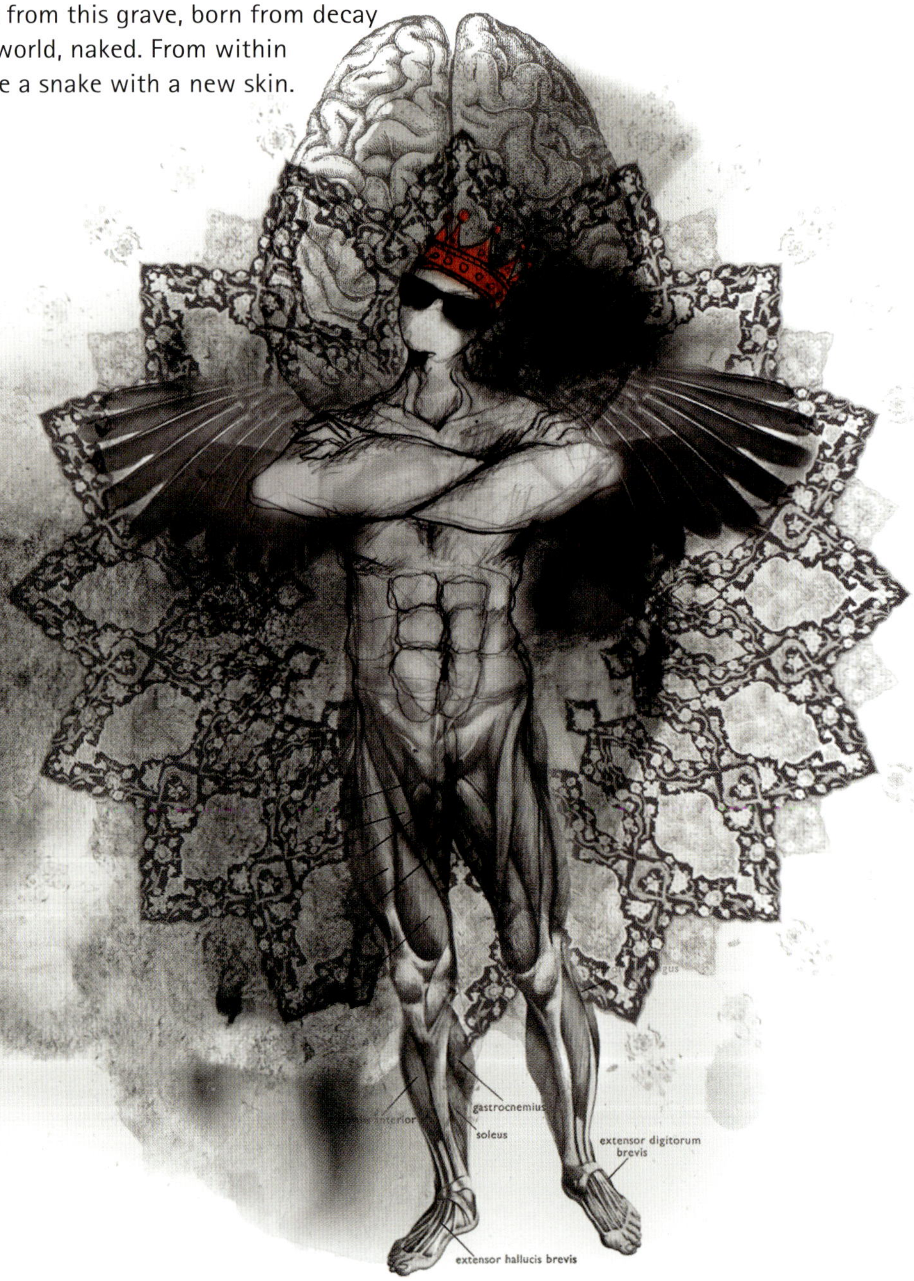

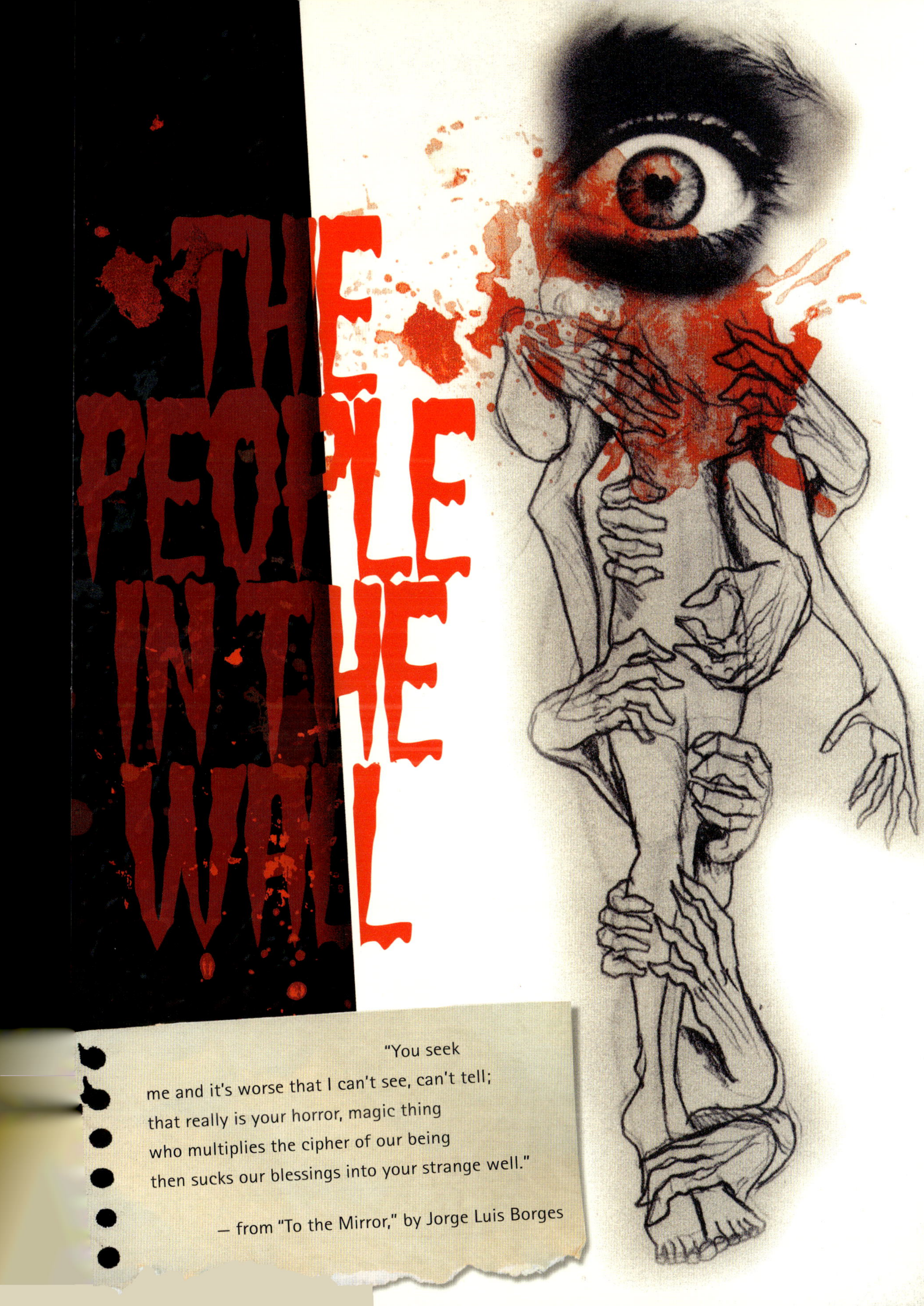
THE PEOPLE IN THE WALL
"You seek
me and it's worse that I can't see, can't tell;
that really is your horror, magic thing
who multiplies the cipher of our being
then sucks our blessings into your strange well."
— from "To the Mirror," by Jorge Luis Borges

1. THE DOORS OF HIS FACE

Beside the rutty black pine road it reared
in antebellum splendor and decay,
the great doors open like a mouth. I feared
the place and Frank knew it. I heard him say,
"A haunted house! I know, let's spend the night
in antebellum splendor, Jill. We'll stay
with ghosts of murderers and slaves." In fright,
I clutched his arm and in my spirit knew
The house was haunted and to spend the night
was death. Frank's face was open as we drew
up to the house. Yes, Frank was laughing, but
something clutched my heart. My spirit knew.
In the great hall I begged him, "Please, let's cut
out, Frank," He smiled. And then the doors crashed shut.

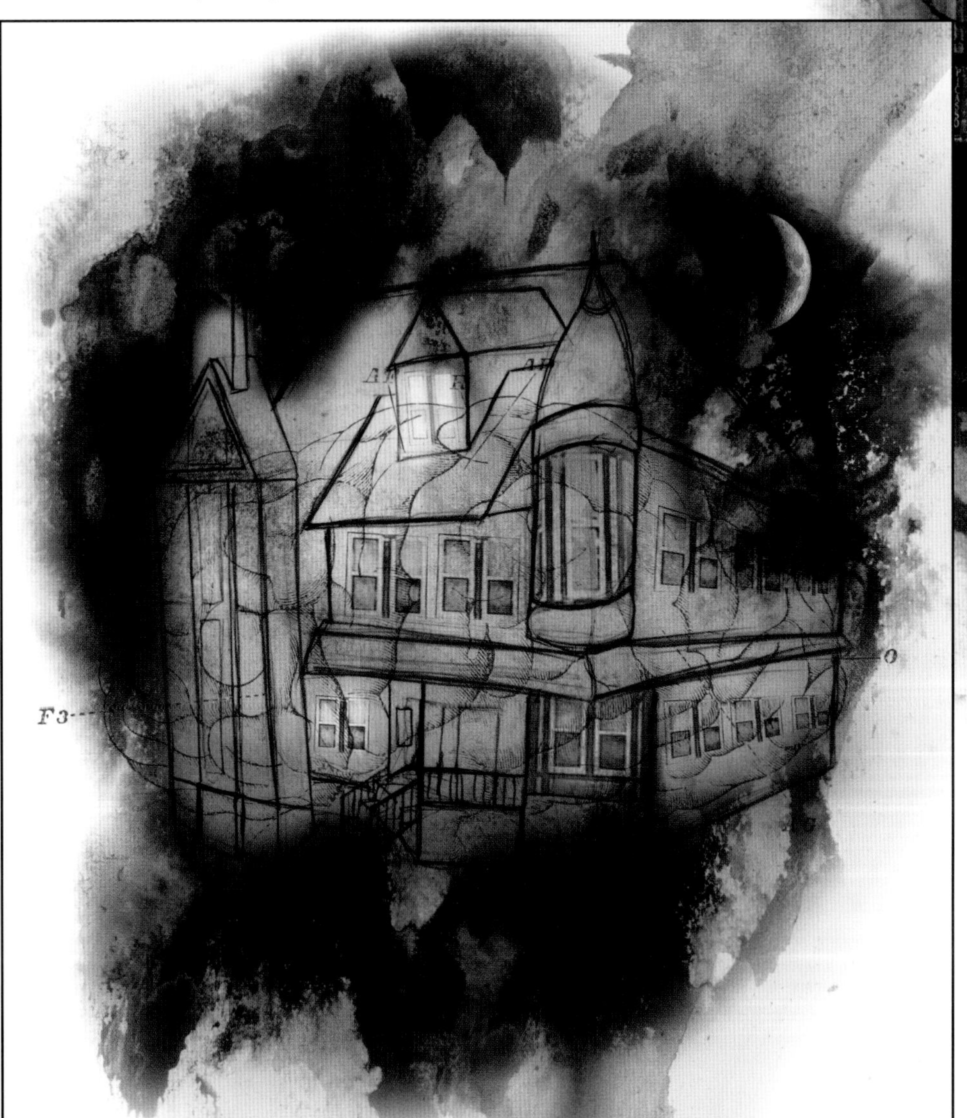

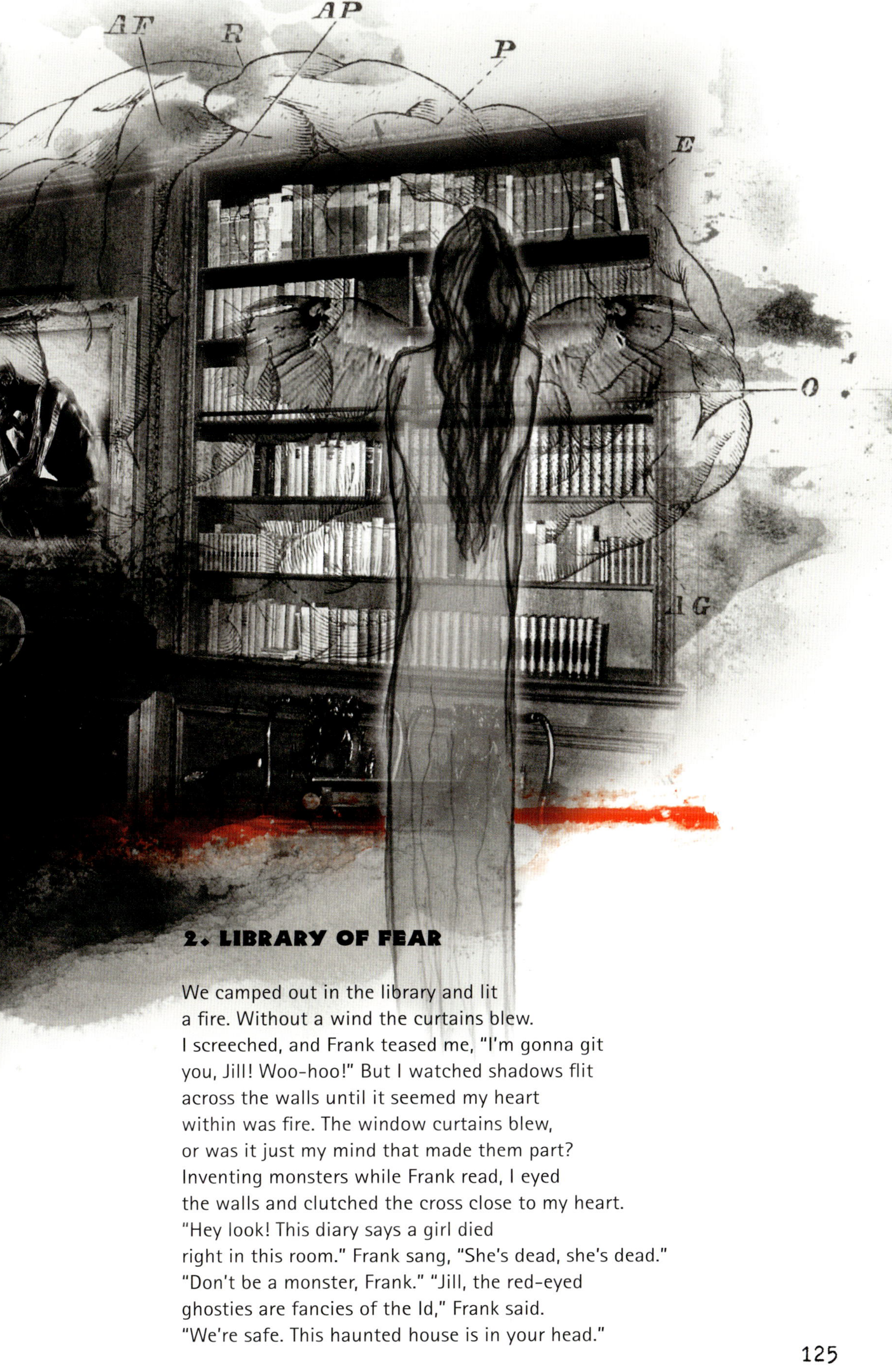

2. LIBRARY OF FEAR

We camped out in the library and lit
a fire. Without a wind the curtains blew.
I screeched, and Frank teased me, "I'm gonna git
you, Jill! Woo-hoo!" But I watched shadows flit
across the walls until it seemed my heart
within was fire. The window curtains blew,
or was it just my mind that made them part?
Inventing monsters while Frank read, I eyed
the walls and clutched the cross close to my heart.
"Hey look! This diary says a girl died
right in this room." Frank sang, "She's dead, she's dead."
"Don't be a monster, Frank." "Jill, the red-eyed
ghosties are fancies of the Id," Frank said.
"We're safe. This haunted house is in your head."

3. THE TURN OF THE SCREW

Franks says, "The grave's a fine and private place,
but none I think do there embrace. Let's hump!"
He's very literary, Frank. His face
spreads in a death-head grin as we go bump
in the night, ghosts be damned. As to my fear,
I cannot think as we embrace, or "hump"
as Frank calls it. Though at our backs I hear
a sudden rushing sound like phantom wings
through the night, ghosts of the damned, screw my fear:
let Frank screw me with rough strife till it stings.
I won't let worms try my virginity.
Again the sudden rushing phantom wings,
the whole house quivers epileptically,
and Frank is screaming as he comes in me.

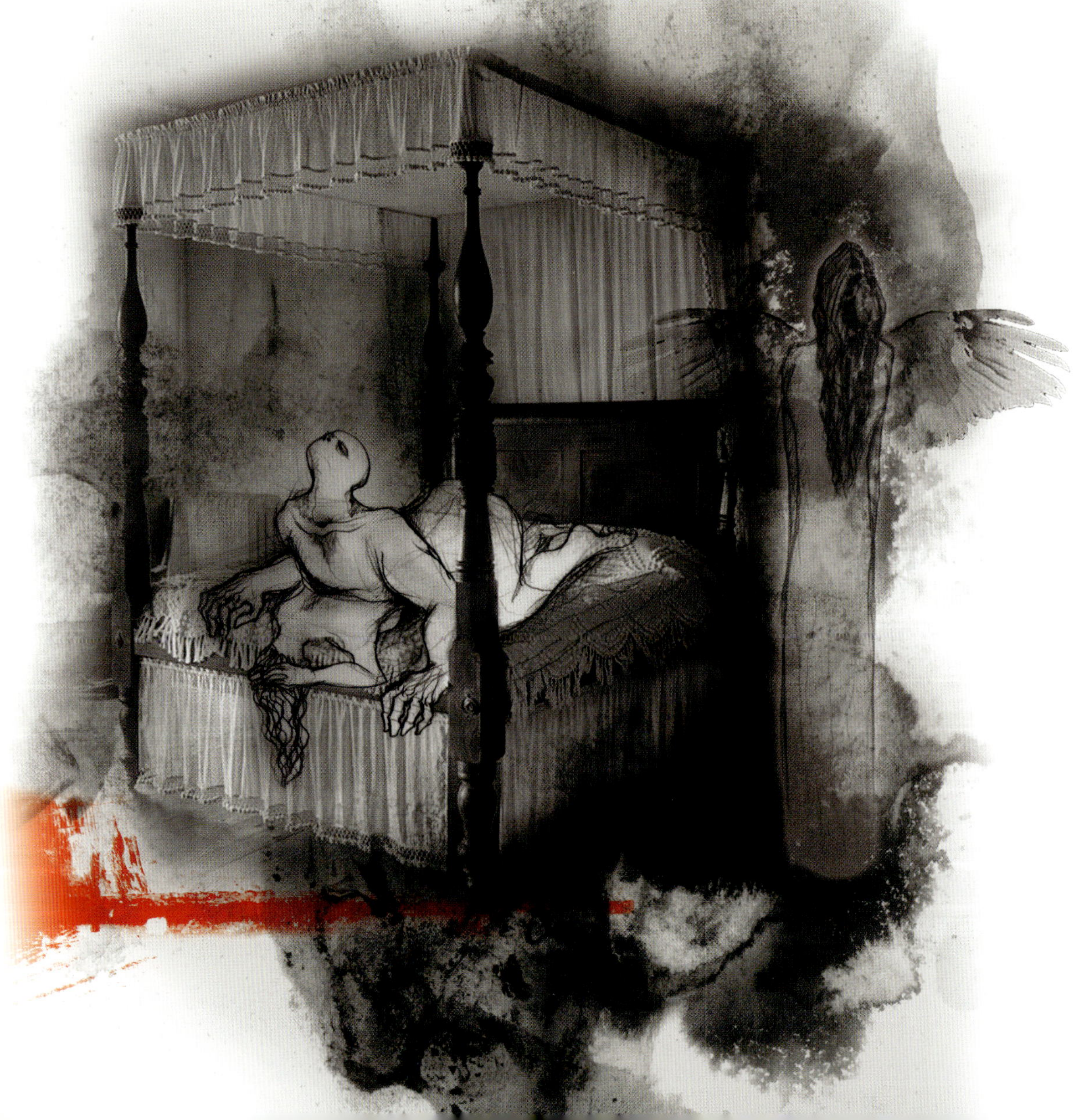

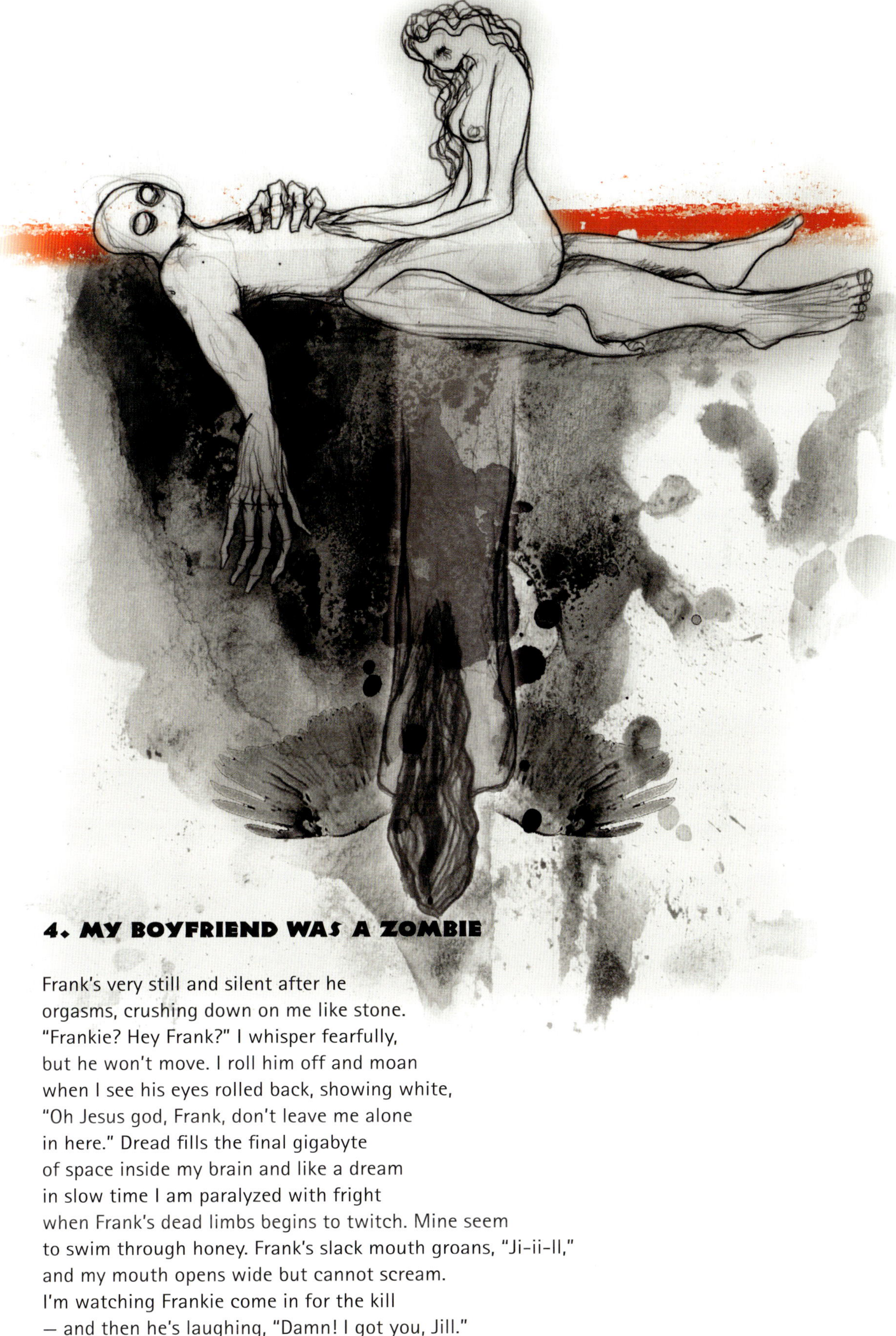

4. MY BOYFRIEND WAS A ZOMBIE

Frank's very still and silent after he
orgasms, crushing down on me like stone.
"Frankie? Hey Frank?" I whisper fearfully,
but he won't move. I roll him off and moan
when I see his eyes rolled back, showing white,
"Oh Jesus god, Frank, don't leave me alone
in here." Dread fills the final gigabyte
of space inside my brain and like a dream
in slow time I am paralyzed with fright
when Frank's dead limbs begins to twitch. Mine seem
to swim through honey. Frank's slack mouth groans, "Ji-ii-ll,"
and my mouth opens wide but cannot scream.
I'm watching Frankie come in for the kill
— and then he's laughing, "Damn! I got you, Jill."

5. THE PEOPLE IN THE WALL

Frank laughs, "I got you! Ha! I got you, Jill,"
but then his face turns quizzical, he falls
down to his knees and gasps as his eyes fill
with awful comprehension, and he sprawls
at my feet, bloody knife stuck in his head.
I scream and run as, bulging from walls,
hands grab my legs, the white hands of the dead,
and bat-faced children beat against the glass.
The porcelain dolls are chattering, the lead
paperweights bouncing on the desk, the gas-
jets in the lamps hiss at me in a fever-
dream, as I run from room to room. I pass
through myself wailing in the mirror and never
can break the glass. The house goes on forever.

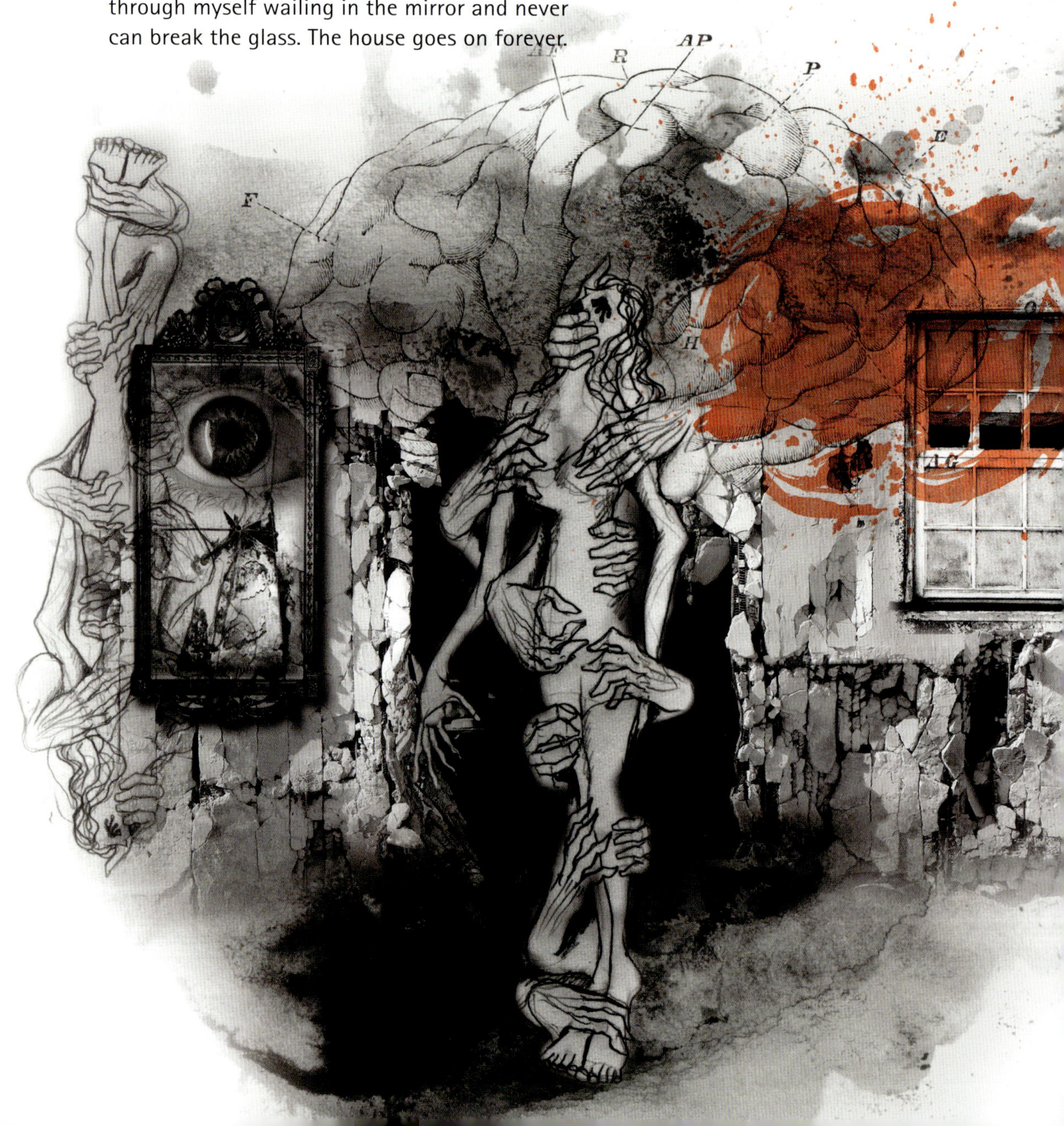

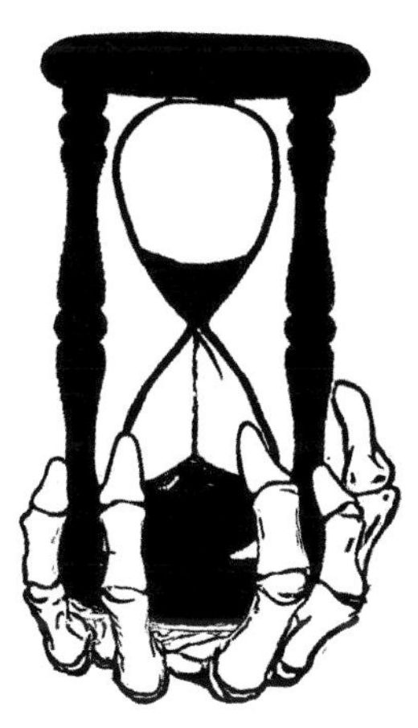

Two Months later

6. MIRROR HOUSE

"She's trapped somewhere inside the mirror glass," says the cadaverous detective who stands by the bedside. He grips her ankles as they twitch in nightmare, but they kick right through his grasp. "You see? She's running in her head, and can't break out." "Okay, but weren't there two who went into that house?" I ask. "He's dead, knife through his skull. Please listen, Steve. If I were you, I'd choose another house instead. That Grishell house is really haunted." "Why, Detective Clark, don't tell me you believe in ghosts." "I've seen fifteen ghostbusters die in there. It's Hotel California, Steve. You can check out, but you can never leave."

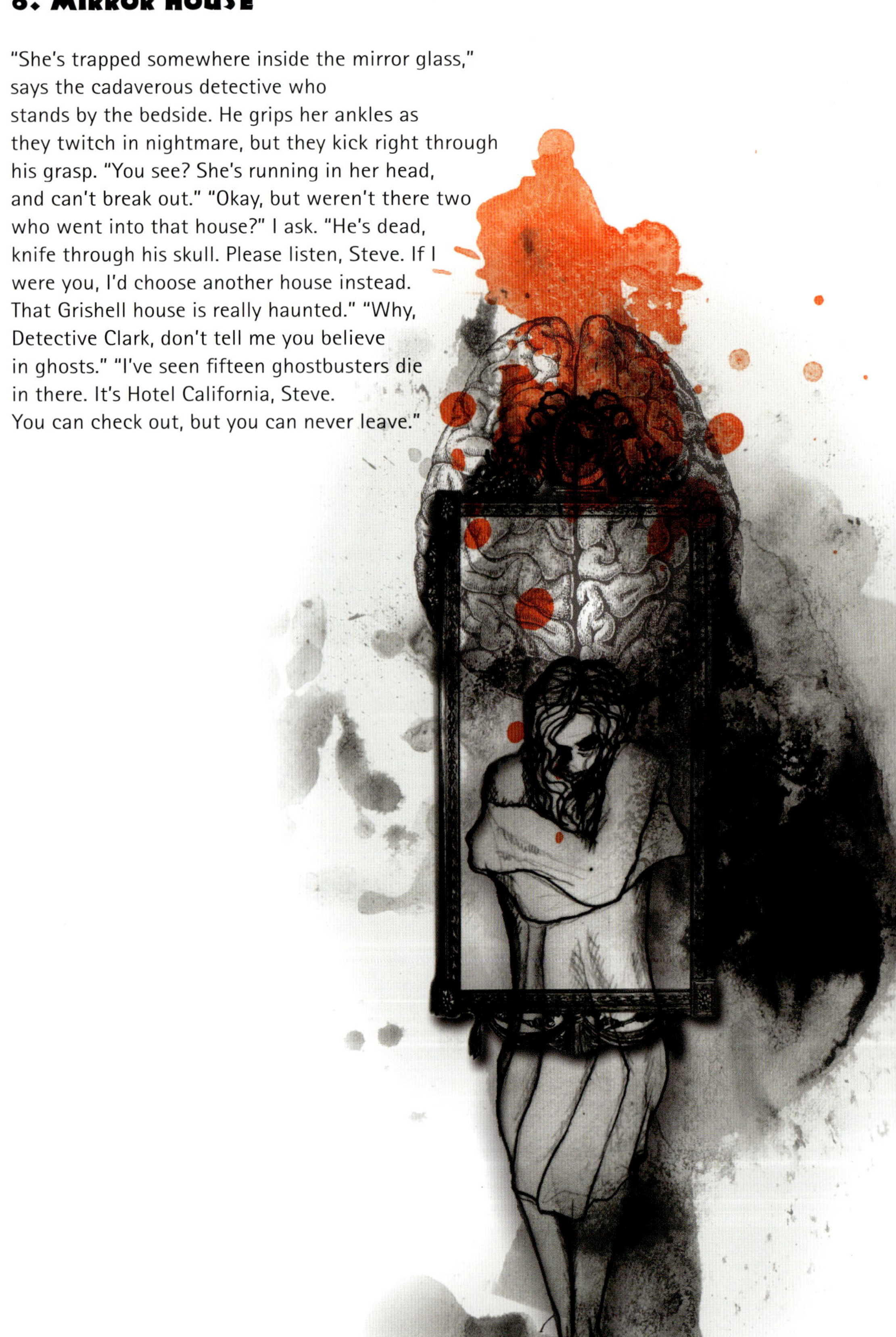

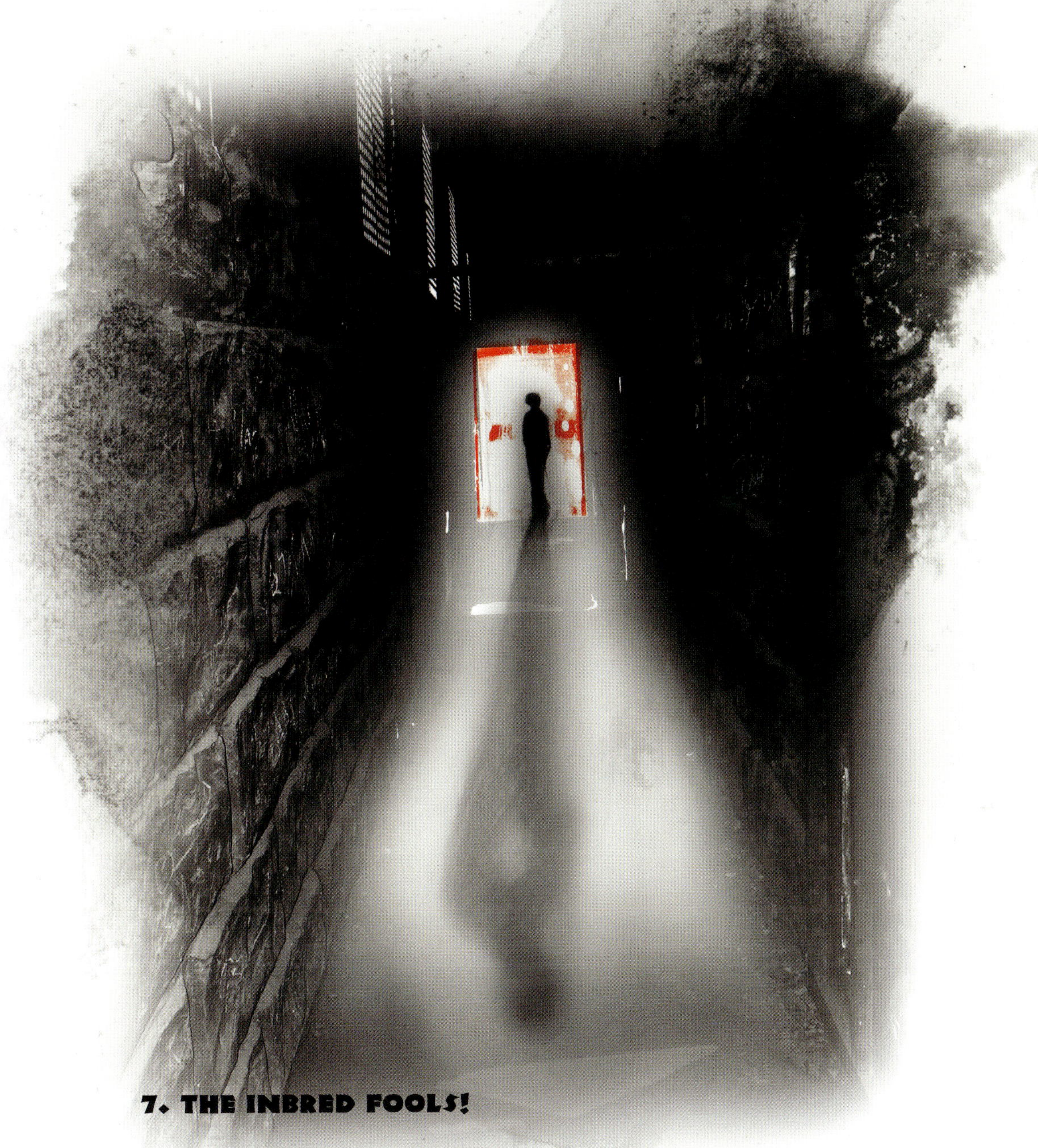

7. THE INBRED FOOLS!

Beside the rutty road I see it rise
in antebellum splendor and decay,
the great doors' mouth wide open in surprise
(it almost seems) to see me with my tray
of chemicals and suitcase full of tools
and scientific instruments. They say
the haunted Grishell house has certain rules:
from dawn to dusk it lets you live. At dark,
you die or go insane. The inbred fools
with their wild tales of couples on a lark
found dead at dawn! I know that someone's lying,
and for a reason I'll find out. I park
my gear in the bedroom. The light is dying.
I will debunk this hoax, or I'll die trying.

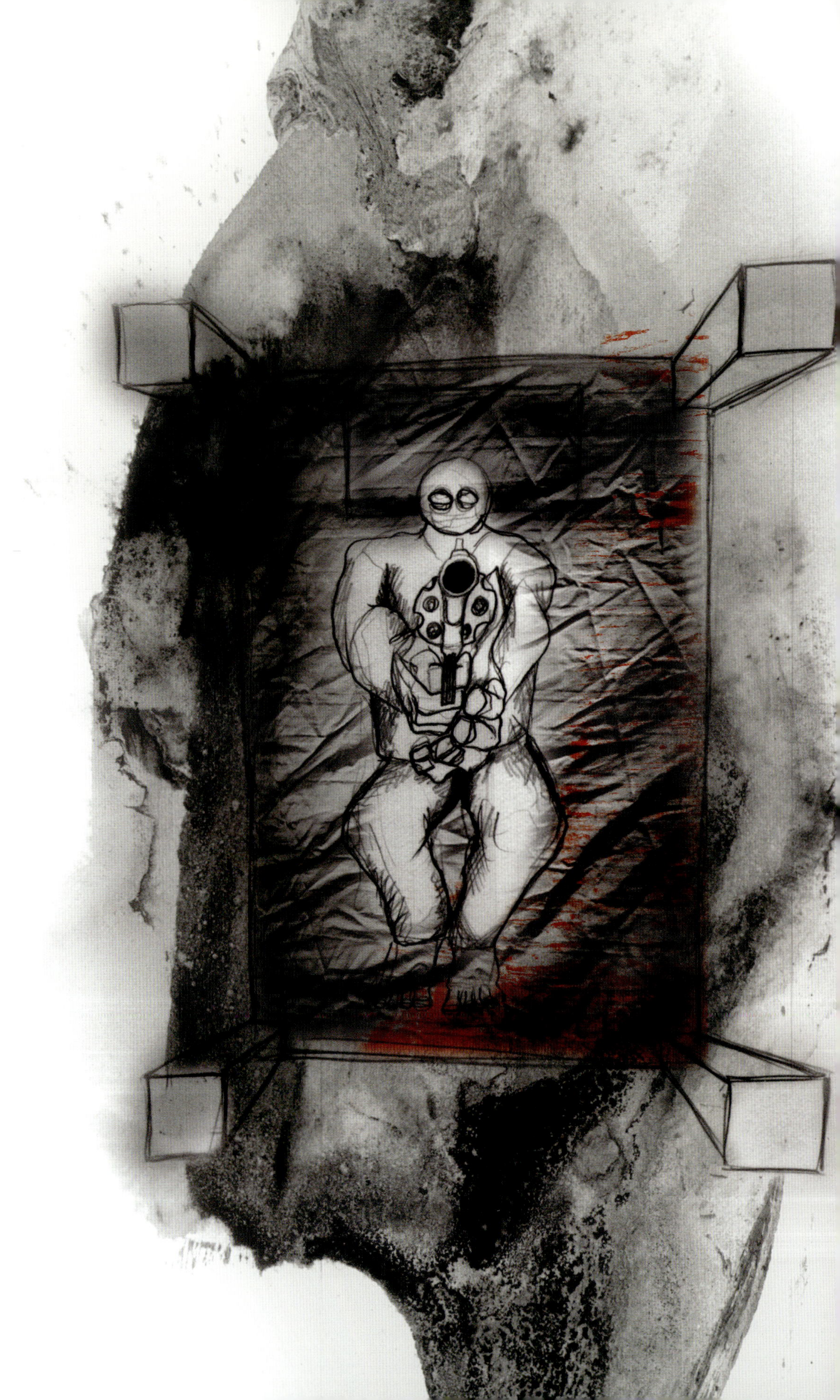

8. THE DEATH BED

My pistol at my side, I go to bed.
The ancient canopy that looms above
on spider legs still hangs a yellow shred
of lace left from its youth (like a dead love,
the lingering clutch of lust). Then in my sleep
I think I see the canopy above
begin to bend its legs. I try to leap,
but dreams are fear, I'm paralyzed — except
one finger, clutching, bang! Now out of sleep
I shoot like pistol shot. I laugh. I've leapt
from sleep, and shot my gun, but what is dead
but dreams and fear (that pair of lies)? Except,
there — in the canopy of this strange bed —
a tiny bullet hole is bleeding red.

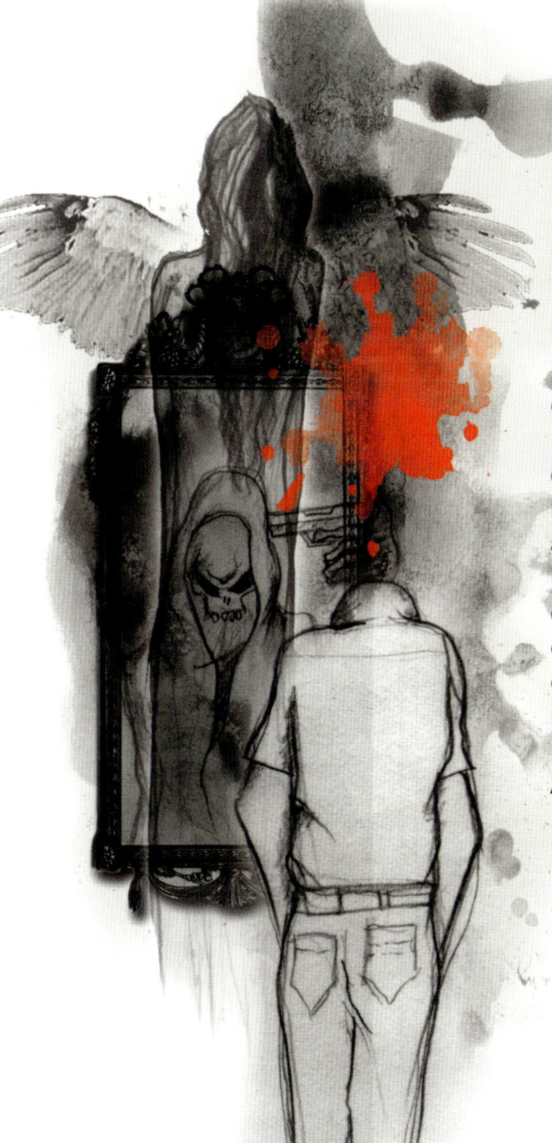

9. THE MIRROR VAMPIRE

Look at that mirror. Why does it persist
in copying me down to the smallest quiver
of my drawn lip and pulsing at the wrist?
In ancient watery crystal, see it shiver
darkly all night, and then at dawn insist
in copying me down to the smallest quiver
again — the tense lips, pulsing at the wrist.
Mirror, you draw me into your weird well
darkly all night, and then at dawn insist
on showing me my ghost trapped in a hell
of glassy planes. You are a vampire other,
mirror, who sucks me in — in your weird well
I see the drowned face of my twin, my brother.
And when I'm dead, you'll duplicate another.

10. THE ESCAPE

The people in the walls are grabbing me
with their white hands, dead hands of all who pass
away in this cursed house, but I wrench free
and run through labyrinths of mirror glass
as bat-faced children with their small sharp claws
snatch at my feet, and find my way at last
to the front doors. "Oh, very faint applause,
you fool," I mock myself, "It's like Clark said,
This place is damned." On the front lawn I pause
and look back at the house where bedsteads bled
and mirrors clutched — then it's no longer there!
Instead I see the top of someone's head
above the back horizon of a chair.
You turn your head as if you feel me here.

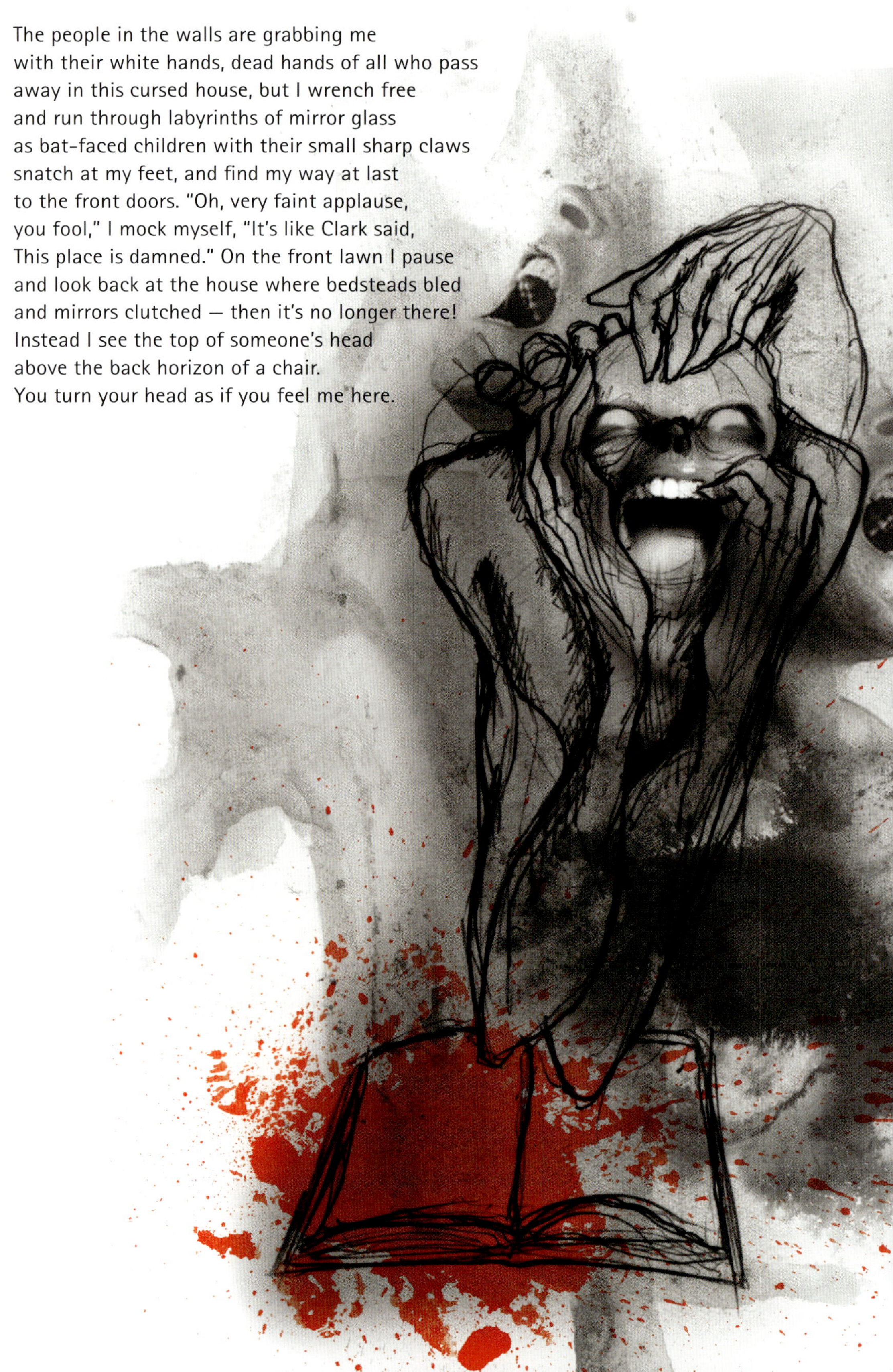

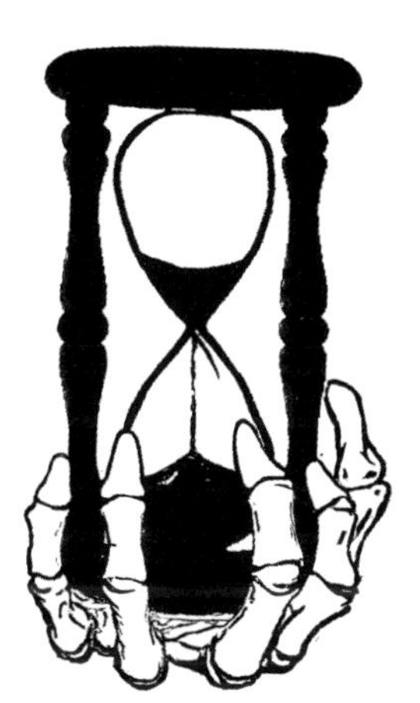

Epilogue

11. HYPOCRITE LECTEUR, — MON SEMBLABLE, — MON FRÈRE!

I wonder if you've ever had the feeling
when reading comfortably in a chair
so deep inside the story that the ceiling
lifts off, the walls peel back, and then you're there
inside the book (some Gothic horror tale
about a couple on a dark road where
they find a haunted house)? Of course they fail
to fend the ghosts off. Genre expectations
determine this, because the cocky male
and frightened girl have sexual relations.
But still, it sucks you in. You know no thing
hovers behind your chair in contemplation
of eating you. Imagining's a book
or mirror, not a friend. Don't look!

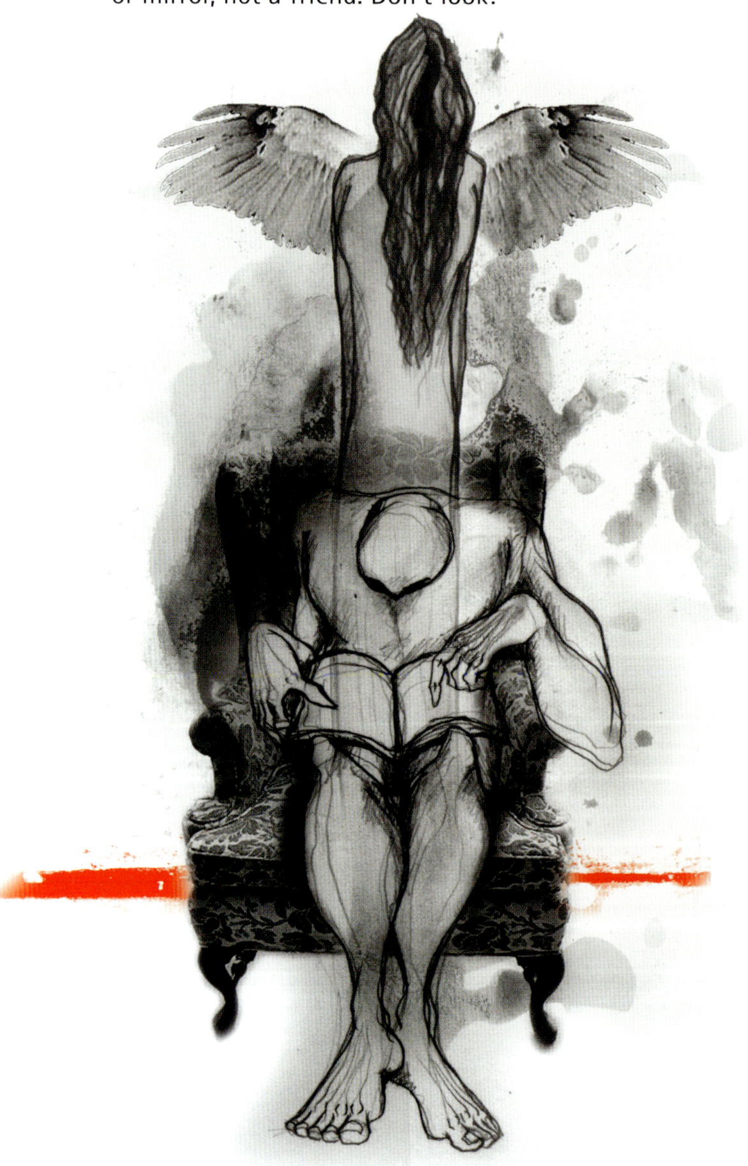

Acknowledgments

Many thanks to Dan Weiss and David Benioff for pointing me towards terrific contemporary genre literature. Thanks also to my collaborators in other arts who have brought this project alive in different forms: Jennifer Sage Holmes (radio play), Dorothy Tunnell (graphic novel), and Beau Blue (animation). And here's to my friends who allowed me to use their names in *The Horror of Haunted Valley*: Dan Weiss, Andrea Troyer, Anthony Miller, John Fitzgerald, Kim Oja, Caroline Heldman, Ron Alcalay, Bilal Shaw, Brian Turner, Kathy Strong, Linda Goldman, Nathan Potter, and Ward Swan. Many thanks to Jeffrey Levine for believing in this project, to Bill Kuch for his marvelous design for the book, and to Jim Schley for his terrific editorial work, and especially his delicate and insightful suggestions on the poems. And thanks to Whittier College for support.

Thanks as well to the editors of the following journals for featuring poems from this book in previous publications:

The Arroyo Literary Review (2013): Seven sonnets from *The Tomb in the Woods,* illustrated by Amin Mansouri: "Prologue," "In a Forest, Savage, Rough and Stern," "Each Open Archway Breathes Out Clutching Dread," "Just Puppets on a Stage of Darkness," "I Hear the Darkness Whispering," "Giant Coils of Darkness Winding," and "The Climb Out of the Underworld."

Carnival (Volume 1, 2012): "The Man with Two Heads."

Measure (Volume 6, issue 2, 2011): "Mexican Movie, 1939."

The Chattahoochee Review (Volume 32, number 1, Spring 2012): "A Woman Like a Bullet."

The Evansville Review (Volume 18, 2008): "New York Blues."

The Ilanot Review (Winter 2015): Four sonnets from "Insects and Cigarettes," with illustrations by Amin Mansouri: "A Fat Black Tick," "Revelation," "The Metamorphosis," and "One Cigarette."

Measure (Volume 6, issue 2, 2011): "Mexican Movie, 1939."

New Letters (Volume 75, Number 1, Fall 2008): "The Revenant," "Claws in the Darkness," and "Worms of the Earth."

Poemeleon (Volume IV, Issue 1, Summer/Fall 2009): Seven sonnets from "The Werewolf of Green Knolls": "Pooch," "Snarl," "Little Piggy," "That Time of Month," "Wolf's Best Friend," "Whine," "Rabbit's Revenge"; and ten sonnets from *The Bent Adventures of India Rubber Man:* "India Rubber Man's Credo," "The Origin of India Rubber Man," "India Rubber Man at the Temple of Sin Adult Novelty Store (the Origin of Miss Elastic)," "The Anthem of Miss Elastic," "Miss Elastic Rescues India Rubber Man from Evil X-Girlfriend," "India Rubber Man and the Fear and Trembling and Sickness Unto Death," "India Rubber Man's

Buddhist Christmas," "India Rubber Man and the Anorexic Doll," "India Rubber Man and Miss Elastic in the Morning," and "India Rubber Man and the Bath."

The Raintown Review (Forthcoming, 2015): Two sonnets from "Ways of Looking at a Vampire," with illustrations by Amin Mansouri: "I Am Legend" and "The Flea."

Rattle 33 (Summer 2010): Twenty-eight sonnets from *Jack Logan, Fighting Airman: The Case of the Red Bordello:* "Acquainted with the Night," "Tricks and Stag Flicks," "The Name of the Rose," "The Trick Turns," "The Act," "Two Black Books and a Stack of Cash," "Angels and Buttercups," "Angel Face," "A Heap of Broken Images," "A Rose by Any Other Name," "Tough Act to Follow," "The Kiss," "The Distressed Rose," "Tough Guise," "The Death Trap," "The City Dead-House," "Dressing the Meat," "From Tempest to Othello," "Spider Cat and Bad Eye," "When It Rains, It Pours," "Animals," "Note Left Pinned to the Pillow (Signed 'Violet')," "Small Fry, Big Fish, and the Dish," "Angels Falling from the Sky," "Taxes and Death," "A Bouquet of Violence," "Violets are Black and Blue," and "Untouchable."

Short Fiction (Number 5, November 2012): Seven sonnets from "The Werewolf of Green Knolls" were adapted into a graphic novel in collaboration with artist Dorothy Tunnell: "Pooch," "Snarl," "Little Piggy," "That Time of Month," "Wolf's Best Friend," "Whine," "Rabbit's Revenge," and "Feeding Time."

Unsplendid (Volume 6, Number 2, April 2015): Three sonnets from "The Ballad of Dottie and Pete": "Greased Chicken Breasts," "Red Pickup," and "Chopped Meat."

The Warwick Review (Volume 5, Number 11, Spring 2011): Eleven sonnets from *The People in the Wall:* "The Doors of His Face," "Library of Fear," "The Turn of the Screw," "My Boyfriend Was a Zombie," "The People in the Wall," "Mirror House," "The Inbred Fools!," "The Death Bed," "The Mirror Vampire," "The Escape," and "Hypocrite lecteur,—mon semblable,—mon frère!"; and nine sonnets from *Operation Ragnarok:* "A Back Alley in Honningsvåg," "Wet Work," "Death and the Author," "At the Fishhouses," "The Job," "The Man with the Glass Eye Speaks," "God Complex," "The Hermeneutics of Spycraft," and "The Poetry of Murder."

In addition, some of these poems have been previously published in the following anthologies:

A Face to Meet the Faces: Persona Poems, edited by Stacey Lynn Brown and Oliver de la Paz (University Of Akron Press, 2012): Seven sonnets from "The Werewolf of Green Knolls" ("Pooch," "Snarl," "Little Piggy," "That Time of Month," "Wolf's Best Friend," "Whine," and "Rabbit's Revenge").

Drawn to Marvel: Poems from the Comic Books, edited by Bryan Dietrich and Marta Ferguson (Minor Arcana Press, 2014): "The Human Torch" and "The Blowfly Thing."

Hot Sonnets, edited by Moira Egan and Clarinda Harriss (Entasis Press, 2011): "India Rubber Man at the Temple of Sin."

Killer Poems: Poems about Murder and Mayhem, edited by Kurt Brown and Harold Schechter (Everyman Pocket Poetry Series, 2011): Two sonnets from "The Chop Shop" ("A Stand-Up Guy" and "Italian Sandwich Meat"), and "The Lover."

Poems Dead and Undead, edited by Tony Barnstone and Michelle Mitchell-Foust (Everyman Pocket Poetry Series, 2014): "Revenant."

Villanelles, edited by Annie Finch and Marie-Elizabeth Mali (Everyman Pocket Poetry Series, 2012): "Mexican Movie, 1939."

The eleven-sonnet sequence *Captain Fantastic, Wizard of Science, and the Quest for the New Universe* was awarded First Prize in the CZP/Rannu Prize in Speculative Literature (2013).